AF352333

ANTHROPOLOGY

and

HISTORIOGRAPHY

of

SCIENCE

ANTHROPOLOGY
and
HISTORIOGRAPHY
of
SCIENCE

········

by D. P. CHATTOPADHYAYA

OHIO UNIVERSITY PRESS   ATHENS

Library of Congress Cataloging-in-Publication Data

Chattopadhyaya, D.P. (Debi Prasad), 1933-
    Anthropology and historiography of science / by D.P. Chattopadhyaya.
       p. cm. − (Series in continental thought ; v. 16)
    Includes bibliographical references.
    ISBN 0-8214-0952-2
    1. Philosophy and science − History. 2. Science − Historiography − History.
3. Anthropology − Philosophy − History. 4. Science − Philosophy − History.
I. Title. II. Series: Series in continental thought ; 16.
B67.C44   1990   89-26582
306.4'2 − dc20   CIP

For
Bimal K. Matilal
and
R. Sundara Rajan

CONTENTS

PREFACE

· · · · · · · · · · · · · ·

WHENEVER I HAVE TRIED TO MAKE CLEAR TO MYSELF THE MAIN REASON OF UNDER-
taking the project of writing this book I have felt a persistent problem
within me. For whom I am going to write it? Philosophers of science know
their job. So do the historians of science. Anthropologists' concern with
science is very marginal and they take the subject as magic or mythic
worldview. Given the situation, have I, as a philosopher, anything of interest to tell to any one of these groups? I wondered. Can I arrange a
dialogue between them that might prove interesting and fruitful to them?
The question intrigued me. I followed it up.

From my intrigued consciousness, on reflection, the answer that
started slowly emerging is somewhat like this. Though reared in Indian
cultural tradition and familiar with the history of Indian philosophy, our
main professional exposure had been to classical European philosophy
and the contemporary analytic school. Two points disturbed me deeply.
First, while we are trying respectfully to familiarise ourselves not only
with their philosophy and science but also, in a way, with their culture
as a whole, how those educated in the Western tradition can afford to
be more or less indifferent to or at best ill-informed about our culture
and its different forms such as philosophy and science? Why do some
of them go to the extent of pronouncing that, being incurable metaphysicians, we Indians can have no sense of history? Historyless Indian
philosophy and science, to most of them, are only of anthropological interest, specimens of a dead past. More disturbing is the second question: why are the analytic empiricist and his Continental phenomenol-

ogist colleague, equally convinced of their common origin in Greek classical philosophy, ordinarily oppressed by a persistent feeling of mutual unintelligibility? The case becomes worse when the former criticizes the latter for his "meaningless verbiage" and the latter accuses the former of his preoccupation with "superficial" issues, neglecting the "essential" ones. A communication gap is not intrinsic to intercultural cases; it is present but avoidable in intracultural cases, as well.

If it is avoidable, to what does it owe its origin and persistence, even within and between the learned communities? Are we to understand, then, that words like *learned* have no community-invariant meaning? Perhaps at this stage one starts perceiving that philosophical issues are invisibly rooted in culture or life.

To strike a more personal note: While mainly working with Popper, Lakatos, and Watkins at London School of Economics in early 1960s, I was simultaneously attending Firth's course on anthropology, Ginsberg's lectures on sociology, Findlay's seminar on *The Cartesian Meditations* at King's College, and Hampshire's seminar on Austin at the University College. What an intellectual feast of diversity! One could not avoid being struck by the depth of group diversity. Yet I for one started thinking about it not only as a metaphilosophical issue but also, perhaps more so, as a living cultural issue. Many of my subsequent publications bear out this continuous concern and query. Rooted in Indian culture, how do I understand and respond to Euro-American philosophy as a whole and to the difference within the latter itself?

Mine is not a study in comparative philosophy. It is basically a philosophical study in the problems of intercultural comparison with special reference to science as a subculture. One issue that has never ceased to intrigue me is that, on the one hand, most of us claim that in philosophy we find a universal solution or, at least, a unified understanding of the problems cropping up in different provinces of knowledge, and yet, on the other hand, we keep on asking others, "Whom are you addressing?" I am inclined to think that philosophy is one of those few forms of subculture that provide us the enabling conditions necessary to open up and carry on fruitfully intercultural, intracultural, or interdisciplinary dialogue. I started working on this book in 1980. But its progress was slow and repeatedly interrupted by several other academic and administrative commitments. A Fulbright Fellowship in 1983 gave me nearly a year's time to spend partly at Harvard and partly at Columbia. My interaction with, among others, Arthur Danto, Erwin Hiebert, Willard Quine, Thomas Kuhn, and Hilary Putnam proved very stimulating. The first two read through a substantial part of the first draft. J. N. Mohanty started taking interest in the manuscript of the book before I could complete it. His interest in and comments on it helped me in very many ways. I have benefited from the criticisms of the publisher's two anonymous readers. In the light of their comments and criticisms I have revised and enlarged my draft. I am grateful for the help of everyone mentioned above.

The material in Chapter 1 has been published under the title "Towards A Philosophical History of Science," in *Philosophy Theory and Action: Essays in Honour of Professor S. S. Barlingay*, edited by K. J. Shah, Rajendra Prasad, and R. Sundara Rajan (Poona: Continental Prakashan, 1980). A version of Chapter 3 was first presented before the seminar on Philosophy in Science at Jadavpur University, February 1980. The material of Chapter 4 has appeared under the title "Remarks on Historiography of Science: Historism and Structuralism," in *Journal of Indian Council of Philosophical Research (JICPR)*, 1, No. 2 (1984) pp.105-135. It was read and discussed earlier in the Friday Seminar, Calcutta. For the comments of the members of the seminar, especially for those of Pranab Sen, I remain grateful. I am equally grateful to my colleagues, Dr. Krishna Roy, Dr. Minakshi Roy Choudhury, and Dr. Chhanda Gupta, with whom I had the opportunity to discuss the themes and arguments of this book time and again. For reading the page proofs and preparing the index Krishna has done so much that I really do not know how to acknowledge adequately my debt to her.

Let me record my thanks to Chandi Ghosh, Satish Bhushan, Asit Dutta, Ajay Kumar, and Renu Bala for their secretarial assistance and much besides.

Apart from my gratitude to the persons named I feel deeply grateful to two institutions, Jadavpur University and Indian Council of Philosophical Research, who have been sustaining me materially, intellectually, and spiritually for a long time.

D. P. CHATTOPADHYAYA
Jadavpur University, Calcutta
Indian Council of Philosophical Research, New Delhi

INTRODUCTION

•••••••••••••••

I

I AM AWARE THAT THE THEMES WHICH I PROPOSE TO SPELL OUT, ARGUE AND establish in this book are rather unconventional.

These days we keep hearing of the philosophy of science, history of science, methodology of science, and the like, but of the historiography of science we hear very rarely.[1] Undoubtedly within the scope of history of science we frequently come across philosophical and methodological problems. But it is to be noted that none of the said disciplines, in either its general or its specialised form, is my basic theme of investigation. That partly explains why my discussion of authors such as Popper and Kuhn is parenthetical and not substantive. I have a theme of my own to explicate, and that is clear from the very explicit (maybe somewhat clumsy) title of the book.

The reason why, in addition to historiography, I am interested in the anthropology of science is an old and influential view that there are certain human societies, tribal ones for example, that are "growthless," that is, have no history to their credit. From the thesis "some societies are historyless" the transition into the next thesis, "some societies are without a history of science," is not very distant. The extremist thesis, "some (primitive) people and their society are prerational and therefore incapable of having any history, still less history of science, of their own," though instructive, has not engaged my pointed attention in this work.

As we know, man has been differently defined by different writers down the centuries, namely, as "(essentially) rational animal," as "tool-using animal," as "sign-using (semiotic) animal," as "existential animal." In each one of these definitions, understandably, the animal nature of man or his biological foundation has been recognised in some way or other. Anthropology, being basically concerned as it is with man, is obviously related to or presupposes one or another of the said definitions. Also the tenability of the claim of the view that man is "essentially historical" is contingent upon the correctness or otherwise of one or more than one definition of man. That by his very animal nature man cannot possibly assume historical dignity is conceded by many thinkers. Naturally the question arises, What enables man to be historical? From Aristotle to Husserl many thinkers have attributed it to his *rationality.* Thinkers such as Marx find in *labour* the seed of human history. Of course, there are many others who refer to God's design as the source of human history.[2]

The distinctions drawn previously between different kinds of history and anthropology and their mutual relation are not to be taken in the strict sense. For example, in the Indian philosophical tradition the distinction between reason and experience is not at all sharp, and in this respect it is markedly different from the Western tradition. Even within the latter the introduction of such terms as *logos, telos,* and *nous* has given rise to immense, not necessarily negative, complexity. It is not a very simple job to explicate the concept of rationality in the human context. Whether reason is paradigmatically human or divine remains a controversial issue. Equally elusive is the answer to the question whether the basic locus of reason is individual human nature or collective culture. Consequently the problems of understanding science, together with its history, are bound to raise a wide range of related issues and problems.

Similarly, the classroom distinction between physical anthropology and cultural anthropology is not as simple as many of us are inclined to believe in our uncritical moments. When we are in our reflective mood we recognise the biological foundation of psychology and the sociological affiliation of the latter. Even the metaphysical dualist feels intellectually obliged to explain the body-mind relation. We go further. In ecology we try to understand how our life on the planet has been shaped by the physical and chemical properties of our environment and also how our life itself, in turn, has been changing our environment, both natural and cultural. Philosophical anthropology tends to blur the dividing edges of physical anthropology and cultural anthropology.[3]

When we reflectively enter into the complexity of anthropology and history we come across numerous problems. Only to a few of them I propose to address myself in this book.

II

If man is *essentially* rational, if every man is an excerpt of *mankind*, whatever he creates or achieves – science, technology, art, society – is bound to bear his imprint. If the *essential* man knows no historical or geographical boundary, his cultural achievements, be those material or spiritual, cannot be absolutely dissimilar. Intriguingly enough, in spite of this "philosophical" assertion, our history is marked by highly uneven cultures. Often we hear of "the dawn of history," "dark age," "the period of Enlightenment," and the like. Similarly in anthropology we find descriptions of different types of society: natural, primitive, pastoral, agricultural or feudal, and industrial. We also hear of "the postindustrial era," "the nuclear age," and the like. Sometimes these different forms are defined in terms of modes of production and distribution. Sometimes relations to our evolving or changing psychological casts are sought.

The labels conventionally attached to different periods of history fail to convey any clear idea about what falls within them. Historical periods and events have in fact been viewed in a highly idealised way or in the reverse, that is, "concretised," way. Analysis shows that both idealisation and concretisation are largely a matter of degree. We cannot get to the events themselves, unless of course we assume that we ourselves literally constitute them, that is, we are their true authors. This extreme view is frequently repudiated and historians and historiographers are often found to be committed to one of the following views:

1. historical events as forming *series*
2. historical events as forming *continuum*, and
3. historical events as forming *unity*.

Again, one may point out, these are ideal types and their different combinations cannot be ruled out. Positively speaking, these are *compossible*.

The same may perhaps be said in the context of an essence-existence distinction. The events that are believed in a rather naive and naturalist manner to be existent, to be "out there in space," are also interpreted as empirical articulations of some essential entities. From one end, what seems to be an *existential* event may from another end well be deemed to be an *essential* event. Whereas writers in the empiricist tradition prefer the naturalist modes of expression, those who follow the transcendental and phenomenological traditions are inclined towards antinaturalist idioms. The latter are unwilling to recognise the existence of "events-in-themselves." To them all events are constituted conjointly by the individual mind and the social mind. In other words, event-identity is a cultural product, that is, is not a natural thing. The phenomenologist tries to show the "concrete unity" between the knowing mind and the known object. In contrast, the naturalist starts with the assumption that there is a gap between the two. The knowing subject and what it wants to know or succeeds in knowing are more or less discrete. This discreteness or distance is primarily rooted in the spatiotemporal difference between the two.

The main debate between the naturalist and the phenomenologist centres around the question whether space-time reality works as a unifying or a differentiating principle in human knowledge. On the outcome of the question depends our view of whether history is essentially anthropological, that is, unitary in character, or whether it is discrete, differential, and distantial. It is in this context that we are reminded of the affinity or otherwise between the synchronic human studies such as anthropology and the diachronic ones such as history. It is not surprising to hear of the view that culture is "sedimented" history or that history is "flowing" culture. It is clear from these metaphorical expressions that human action, understanding, and disposition may be, in fact are, viewed from different ends, spatial and temporal. The events spread over centuries may be viewed as a simultaneous totality. This is evident from the concept of "contemporaneity of history" propounded by such philosophers as Hegel, Croce and Collingwood. One is reminded of the same concept when Husserl speaks of ego's ability to "constitute" other egos, other "things," and all other constituents of culture.[4]

Conversely speaking, the event or thing existentially occupying the same space may be differently discovered or disclosed at different times. The spatial identity of every thing, of every being, lends itself to different temporal articulations and interpretations. Every bit and every chunk of social reality may be understood both historically, that is, as unfolded and flowing reality, and anthropologically, that is, as enfolded within the *essential* nature of man. Related to the question of the relation between history and anthropology is the equally important question of the relation between ontology and epistemology of the social events. The structures of the events are not presented to us as accomplished facts.

Unless the events are structurable, they are not cognitively available to us. The same event may be differently structured. What is part of a local history may also be a constituent of national history, even of global history. But in the enlarged (or reduced) contexts the identity of the event undergoes significant changes. The identity of social reality is hardly context-insensitive. Positively speaking, this context sensitivity of social events, viewed historically or anthropologically, is nothing but a round-about recognition of the underlying human factor, the role of human understanding, interpretation, or, to use another term, constitution.

One of the main questions I intend to answer in the following pages is this: Are the event-structures, structures of scientific events of historical significance, purely local or context-bound? Or have they some global or transcendental import in them? In a sense every scientific achievement is basically individual or intramonadic in character. But this seems to be only one-half of the truth. Had a scientific theory or discovery been exclusively intramonadic, how could it be appreciated, communicated, shared and tested intermonadically, that is, objectively, if not universally? So, although, on the one hand, I shall try to show the context-bound or, at any rate, the context-sensitive character of science, simultaneously I shall also try to show the conditions under which it assumes transcendental character, appreciation, and at times even validation. However, when it comes to the question of transcendental validation, I propose to argue to establish the basic anthropological roots of science. My intention is to explain that a transcendental validation-claim is bound to have an element of imperfection in it. Because man is basically (I am deliberately avoiding the expression "essentially") finite and fallible, his transcendental-cognitive achievements, though in principle recognised, are bound to remain questionable and corrigible. In other words, in opposition to the strong Husserlian thesis, I shall maintain that even the all-comprehensive philosophy as rigorous science constituted by transcendental subjectivity is incomplete and open-ended. Untenability and rejection of the naive positivist view of science, specialised or unified, by themselves do not substantiate the claim of correctness of the transcendental phenomenological view of science. Though well intended, this view is unsustainable in the way it has been formulated. For even within the latter one discovers endless tension. Husserl himself speaks of the necessity of taking philosophy as a perpetual self-critique.[5] Why is this necessity felt at all? If the dream of all comprehensive rigorous science is humanly realisable, why speak of this self-critical necessity? Should we take "critique" as investigation into justificationary principles? Can all the elements of criticism be completely internalised?

III

I will try to draw what seems to me an important distinction between the internal view of science and the external view of it. Every human event, every historical event, may be viewed both ways. If all external views are lightly dismissed as naturalist, the critic may argue that the internal view is vitiated by a sort of solipsism, personal or social. Further, summary rejection of the external view amounts to refusal to recognise the presence and interpretation of other human beings, others' points of view, others' understandings (including misunderstandings). The self or ego by its unilateral authority cannot create or constitute others, their diverse views and values. In brief, the self is not the author of the Other in general.

Underestimation of the external view has another unintended danger. If we keep on arguing that other people belonging to different or alien cultures would never be able to understand our views and actions—science and technology, for example—on the alleged ground of their irremediably subjective character, we concede, perhaps unwittingly, that we ourselves would not be able to understand theirs on the same ground. Though we often entertain a prereflective view that "experimental science," unlike "speculative metaphysics" or "irrational myths," is equally recognisable and acceptable by all people irrespective of their different cultural and historical affiliations, we tend to forget that "myths" of today were "sciences" of yesterdays. We also forget that what is "metaphysics in one culture" is "science in another." Even evaluations of "science" and "metaphysics" are not universalisable. It is no wonder that the phenomenological method is given precedence over the experimental one by some serious philosophers such as Hegel and Husserl. It is equally instructive to note that there are some pronaturalists such as Duhem and Quine, who are not prepared to accord a privileged status even to what is said to be crucial experiments. Given this seemingly anarchic methodological state of affairs, we find that some philosophers, somewhat in despair, resort to transcendental methods purported to do away with epistemic scepticism and methodological anarchism. I would try to show by examining the views, among others, of Kant, Hegel and Husserl that their uses of transcendental arguments have not yielded the desired results. When they claim that they have chased away the ghost of scepticism and achieved certainty, their claim is tainted by a sort of fideism or uncriticisable dogmatism. But I would not enter into exegetical details. That is not my task in this book. I have done it elsewhere.[6]

The question that bothers me time and again is the relation between transcendental idealisation of the given, on the one hand, and natural recognition of the given, on the other. If the exaggerated fear of naturalism and the resulting scepticism goad us to go far in the transcendental direction, we start losing touch with the lifeworld. On the contrary, if we get very close to the given and bogged down into it and fail to raise our head and eyes to gaze distant horizons (of knowledge), our epistemic achievements not only become very modest but also leave us uncertain about their relation to other possible objects of knowledge belonging to distant domains and alien cultures.

In other words, I do recognise the necessity both of transcendental idealisation and the importance of the factual given. At the same time, I see that if the limits of their role are not critically borne in mind, we are likely to derive highly idealised scientific pictures of the world that are not fair and answerable to the insistent facts of life. Alternatively, we may get lost in the naturalist naivete, trying in vain to convince ourselves that we have reached the rock-bottom certainty of experience, and about the rest of the world we may resort to the strategy of "free creation," a sort of instrumentalism, and prefer silence on all "metaphysical" issues. In order to avoid the above extremist views and also, perhaps more so, to be fair to the experience of life I find myself favouring the view that we must start with our own experience, own culture, and the cues provided by them. This "prereflective" starting point, when critically reflected upon, does not appear to me either incorrect or dispensable. To minimise the miseffects of rightly dreaded cultural relativism and to have a *relatively* firm ground of reference where we can repeatedly (but questioningly) return in the hours of needs, theoretical and practical, we must have a *locus* of our own wherefrom we can meaningfully try, go on trying, to understand the larger world around us populated by other things and other beings. In fact, the locus we "choose" is in a sense given to us. We are culturally situated in it. But this situation is neither fixed nor undisturbed.

We are continually being invaded by "alien" ideas and forces, visited by welcome and unwelcome strangers, and, what is more, disturbed by "internal" questions and findings. I will try to show the necessity and problems attending our position in a particular cultural milieu. When we go into the historical details of different cultures and the subcultures such as science and technology within them, we come across parallel problems and comparable enterprises, both theoretical and practical, to solve the same. To substantiate the thesis of cultural evolutionism or parallelism, as distinguished from diffusionism, I would try to make use of one or two well-known examples drawn from the recorded history of science. I refuse to accept cultural absolutism not only because it is somewhat uncritically speculative but also because of its imperviousness or indifference to testing details and hard empirical findings. For these reasons if I allow my view to be moderately relativist or contextualist, I find nothing wrong.

I attach great importance to the testing details of experience, of our own culture and those of other cultures. Broadly speaking, three different levels are discernible in the understanding of cultural details, namely, the descriptive, interpretative and transcendental. At the bottom or descriptive level informative contents are allowed to retain and represent their specific features. At the interpretative level some sort of conceptual reorganisation or "eidetic reduction" is brought about. At this level details are somewhat deliberately ignored and their unitary features highlighted. At the third or transcendental level we try to portray a unitary picture of the details. An attempt to show the meaningful unity of all details is made. Each one of these levels of understanding has its advantageous as well as problematic features. For example, unless we go to the bottom or descriptive level of culture, we fail to explain why in some cases we are culturally blind to the meaningful events and actions of alien cultures. If the unitary features of different cultures are not kept in view, it becomes difficult for us to understand how cross-cultural identification of objects and communication of ideas become possible. From this I am not proposing to jump immediately to the postulated existence of cultural universals as abstract entities. For there are other details to be looked into before we make up our mind on the issue.

IV

I find an instructive parallelism between the problem of understanding an alien culture and that of translating the language of that culture into ours. Basically it seems to me that it is not easy to transplant the "meanings" of one culture into another without any loss or damage in the process. Cultural objects in all their forms are meaningful. Indeterminacy of translation and inadequacy of cross-cultural communication are kindred problems. These problems are felt more acutely at the higher (eidetic-transcendental) levels and less acutely at the ground (descriptive-narrative) levels.

Another related problem which bothers me and engages my attention is the alleged careless attitude of philosophy to history. Why the philosophy at the higher reaches is not disturbed by what goes on "below" them? Why it is so that transcendental philosophy, "rigorous science" at its best, claims to be absolutely binding on whatever falls within its scope? Why it is claimed that the "First Principles" or "Absolute Presuppositions" are not answerable to anything and anyone? I am afraid that unless philosophical principles, in spite of their "transcendental supremacy," are made answerable to the findings of natural science, history and anthropology, what we end up with is an elegant but empty speculative system. By its very nature it forecloses criticism and question. Claiming itself to be a transcendental critique, in effect, it turns out be an essentially justificationist framework. Everything external and critical of it is sought to be internalised and assimilated within it. Its hegemonistic approach and self-validational stance leave nothing in the world or even beyond it which can possibly be its falsifier.

My investigations suggest that this self-righteous transcendental philosophy of First Principles cannot defend itself for long. Because basically it remains a human achievement marked by its necessary attending limitations. Human presuppositions, whatever might be their domain or level, cannot hang awkwardly in the air. Nor are they, strictly speaking, absolute. They are based upon some or other forms of the life-world and addressed to some or other life-problems. History of philosophy and scientific method make it abundantly clear that, rightly understood, the so-called absolute presuppositions are relative and of different levels. They are used sometimes explicitly and sometimes implicitly, depending upon the levels of understanding of the persons concerned. By implication, I propose to contest the view that there may be a form of science or superscience that is absolutely presupposition-free. Neither individual nor society can have a mind that is literally tabula rasa. Influenced by both Kant and Hegel, Collingwood has rightly pointed out that the absolute presuppositions, despite their absolutistic claim, are actually embedded in historical epochs.[7] Though, formally speaking, one may draw distinctions between different levels of presuppositions—logicomathematical, empiricoscientific and philosophicotranscendental—that does not prove that they are not rooted in human history. However, this is not to deny that there are different routes to the roots. This can be persuasively shown by quoting from the works of Husserl, the later Wittgenstein, and Quine on mathematics, science, and society.

The sign-using man, that is, the semiotic being, never ceases to be historical and therefore culture-relative. Every form of his linguistic identification and representation of objects and states of affairs remains more or less indefinite. His definitions work mainly because of some shared forms of life and conventions. If what he ostends is understood correctly by others it is because of their "common intracultural understanding." If objects and persons turn out to be properly nameable, it is not because of some unalterable and *essential* nexus between names and nominata but because of culturally *stable* relationships obtained between them. If the so-called basic statements succeed in serving some basic cognitive purpose, that is mainly due to the human ability of commonly sharing certain (repeatable) experiences of objects under identical normal conditions. Basic statements work because of the efficacy of common conventions, traditions, customs, and so on. In other words, the (ontological) realistic claims even of verifiers and falsifiers, the so-called self-evident statements often believed to be ultimate and unquestionable, are on scrutiny found to derive their authority from social conventions or sedimented history. If these vagaries of indefiniteness or inconsistency disturbingly affect the uses of language within a culture, we can well imagine what will happen to the role of language in the cases of cross-cultural, that is, bilingual and multilingual, communication. It seems that from the paradigm of logical proper names and rigid designators we are thrown back to the complex but rich forms of life.

But then we face another predicament. What we gain in terms of richness from the life-worlds or forms of life seems to be substantially taken away by their natural complexity. Although we are asking, maybe ill-advisedly, for something quite self-evident, we get nothing more than what is complex and conditional. When we, as human beings, crave for "logical neatness" we are condemned by the life-world to some "prelogical clumsiness," especially in our relation to the understanding of alien cultures or subcultures such as science and metaphysics. For example, the science of primitive culture appears to many of us "prelogical" and "bizarre." Even those of us who belong to the "same" philosophical culture are not unanimous in our appreciation of science and metaphysics. Some scientific philosophers find metaphysical statements meaningless. Some metaphysicians are surprised by the learned naivete of the logical positivist or the scientistic philosopher. Of course, there are some philosophers of larger sympathies who find no kind of antagonism between factual details of science and experimental reasoning, on the one hand, and speculative metaphysics and transcendental method, on the other.[8] When I mention all these problems in the context of man as a semiotic being and his linguistic competence what I try to emphasise is that performance of language as an institution cannot be understood and assessed in an abstract and independent manner. We have to look carefully into how it is used, how it is interpreted and reinterpreted. Abstracted from the lifeworld, practical life, the ideal of linguistic clarity is bound to prove elusive.

In my investigations I consciously give some special attention to some aspects of the philosophy of language. I look into different models of language use. I seek to build some models by deliberately disregarding the underlying human factor. Although I do not rule out the possibility of construing language for some specific purpose as *technical* tools, I am mainly interested here in understanding language as both an epistemic and an effective articulation of man's perception of the world within and around him. That leads me to emphasise the role of interpretation of language by language users. Language is used not only for the purpose of interpreting other things and other beings but also, and primarily so, for the purpose of man's self-interpretation. Since man is situated in some or the other cultural milieu he is continuously engaged in interaction with others, in assimilating or rejecting what others have to offer him. In the process man's self-interpretation becomes deepened and enlarged, but not necessarily so. In any case, the self-enlargement of man ceases to be *critical* while he refuses to learn from others' experience, from detected mistakes of his own experience. The uncritical enlargement of man's cognitive horizon becomes uninformative or vacuous if it is not genuinely critical. If every critical or negative component of our knowledge, a sort of self-explication, is sought to be assimilated within the self by favourably reinterpreting it, we may derive a wrong-headed self-satisfaction but not genuine horizonal expansion of knowledge.

In the technical use of language we can of course freely choose our axioms to organise a particular domain of experience, a particular set of objects. But in what lies the rationality of exercising this freedom? Certainly in the sphere of social knowledge we are not basically interested in axiomatising uninformative statements. At some point or other of our cognitive inquiry we feel impelled to examine the adequacy of what we have axiomatised. Conversely speaking, we want our axiomatic system, when it is interpreted, to prove to be consilient with, not negated by, the objects of experience of the domain concerned.

The problem that I raise in connection with the axiomatisation of cognitive domain is a pointer to two other related problems. First, as I have mentioned earlier, signs and symbols by their very nature purport to connect one with many. By one sign we want to signify many similar things. Similarly a symbol seeks to symbolise many things of similar nature. Since similarity is not identity, in every specific case of sign-signified or symbol-symbolised relationship there is bound to be a problematic feature, an element of indefiniteness. Although this is true, one does not know how to get out of it completely. In terms of practice and interpretation, more practice and reinterpretation, we try to minimise the effects of this problematic aspect of language use. Second, this point also proves central in another way to the basic issue dealt with in this· book. We are examining the claims whether different societies – primitive, medieval, modern, and future – and their one particular sub-culture, "science," by whatever name we call it – magic, metaphysics, science or superscience – can be brought under one unitary cognitive structure. In other words, we are critically looking into the transcendental hypothesis that there is a valid way of viewing (or constituting) different societies and their different sub-cultures from a unitary standpoint. This epistemological question, as one can see it, is also bedevilled by one-many relationship, one transcendental cognitive structure and many societies and their subcultures.

V

This epistemological question, like the previous linguistic one, assumes added significance because of its human roots. The problem may be put in this way. Can man, being finite and fallible as he is, really have in him a cognitive ability which is so comprehensive and authentic that by it he can not only understand all different societies and their sub-cultures but also succeed in relating them as a single meaningful whole. This question may be formulated both synchronically (anthropologically) and diachronically (historically). The historiographer raises the question using his own idioms: how a historiographer of science, situated as he is within a particular culture and its particular language, can possibly go back into the vanished societies of the past and correctly recapture their different sub-cultures? Is he not prevented or handicapped by the logic of his own situation, by the physics of his own space-time framework and the latter's distance from the past societies and their cultural achievements? Unless history can somehow be effectively dissociated from the space-time frameworks of the past (and the future) societies, it is difficult to see how a historiographer of today can correctly understand the sciences of yesterday and those of tomorrow. To put it differently, to make the ideal of transcendental history actually available, *time-bound* history needs to be dehistorised, that is, de-temporalised. Can the transcendental historiographer of science perform this humanly impossible feat? To what extent can he transcend his time and place, culture and language, within which his own standpoint is located? Is self-transcendence a mere ideal or gradually achievable programme? Do the executor of this programme and his collaborators know the end to which they are aiming? If the end is not substantially available to them, how can they possibly assess and evaluate their cognitive achievements? Since the ideal of rationality defined in terms of correspondence theory of truth is not available to them because of their endwise approach, and since they have to go by the ideal of rationality defined in terms of consistency or the logic of noncontradiction, it is difficult to see how their transcendental claim could be anything more than very partial and modest. Yet it is rather surprising that the defender of transcendental historiographer keeps on claiming that his programme is best and is free of all the traces of scepticism and relativism that allegedly bedevil the positivist account of the history of science.

How is history possible? Must it be factually detailed and narrative? Or, is history more intelligible and meaningful when it is transcendentally structured and unified? These are the basic questions that I shall be trying to answer in the book from different points of view. While delineating the answers, generally speaking, I have consciously decided to concentrate more on the main arguments and less on their concerned authors. But, in the case of examining the rival claims of historism and dialectical reason, on the one hand, and structuralism and analytic reason, on the other, I feel it necessary to refer to the authors themselves in details. Is there any dichotomy between self and other? Do they form a continuum? Or are they articulations of one and the same unity? In their answers to these basic questions I find that Sartre as a historiographer and Lévi-Strauss as an anthropologist have very interesting things to say, which are very close to my own approach to the main themes of the book.[9]

Sartre's commitment to dialectical reason leads him to emphasise the developing and continuous character of history. Time and needs are the basic concepts used by him to explain the formation and transformation of cultural totalities as developing historical units. Since the Sartrean self is practically free and the main dynamic of history, Sartre is obliged to recognise the existence of both conflicting and cooperative elements in every cultural totality. The same dynamics accounts for detotalisation and retotalisation of different historical units. While he emphasises the continuous (creative and occasionally degenerative) character of the historical process of totalisation, detotalisation, and retotalisation, Lévi-Strauss tries to highlight their unitary-structural character. Unless this structural approach is followed, it is argued, we fail to understand that the distinction between different cultures is only contextual and not qualitative. The naturalist view that some societies are "primitive and prelogical" and some others are "civilised and logical" cannot be convincingly combated unless the unitary-structural approach is understood and followed. This sort of distinction is to be traced to the qualitative approach, leading us to believe that some societies are indeed more developed and some others less so. According to the structuralist, the distinction between a "modern" tool (steel axe) and a "primitive" one (stone axe) is misleadingly comparative. The issue should be viewed as one of culture-bound objects and in terms of some "cultural universals" that are not circumscribed by local or regional histories. But in and through the latter the former are expressed and become intelligible. Once we follow the real import of cultural universals, it is claimed, we will not draw any arbitrary distinction between, say, "myth-logic" and "math-logic." This and other similar distinctions are traced by the structuralist to Sartre's pro-Cartesian ontological dualism between Self and Other.

Predictably, Sartre pleads not guilty to the charge and argues that the distinction between self and other is being historically narrowed down through development and practical effects of dialectical reason. Instead of viewing self and other as constituents of a unitary structure, it is claimed, in the course of satisfying our needs and exercising our freedom we are narrowing the gap between the two. Taking the war to the enemy camp Sartre critically points out that the Straussian cultural universals are mere "constructs of analytical reason," unfair to the ethnographic facts and basically unhistorical in character. In order to work out a rational history of science Sartre advises us not to rely upon the structuralist's analytical reason but to consult details of other cultures and of other epochs. The main problem one has to tackle here is whether I or we constitute or recognise the details of other cultures. If the individual self (or even the social self) is credited with the freedom and competence to constitute other cultures as totalities to be studied, by implication, the structuralist critically points out, the historian denies himself what he does claim to have. In that case the historian of the Sartrean persuasion, according to Lévi-Strauss, is unable to entertain any external criticism. All criticism then turns out to be self-criticism, self's free criticism. This unilateral freedom of criticism is opposed by the structuralist. How the human cogito (I or We) can be as doubt-free and as certain as the Cartesian cogito, berating, if not denying altogether, the existence and free actions of *other* I's and *other* We's, that is, their cultural praxis, the basic stuff and dynamics of history. Further, the structuralist denies the charge that he is antihistorist. On the contrary, he claims that his approach is doubly historical, both germinally and terminally, that is, initially and finally. But he hastens to add that whereas history is merely informative, anthropology is comprehensive. What is more, the historian himself, maybe unconsciously, is also a structuralist of a sort. The details he frequently speaks of are in fact structured and therefore meaningful. The historian's continuum, in the structuralist's view, is a flattened unitary picture.

The rationale of the Sartre-Strauss debate brings us back to the old distinction between narrative or unfolded history and transcendental or enfolded history. One feels that in spite of Lévi-Strauss's prohistorical self-defence, in his structuralist scheme of unitary history time gets frozen. If "comprehensive" anthropology is not in any way disturbed by historical "information" or ethnographic findings, one is somehow led to believe that cultural universals are indeed analytical constructs and mere explanatory heuristics, not historically testable hypotheses. How can the structures which make history possible and intelligible be tested or criticised by it? Whether this is a one-sided view or not can be decided only when we go deeply into the details of the related issues.

When anthropology is described as a branch of semiology, we notice two complementary aspects of it, namely, (1) man interprets himself in terms of certain definite signs and symbols and (2) his culture itself is also a system of signs and symbols. Man cannot interpret himself without using the signs and symbols by which he is environed or in which he is inducted by virtue of his affiliation to a particular culture. To put it differently, his self-interpreting signs and symbols are derived from others and not entirely invented by himself. He, in isolation, cannot legislate the relation between a sign and what it signifies. Others' appearance in the scene of significance is inevitable, that is, an integral part of man's social affiliation. However, to say this is not to deny man's capacity to constitute new signs and symbols or to bestow new meanings, referential or sense, to the existing ones. It is well known that meanings of words undergo change over time. Larger dictionaries of different languages convincingly show us how the same words keep on assuming new meanings and losing the old ones. Semiology or semantics is therefore to be distinguished from the archaeology of meaning. Not only word meanings but also grammatical rules undergo slow historical change.

What I am asserting in the context of linguistic signs and symbols may easily be extended to other areas of culture. The meaningfulness of cultural objects is not a static thing. It is basically historical. Since human beings are the main authors of history, one might say, the meaningfulness of cultural objects is rooted in human nature, that is, anthropological in character. My reflections suggest that the complementarity of history and anthropology is to be understood in terms of human nature. But, as indicated before, on the very question, what "human nature" is like, philosophers hardly agree. In order to understand how history and anthropology are related in the context of science as subculture I propose to examine some received models of sign-signified relationship. My researches in this area have gradually convinced me of the inadequacy and imperfection of the "fixed" and "rigid" models. Their main defect lies in their insufficient recognition of man as the author of the *changing* systems or totalities of signs and symbols. Once the basic human roots of semiotic systems are deeply understood, the creative, dynamic, or historical features of cultural objects as signs and symbols become increasingly clearer. That helps us to get rid of the Platonic views that "meanings" are abstract entities, "propositions" are eternal unities, and the like. Once our mind is purged of these fallacious notions, we are able to follow clearly the intimate relation between the life-world and its idealised view, between anthropology of science and history of science – and between different levels – narrative, structural, and so on – of history.

VI

Finally I will attempt to show that the supposed distinction between structuralism and historism is untenable in its strict form and in the context of understanding of science. Neither the antihistorism of the Cartesian-Kantian tradition nor the antistructuralism of the Marxist-Heideggerian tradition is tenable in its purely exclusive form. My detailed examination of the Sartrean and the Straussian views is intended to drive home this basic point.

I approach the same issue from another end. Success and even failure of communication and conversation indicate that we can overcome the postulated Self-Other dichotomy. The historian's ability to write the history of science of past and distant cultures is indicative of his success in communicating, conversing with their authors, and understanding their thoughts and actions. In spite of (and also because of) the historian's rootedness in one culture, he can rethink and reenact in his mind what was thought of and done by other people in other past or alien cultures. This fact gives credence to different sorts of universals: biological, psychological, linguistic and spiritual. While I examine these views I speak of *human universals* in terms of which I find it very plausible to understand and explain intercultural identification of objects and communication of ideas.

In the process I will try to defend a sort of internal realism that attempts to show plausibly how "the same" world (consisting of different cultures) may be differently, and yet truly, grasped. My version of internal realism aims at disclosing the anthropological roots of science. It purports to explain how different worldviews, "factual" as well as "fictitious," scientific and mythic, are constituted and understood.

In this connection, I criticise and reject different forms of external realism often alluded to as naive naturalist or positivist modes of thought. At the same time, I would like to point out why the transcendentalist response to it, unless critically qualified, runs into heavy weather. Unduly scared of the different conceptual frameworks and the divergent worldviews, we need not resort to a sort of transcendentalism that tries to show that every point of view, and every form of science based thereon, is a mere articulation of one, and a universal, transcendental standpoint.

It is in this context that I specially refer to the seminal view of Husserl. Against the background of his understandable anxiety to do away with scepticism and relativism I take his defence of transcendental philosophy, particularly the concept of transcendental subjectivity, as the supreme constitutive principle of an "all-comprehensive rigorous science." While I do appreciate Husserl's ingenious effort to construct a full-fledged transcendental philosophy, and take due notice of his improvement upon the Kantian transcendentalism and his significant reference to the life-world, simultaneously I try to indicate the point where it fails to be genuinely critical and self-critical. Called upon to perform the double duty of *idealising* the life-world in science and of *concretising* the transcendental self-experience in the life-world, I find, to my dismay, the constitutive principle of transcendental subjectivity encounters no difficulty and faces no criticism whatsoever. To me, this "success story" appears surprisingly anticritical. All critical elements are dubbed as "external" and "naturalist" and sought to be internalised effortlessly. Hence, I critically refer to Husserl's hybrid concept of "historical a priori," reminiscent of Kant's "synthetic a priori." I hear the echoes of a priori justificationism of Kant in Husserl, despite the latter's commitment to the life-world. I would argue that the weakness of Husserl's transcendentalism lies mainly in his inadequate recognition of the critical significance of the life-world.

At this point, I briefly refer to some post-Husserlian thinkers who are sympathetic to his position and yet perceptive of the shortcomings of transcendental subjectivity as a critique as well as an explication of human experience.[10]

Notwithstanding my criticism of Husserl I also try to demonstrate where the basic strength of his transcendental philosophy lies. I refer to some modern philosophers of science such as Popper, Quine, and Kuhn, whose views are not ordinarily, even remotely, associated with transcendentalism. I would argue, referring to their views, to the effect that some moderate form of transcendentalism or other is absolutely necessary for making science and its history possible and intelligible. Even minimal science needs the principles of systematisation that are bound to be relatively independent of what they are required to systematise. And these are the principles that are responsible for the intelligibility and the intercultural communicability of what science is. Despite their abstract and general form I try to point out why they should be regarded as both anthropological and historical, anthropological because of their rootedness in human nature and historical because of their changeable, criticisable, and yet identifiably continuous character.

To the reader of this study of mine it will be clear that, though initiated in and familiar with the Western analytic tradition of philosophy, particularly philosophy of science, I have been trying to tackle some problems by using some basic concepts of phenomenology and existentialism. If my familiarity with the history of Indian philosophy of science has not been extensively brought to bear upon the themes of the book, it is mainly because of my feeling that many of these problems owe their origin to the bifurcation of epistemology into empiricism and rationalism. Since, fortunately, in Indian philosophy mutual exclusivity of reason and experience is not generally recognised, most anthropological and historiographical problems pertaining to the knowledge of other minds, other times, and cultures are not prominent. This, however, does not mean that the problems of science did not engage the attention of Indian philosophers or—as has been said by some uninformed critics—that Indian thought has no articulate philosophy of time or history. If we believe in cultural parallelism, that is, that fundamental problems of theory and practice are more or less found in all cultures, it would be difficult to conclude that only the people of certain cultures have a privileged access to the basic issue of human life and living.

In fact, one of the aims of this book is to show that the problems of the life-world are more or less similar and that their difference lies in how they are *thematised* and sought to be solved in diverse ways by the people living under different natural and cultural conditions. What I mean, philosophically speaking, is this: as members of the same species all human beings have something in common but that does not negate their cultural difference. It is in this context that one has to understand my concept of *human universals*. These are neither abstract entities nor innate ideas. The very fact that all human beings, in spite of their difference in different spheres of life, can more or less communicate among themselves strongly suggests that they have the necessary *capacity* within them. One need not describe this capacity as innate in the sense that it is self-operative or self-actualisable irrespective of our circumstances of life and our actions Our self-enlargement, both within and without, both in theory and in practice, is largely dependent upon how we act vis-à-vis the problems of our life-world.

Human universals are simultaneously presupposed, authored, and used by ourselves. Both documented history and anthropology lend abundant support to this view. It is for this reason that I have tried to work out how the complementary perspectives of anthropology and historiography help us enormously to understand some basic problems of science both as an institution and as a cognitive enterprise. This work is partially born of my feeling that contemporary philosophy of science in the analytic tradition is unnecessarily abstract and contaminated by extratheorisation. However abstractly it may be problematised, thematised and formulated, science continues to be a basic form of life-activity. Unless this fundamental truth is understood by us, our analytic-theoretic refinement cannot substantially help us to solve the well-known problems of philosophy of science.

CHAPTER ONE

A Historiography of Science: Some Preliminaries

LET US THINK OF A SOCIETY CALLED PRIMITIVE SOCIETY (PS) AT A TIME T1 with a number of wise men called Magicians (M) in it. Let us think of another society called Medieval Society (MS) at a time T2 with a number of wise men called Philosophers (P) in it. Let us think of still another society called Contemporary Society (CS) at a time T3 with a number of wise men called Scientists (S) in it. Let us take PS, MS, and CS as *ideal types* of historical societies, that is, not descriptions of this or that actual society. T1, T2, and T3, the time-addresses of PS, MS, and CS, are also ideally sliced segments of history, that is, not photo-mnemonic reproductions of this or that particular time. PS(T1), MS(T2), and CS(T3) are, from my point of view, only conceptually successive, and I need not suppose that they are successive in the objective time-order.

Ideally sliced segments of history can be simultaneously pictured before the eye of the mind and studied as separate parts of one single unrolled carpet of time, or, should I say, slightly curved canvas of space. Simultaneity and history of PS(T1), MS(T2), and CS(T3) are not intrinsically incompatible concepts. The "same" phenomena, in this case societies, can be studied from two different but complementary points of view, historical and sociological. History may be sociologised and sociology historised. Different and separate societies, such as PS(T1), MS(T2), and CS(T3), may also be looked at as ordered in the scale of time. When I see segments as segments I have already in a sense spatialised time.

And it is no wonder that one raises one's eyebrow when one hears for the first time the theoretical term *contemporaneity* of history. To break the spell of wonder one must be reminded that it is impossible for one's understanding to escape its basic affiliation to its cultural environment, which includes, among other things, theories, beliefs, norms, and forms of action. For example, when I am trying to understand diachronically, that is, historically or synchronically – that is – sociologically, science as a particular set of activities, or a corpus of beliefs, or both, I and others as well must reflectively bear in mind that my understanding itself is culturally affiliated to one or other CS(T3). Affiliated as I am to CS(T3), in certain respects I may be enjoying more advantages than you of MS(T2) or he of PS(T1) in the matter of understanding the ideas of the wise men, S, Scientists, but, with my understanding embedded in CS(T3), it often proves very difficult for me to turn my understanding on the presuppositions, assumptions, shared beliefs,and so on,etc. that are *almost* constitutive of CS(T3). Moreover, culturally at a distance from, or being somewhat alien to, MS(T2) and PS(T1), I cannot easily get into the structures of the ideas of the wisemen of MS(12), that is, P, and those of PS(T1), that is, M. The structures of the activities and ideas of S, P, and M are not only conceptually successive but also partially overlapping and mutually inclusive, and, therefore, cross-cultural identification, cognition, and communication are possible.

Let us think of a society called Future Society (FS) at a time T4 with a number of wisemen called Superscientists (SS) in it. It is also an ideal-type society that can only be structurally (and not specifically) described. Our forecast about the activities, achievements, and beliefs of the laymen, especially of the wisemen or SS of FS(T4), is bound to have a ring of fictionality around it for my ear, which is used to the tune of S of CS(T3) for years.

Fact=fiction dualism is primarily, but not entirely, intellectual and contextual. The net of fiction is cast to catch the elusive but supposedly existing fishes of facts. The cast of the laymen is wide and that of the wisemen narrow, for the former knows only vaguely what fact he is after, whereas the latter knows pretty precisely. The line of demarcation drawn between facts and fictions or that between science, on the one hand, and nonscience, comprising myths, metaphysics, and other forms of speculation with thin content, on the other, and the criteria used for the purpose of drawing the lines are somewhat peculiar to the concerned society or even community within it. The nature of the problems under consideration suggests the line and criteria of demarcation. As already stated, the wisemen=layman distinction should be understood in a culture-relative way.

I may be accused of indulging in an extreme form of relativism and my proposed theory of the history of science and philosophy criticised as a purely contextualist and therefore ad hoc one. I plead not guilty to the charges. I would submit that to avoid the more serious charges of anthropomorphism, cultural hegemonism, ethnocentrism, or even absolutism one is perhaps well advised to be a critical contextualist. When I say "my understanding" of other societies is bound to be shaped by the structure and capacities of my understanding which in their turn are influenced by my culture, I am giving a mere reflective description of a complex situation and trying to avoid the fallacy of the absolutist rationalist whose unilateral "cognitive" verdict on other cultures seems to suggest that he has a privileged access to the meanings and aims of the activities and beliefs of other persons, such as, M of PS(T1), P of MS(T2), S of CS(T3), and SS of FS(T4). My question is: who am I or, for that matter who is absolutist to say that they do not know what they mean when they say, do, and believe something, or, what is worse, that they are not logically equipped for the purpose. It is better we recall that not only ethics and economics but also geometry and logic have behind them long historical careers. We should also remember that the culture-oriented character of one's understanding is no hindrance to one's understanding of others' activities and beliefs, that is, magic, philosophy, or science. It is evident from numerous perceptive histories of science written from articulate or inarticulate sociological or anthropological points of view. Of course, there is always a difference between a good history of science and a bad one whatever might be the author's point of view. All factors being equal, a historian who is reflectively and critically conscious of the sociological, linguistic, and other cultural factors that influence his understanding is expected to give more correct accounts of others' achievements, scientific or otherwise, than those who are not so conscious. Contextinvariant and theory-neutral history and pure-observation language are chimeras.

Every society has its own models of layman, wisemen, physician, priest, philosopher, scientist. But the words do not mean the same things everywhere: PS(T1) or MS(T2) or CS(T3). Even within our own society these words are used to mean different things in different contexts. Sometimes the layman thinks and acts as the wiseman does; the opposite also happens. Sometimes the philosopher performs the duties of the priest and also those of the scientist. What is very important to bear in mind is the precise time context we are talking of. In PS(T1) and MS(T2), for instance, the roles of the wiseman, the physician, the priest, the philosopher, and the scientist had not been sharply defined; rather they all had been practically rolled into one. Compared to what one sees in the CS(T3), the principles of division of labour were much less carried out in PS(T1) and MS(T2) and, given the present trend, are likely to be even more practised in FS(T4). The authors of the Vedas had various qualities admirably harmonised, namely, poetic-artistic talents, scientific insight, philosophical vision, and power of thought. The early Greek cosmologists—Thales, Anaximander, and Anaximenes—were also both scientists and philosophers. The point has been persuasively argued by, among others Ueberweg, Windle-band and B. N. Seal.

> If by science we understand that independent and self-conscious work of intelligence which seeks knowledge methodically for its own sake, then it is among the Greeks . . . of the sixth century B.C., that we first find such a science,—aside from some tendencies among the peoples of the Orient, those of China and India partic-ularly, only recently disclosed. The great civilised peoples of earlier antiquity were not, indeed, either in an abundance of information on single subjects, or in general views of the universe; but the former was gained in connection with practical needs, and the lat-ter grew out of mythical fancy, so they remained under the con-trol, partly of daily need, partly of religious poetry. . . .[1]

It is instructive to bear in mind that the great names in Hindu medicine, Susruta (fifth century B.C.) and Caraka (second century B.C.), and those in Graeco-Roman world, Hippocrates, a contemporary of Susruta, and Galen, a contemporary of Caraka, mastered several other branches of knowledge than the one with which their fame remains most intimately associated. All of them had thorough grounding in the First Principles of Knowledge, or what we can term *philosophy* these days. Leonardo da Vinci (1452-1519) and Leibniz (1646-1714) were versatile genius of the very rare type: the former was not only an extraordinary painter, sculptor, architect and engineer but also a gifted scientist and a philosopher; the latter left his marks on such diverse fields as logic, mathematics, mechanics, geology, jurispru-dence, history, linguistics, and theology. Neither in the early ages nor in the Middle Ages was the principle of the division of labour prevalent in the field of knowledge as we see it practised today. Every age, as I have said, has its own intuitive, that is, undefined, notions of the layman, the wiseman, the physician, the engineer, and so on, and operates with the same. Of course, the notions change slowly over the centuries, over the decades, but at times the notions change fast and almost in a revolutionary manner. I say "almost" because the revolution itself has its own seminal history and, once it is brought about by the genius of an Archimedes, or Arya Bhatta, or of a Copernicus, or an Einstein, it does not take at least the informed by stupefying surprise.

Another point that is very important and of which we can be easily conscious on reflection is this. We tend to accept most of the parts of our cultural heritage, except those about which we can claim to have firsthand or professional acquaintance, almost as a matter of course: without serious questions or criticism. As I happen to be a professional philosopher, my questioning attitude and critical outlook are almost entirely confined to currently influential philosophical theories and arguments. Insofar as other areas of knowledge, such as, medicine, meteorology, economics, engineering, physics, and especially their higher reaches and latest findings are concerned, we generally accept, rely, and act on the specialists' views. To us, the outsiders and the laymen, specialists' views are an integral part of culture. Unless these views prove inconsistent with or problematic to our otherwise conventionally accepted culture, we do not turn our critical queries on them.

Ordinarily one is not critically disposed to the whole of one's culture, whether that culture is PS(T1) or MS(T2) or CS(T3) or whether that one is a layman or a wiseman or a specialist in the context concerned. One tends to believe and accept all nonproblematic elements or aspects of one's culture as almost inseparable parts of one's own being. Language and all that is preserved in it, customs, myths, conventions, and so on, not only surround us but also penetrate deep into our personality structure, obviously not in a uniform or repetitious way. The problematic features of a culture can hardly be identified and communicated in a person-invariant, or purely objective, manner. The symptoms of a person's bodily behaviour that appear to me absolutely normal may immediately disturb an expert diagnostician who can read in them a danger signal of a grave illness. A problem is an objectively disturbed area of one's conceptual network enabling one to truly think of, and successfully act in, the world in which one lives.

Generally speaking, we take only certain practical problems, war, strike, epidemic diseases, energy crisis, and inflation, for example, as universal or at least near universal in their scope. In respect to theoretical problems the scope becomes universal only in those rare cases when the proposed solutions result in revolutionary changes in the prevalent worldviews, the sort of revolutionary changes associated with the names of Marx, Freud, and Einstein in CS(T3). One is advised to bear in mind that there are some theory-intoxicated men who take their theoretical problems more seriously than the seriousness which characterise the common man's approach to each practical problems as the runaway rise in the consumer's price index, transport strike, or energy crisis. Theory-intoxication may be of a different sort resulting in distortion beyond recognition of other cultures in one's own culture. I have argued the point, the theory-practice dialectic, elsewhere.[2]

That nearly all of us accept our culture, at any rate most of its elements, rather uncritically, and think and act conventionally has been very persuasively analysed by, among others, Hayek in a somewhat different, although related, context. In the course of giving his view on the nature of the subject matter of social studies he says, "A medicine or a cosmetic, e.g., for the purposes of social study, is not what cures an ailment or improves a person's look, but what (the concerned) people think will have that effect."[3] To say this is *not* to suggest that the subject matters of all social studies are equally and irremediably subjective or remain identically so over a long period of time; still less does it mean any offence to a realistic worldview, that is, that the World (in a sense) is there independently of how it is thought of, for instance, by M of PS(T1), P of MS(T2) or S of CS(T3). A word of caution. The ontological question, Whether there is World independently of its being perceived or conceived by a man or a group of man? is logically different from the epistemological question, How that independent World is perceived or conceived? True, to make the answer to the ontological question clear and intelligible it has to be brought closer to, and perhaps formulated to a great extent in terms of, the answer to the epistemological one. Conceptual inseparability of the answers to the questions does not logically oblige one to believe that the imports of the questions themselves are identical. Laying too much emphasis either on the slogan of *esse est percipi* or on that of *esse est concipi* we are avoidably caught in an erratic and almost endless swing between the two extreme forms of constructivism. I am not opposed to constructivism in every form. On the contrary, some persistent features of *every* cultural life, namely, interpersonal and intercultural communication of ideas and experiences, cross-cultural identification of objects, and so on, are indicative of the *general* truth of methodological constructivism. Methodological constructivism is *not* inconsistent with ontological realism.[4] But, unfortunately, often the one-sided advocacy of the case of constructivism tends to make us blind to the fact that its *general* truth-claim is ontologically warranted and sustainable. And this would be evident from both critical reflections on the findings of the working anthropologists and conclusions of the historians of science.

The concepts of relativism, contextualism and constructivism are closely interrelated. Theories and practices, science and technology, of a society are best understandable in the context of that particular society, relating them to the coherent system of beliefs accepted by the people of that society. And on demand the concerned people can also produce or indicate a body of evidence in support of their beliefs. The evidence-relative character of their beliefs sets a limit to the subjectivity of the beliefs and somewhat insulates the same from the biases and prejudices of the individual human being. Close scrutiny of the evidence forming a coherent system and on which one is obliged to fall back in defence of his beliefs, theories, practices, and so on, reveals that they themselves in turn, that is, at a different level, are questionable and corrigible. Thus the history of science and technology of a society, questioned and corrected in the light of disturbing and testing evidence, changes, at times slowly and at times rapidly, over a period of time.

The questions and corrections affecting the course and career of science and technology need not be necessarily internal. They may be external as well. For the people of other societies, belonging to other cultures, in spite of their initial handicap due to what may be called cultural distance, can and do understand the ideas and actions of our society. Contextualism does not mean cultural solipsism. Every society has its two complementary images: how it presents itself to itself and how it appears or projects itself to other selves. The projected image may be an appearance in the sense that it may not have a point-to-point correspondence with the self-image of the society, but that does not mean that its personality is split. In other words, ontological unity and identity of a society are quite consistent with its dual or even multiple images. By implication this also suggests a limit to the thesis of constructivism that I accept partially and only partially.

The burden that new information generally imposes on a rational man is that the relation of the new information to the other organised information with which the latter operates has to be defined, however provisional that definition may be. I draw a distinction between *knowl-*

edge and *information* in this context. Knowledge is more demanding than information in the matters of seeking and accepting its place in one's world of beliefs and activities. As I have said, this is generally, and not, in all cases, true. For some people information provided by a particular source or authority carries the weight of knowledge. "Who accepts whose authority?" illustrates a sort of question that cannot be answered in a universally acceptable form. The norms of acceptability cannot be defined in a context-invariant manner. The same point holds good in the case of the concept of rational man. There is no single or unique rational man by reference to whom one can uniquely define the relations between information and knowledge.[5] PS, MS, and CS have their own models of rational man, relation between knowledge and information, and criteria of acceptability. Each one of these models, we must bear in mind, has logical room for several submodels within it. The rational man, Magician of PS, may accept a particular piece of information, such as, a message of God conveyed through a priest, as quite consistent with what he accepts as a system of scientific knowledge, Magic, whereas the rational man, Scientist of CS, may think either that the said information is inconsistent with his system of scientific knowledge, S, or that it and S are consistent provided the terms *message of God, priest,* and *conveyance* are interpreted in a way which is consistent with S. In the latter case the acceptability of the information is contingent upon its interpretation's meeting the requirements of S. In principle it is, then, open to several interpretations meeting the requirements of different systems of scientific knowledge, such as, Magic (M), Philosophy (P), Science (S), and Superscience (SS).

This line of my argument may lead one to believe that, in spite of my denial, I propose to defend a strong thesis of contextualism. The defender of this thesis, it is suggested, encounters many difficulties in answering such questions as, which one of the interpretations of a particular piece of information is to be accepted and which of the available criteria is actually useful for the purpose? Besides, such ontological questions as, What is there behind the information? are also bound to raise difficulties. The major difficulty that bothers one is perhaps this. All these questions can be answered, broadly speaking, in two different ways: internally, from within a particular society and consciously bearing that society alone in mind, and externally, from within a particular society but bearing well in mind the views entertained on the matter by other societies and trying to understand them coherently. I prefer the term *understanding* to *rational reconstruction* because of its flexible logical connections. Although I try to understand the ideas and activities of other persons belonging to other societies, I cannot completely rise above the influences of the society to which I myself belong historically, linguistically, culturally, and in various other ways. This relation of my belonging to my society can never be completely fathomed and clearly expressed. In this sense every answer to the preceding questions is bound to be internal. There is a limit to the sense in which a person can be exclusively preoccupied with the ideas and activities of his own society, completely ignoring those of others. For every society is culturally more or less open-ended, without any *culture-neutral protective belt* thrown around it, ensuring its autonomous existence and growth. Stated differently, *in real-life situations cultural interaction is inescapable.* But there is a significant difference between *entertained cultural interaction* and *imposed cultural interaction.* Under the conditions of imposed cultural interaction one has to react almost without freedom to external cultural stimuli. Consequently, the nature of the reactions tends to be clumsy, ill-formulated, vaguely or loosely connected with the rest of one's cultural acquisitions. The external cultural stimuli with which one is obliged to interact are of diverse sorts: a flying saucer, a strange object; a talking tiger, an incredible story; an act of rising again to life from the dead, a strange episode; an infallible future-telling machine, an unbelievable "invention"; a physician who can cure all diseases, a god who is all-knowing and all-powerful. From one's point of view each one of these examples may appear extraordinary. Little reflection is necessary to convince ourselves that this is not necessarily the case. Even to what we regard as ordinary external cultural stimuli our reactions are almost compulsive, although the consequences thereof on our system of ideas and activities may not be conspicuous or serious. The entertained cultural reactions are in most cases anticipated, selective, orderly, well-formulated, and more or less clearly connectable to the rest of our cultural acquisitions. If the full implications of what I call the inescapability of cultural interactions with or responses to the external stimuli are adequately realised, I think, the idea that I propose to defend a strong version of contextualism will be quietly abandoned. It is a sort of conversationalism or communicationism that involves the "presence" of both Self and Other, we and they.

The case and strength of contextualism as I understand it will be clear to one if one carefully studies how cultural interactions internally work. *Culture*, like *language*, is an umbrella term. It refers to certain nonuniform, developmentally uneven, and culturally interacting units.

The relation of these subcultural units to the concerned overall culture is like that of the dialects of a particular language to the language itself. The borderlines of the subcultures are overlapping, interpenetrating and changing. Subcultures may be viewed in two different ways, vertically and horizontally. Vertically, a culture, such as the Indian, may be viewed as the totality of several subcultures, communities, of Bengal, of Gujrat, of Punjab, of Tamilnadu,and so on. Horizontally, a culture may be understood as a totality of different strata of subcultures, of arts, morals, religion, technology, language, and so forth. A map of a language showing the relations and ranges of its dialects cannot be neatly drawn, at least not correctly, using only one colour or type of marking: vertical, horizontal, or diagonal. One experiences comparable difficulties in drawing a map of a culture showing correctly the relations and ranges of its subcultures. What is even more difficult to show by drawing is the tie that binds the subcultures together. Political administration may be referred to as a well-recognised unifying tie. But history abounds with illustrations showing the impotence of polity to define intersubcultural relations. Culture has often been found to have defied and crossed the boundaries of polity. It is equally difficult to show the *depth dimensions of culture* – aesthetic, ethical, and religious – encompassing all the subcultures. These difficulties are inherent in the very character of culture. Needless to say, the act of drawing a map of culture or language is itself a cultural act. Nature knows no mapping, no border or boundary on its geophysical surface. Even a "physical boundary" is a human artefact.

The interactions of the subcultures among themselves generate a *conflict-cooperation situation*. The unevenness of the depth dimensions also generates a similar situation. Industrial culture promotes individualism, petrifies interpersonal relations, and creates the conditions of alienation. The dominant force in CS is industrial culture. Agrarian culture lays emphasis on the community life, favours the joint (that is, molecular) family system and face-to-face relations, and frowns upon the individual's right to question the community ethos. The dominant force in MS is agrarian culture. At times industrial culture is taken as a synonym of city culture and agrarian culture of village culture. Almost all cultures are composite in the sense that some of their subcultures are dominantly agrarian and some others dominantly industrial. The dominant forces of PS are generated by hunting, fishing and fruit-picking. As I have said before, the same society is often found to be an unplanned locus of different cultures, different subcultures, each known by its dominant force or the *mode of production*. The dominant mode of production is not the only way to understand the identity and function of a culture. At certain stages the cultures of a society are better understood in terms of religious movement or warfare. The role of ideas in shaping the course and career of a culture must not be assimilated under the role of the mode of production. The interaction between these two roles is not one-sided. The normal dominance of the mode of production is occasionally interrupted by a novel and very influential idea or a set of ideas.

Ideas are both products and producers of culture. The course and contents of a culture, normally expressed in its ideas and ideals, are at times questioned, criticised, and corrected by newly found ideas. When the culturally inherited ideas and ideals of a society fail to satisfy the growing needs, material and intellectual, of a sizable section of its members, an objective situation necessitating the search for discovery and acceptance of new ideas and ideals is created. The said needs are generated by interaction between culture and culture, that is, externally, and, also, perhaps more so, by interaction among the subcultures, that is, internally. The needs are expressed in the forms of problem and even crisis.

In PS(T1) the external stimuli prove really disturbing, almost disruptive. But, in the absence of a *culture-neutral protective belt* around it, every PS(T1) has to learn to live with the "disturbances" of the external origin; gradually in the process it partly adjusts itself to the stimuli, partly internalises the latter, and partly resists and rejects the same.[6] Having learned how to respond to the external stimuli and having internalised the messages of the external cultures, MS(T2) and particularly CS(T3) are better equipped in terms of materials and intellectual apparatuses than PS(T1) to turn their critical and pointed attention to the problematic features of internal stimuli produced by the interactions of the structurally heterogeneous and functionally uneven subcultures. The veiled comparative evaluation of the cultural acquisitions of PS(T1), MS(T2), and CS(T3) as implied in my preceding, sentence shows my own cultural grounding or point of view, which, as I have already said, may be concealed up to a point but cannot be logically disowned. However, I would like to add, this does not amount to giving up contextualism as I understand it. It involves endless *dialogue* and *interpretation* between the "insiders" and the "outsiders." It is an open-ended hermeneutic enterprise and exploration.

Openness of a particular culture of a society to external stimuli produced by other cultures of other societies sets a limit to its *autonomy* and to the extent of its autonomous growth. History and analysis would show that different subcultures, such as, religion, polity and science, are not equally open to external stimuli or what may be called occasions of criticism. The subcultures less open to external criticism are generally also found to be less responsive to internal criticism. In the scale of stimulus-response or that of successful interaction experimental sciences such as physics and chemistry come up at the top, religion occupies a bottom position, and polity figures somewhere in between. Science as a subculture of a society, of India for instance, can hardly be indifferent to the newly established scientific theories of other societies, of the United States and the Soviet Union, for example. Science as a spectrum of subcultures of different societies spread over the whole world is in a sense a community by itself. One might say that scientific culture of today in CS(T3) is really international, cutting across the political boundaries of different nations or societies, and that the problems of translation are felt least in this area of men's cultural acquisition. Given the common rules of the game of science, its methodological uniformity, abstractness, and "hegemonism," one might perhaps rightly assert that in the next few centuries, in FS(T4), the character of science would acquire more homogeneity and many other branches of knowledge not yet known as strict science would be brought under its expanding scope. Polity as a subculture of a society, of India, for example, is less responsive to the structures and functions of the polities of other societies, of the United Kingdom, the United States, China, and the Soviet Union, for example. Not that interactions between these polities are not taking place; but compared to those in sciences, their level is lower. Politywise human societies are somewhat conservative. In respect to religion they are even more conservative. While I am saying all these things, one can easily find out my own point of view: the cultural background of my mind in CS(T3), which partly accounts for the comparative placements of science, polity, and religion in the scale of interaction indicated previously.

It is absolutely necessary to bear this point in mind. Otherwise one might be deluded to believe that the position of science, polity, or religion defined in terms of its openness or lack thereof has been alike in all societies—PS(T1), MS(T2), and CS(T3). The demarcation between science and religion in PS(T1) was not as sharp as we find it today in CS(T3). Not only in PS(T1) but also in MS(T2) polity had a close relation with religion; in CS(T3) this relation is becoming increasingly loose and formal. Another point that we should bear in mind is this. At times following external aggression or annexation the victor's polity is formally imposed on the total culture, including such subcultures as religion, polity and science, of the vanquished. I say "formally" because the impositions in the case of culture, especially in its nonmaterial aspects, cannot be effectively total. The room for interaction, retreat, or withdrawal is always there. The victor in one respect of culture, such as, political organisation or warfare, may through interaction prove vanquished in another, for example, religion or science. The subculture that dominates a society in war generally cannot dominate it in peace. Those who wield arms, military leaders, dominate during warfare but yield their position to the masters of ideas during peace or act according to the latter's advice: allow them to play their role in effect. The basic features of a conflict-cooperation situation even pertain to the relation between culture of the victor and that of the vanquished. It is never a case of all-conflict-and-no-cooperation or of all-cooperation-and-no-conflict. The grey area of cultural interactions marked by varying degrees of assimilation, resistance, rejection, modification, and acceptance is almost universal and very instructive.

It is interesting to note why a working scientist of a society at a particular point of time wants to resist the acceptance of a particular piece of information as true, even though he recognises that it satisfies the logical and experimental tests he accepts. He wants to resist its acceptance because he realises that its implications immediately disturb and may later on irreparably damage his "disciplinary matrix" or "set of paradigms."[7] Unless information embodies the result of crucial experiment – crucial to the accepted set of paradigms – it cannot be taken as a threat to the set of paradigms as a whole. Information obtained from that sort of experiment brings about a decisive or revolutionary change in the history of science. But revolutionary change in the conceptual framework of science may be interpreted in a conservative manner in order to minimise its "damaging" or "destructive" effect on the framework concerned. To what extent crucial information can change the conceptual framework of science depends, aside from the nature of interpretation, conservative or radical, on the nature of the social background of science – whether it is PS(T1) or MS(T2) or CS(T3) – and the logical rigours which define its systematic character. Certainly in PS(T1) and MS(T2), a logical system of science did mean something different from what it does in CS(T3) or will mean in FS(T4). Science as a subculture in PS(T1) or MS(T2) was much less autonomous and systematised than it is in CS(T3). Systematically incorporated in philosophy and religion, science and its logic shared the strength and weakness of the said two disciplines in PS(T1) and MS(T2). Let us not forget that the separateness of these disciplines is the result of the evolution of culture and increasing intellectual division of labour. But the said separation is not irreconcilable.

Notwithstanding the previously mentioned division of labour and cultural distance, a continuous dialogue among PS(T1), MS(T2), CS(T3), and FS(T4) is occurring. We cannot help it. As human beings we stand *disclosed* both forwardly, or futuristically, and backwardly, or historically.[8] Thus we *interpret* ourselves to ourselves and also to otherselves. All our cultural achievements and failures, scientific and otherwise, are also undergoing this endless process of interpretation. By no act of will or decision can a human being or culture withdraw and disengage himself or itself from this anthropohistorical process. To understand the history of science the concerned historian, irrespective of his cultural affiliation, has to try to get to the anthropological roots of science of his chosen area. He has to enter into a dialogue with the people whose science is the object of his understanding and interpretation. In effect the historian is called upon by his task to reread the texts of science with their authors and to see to what extent their context or horizons of intended meanings fuse or come together.

CHAPTER TWO

Understanding Science of an Alien Society

THE RELATION BETWEEN SCIENCE AND PHILOSOPHY IN THE PAST WAS NOT QUITE how we view it today. But it is reviewed and refined from time to time. An imperceptible change in it always takes place. The traditional distinction drawn among "ancient," "medieval," and "modern" or "contemporary" is, as I said, typological and followed for methodological convenience, not for any substantive consideration. Review of the past, in general, and of the past science, in particular, is necessitated by the state of present science and social needs, both theoretical and practical. The "answers" of the past are largely determined by the "questions" raised by the present. In this connection one recalls the question-and-answer method proposed by Collingwood.

In this chapter, I would like to show (1) that our *understanding* of other societies, their paradigms of wisdom and wisemen, is objectively grounded in our own paradigms, which are either consciously chosen or prereflectively accepted; and (2) that the logic and psychology of choice-acceptance are shaped by a very complex process of social interaction marked by both conflict and cooperation between and within cultures and subcultures. In this connection to clarify my view (3) I would very briefly refer to two important case studies often mentioned in the histories of science: the concepts of (a) irrational number and (b) the atom in ancient India and Greece.

It would be interesting to try to understand the reasons leading to the gradual independence of science. Philosophical reflection and analysis of the history of science reveal that speculative, mythical, and experimental elements were mixed up in it. This mixup may be viewed as either logical and systematic or prelogical and presystematic. Why one views the composite elements of speculation, myth, and experiment in one particular way rather than another largely depends upon one's own point of view. The concepts of logic, logical laws, and system are not identical in different societies. Also widely different are the techniques and formulations of experimental findings. What was once recognised as a *logical system of knowledge* in PS(T1) is perhaps regarded today, in CS(T3), as an *indefinite whole of ill-assorted information, beliefs, and fancies* brought together by untestable speculative links. Even the basic laws of logic –"basic" to "us"– do not convey the same sense to the widely different cultural groups. The things that present themselves as distinctively different to the "naked" eye may appear basically the same to the "tutored" mind. Questions such as, Whether eyes see in effect nakedly? and Whether the mind can act or be applied in a totally untutored way? are not peculiar to the philosopher of CS(T3). Needless to say, the proposed answers to the questions, closely analysed, reveal their different cultural parenthood.

The said cultural difference seems to operate at two different levels, primary and secondary, or, to put it differently, *descriptive* and *interpretative*. The levels may be more but not less. By the *primary levels of intelligibility* I mean the way a wiseman, Magician, of PS(T1), understands and describes his own society: that is, from within. By the *secondary level of intelligibility* I mean how a wiseman, Scientist, of, say, CS(T3), understands and describes PS(T1) or MS(T2). The way a wiseman, Philosopher, of MS(T2) understands and describes PS(T1) may be a matter of understanding and description for a wiseman, Scientist, of CS(T3). Thus more than one level of understanding or several levels of understanding may be simultaneously object(s) or matter(s) of one's understanding. A history of ancient science and philosophy written by a contemporary historian is almost bound to be different from one written by a medieval historian. The difference is due not only to the *informational contents* but also to the *conceptual frameworks*. The conceptual framework with which a historian works has an important role in the determination of the contents and also in the definition of the scope of history in question. It may be pointed out that at every level the historian is obliged to work with one or another conceptual framework for the purpose of organising information and also perhaps of determining what is considered to be information. And because of this basic feature of thought even at the primary level, the information, correct as well as fancied, that a historian claims that he is "objectively describing" is found to be mixed up with interpretation. Interpretation, however, does not mean distortion of facts beyond recognition. The question of "distortion" is generally raised by those naive realists who believe that "pure facts" can be seen by "naked eyes" and "pure information" understood by the "untutored or clear mind." The contribution of the conceptual framework and that of *the given* can be separated at least for the limited *analytic purpose*. The separation, however, can never be clear-cut because of the continuous dialectical relation between the two. Of late, the point has been persuasively argued by Davidson in a related context.

As there cannot be a circumference without a point, there cannot be a view without a point of view. This may sound trivial. But it is not. Once we closely look into the dialectical relation within the analytic purpose, we find two elements and designate one as "conceptual framework" and the other, in the absence of a better expression, as "given," and we also discern different levels of "operation" or "working" of the said relation. The level difference may also be observed in the relation between the eyes and what the eyes see. The ocular structure of *normal* human beings is the same, yet their observation reports vary, differ, and at times even conflict. For the time being let us forget the difficulties involved in the attempt to define "normal human being." Frankly speaking, I do not know whether the ability of all normal human beings to see is the same irrespective of different ecological factors. I strongly suspect it is not. The power of vision of people used to bright electric or tube light and that of the people used to wick lamp or no lamp at all after the sun sets is perhaps not the same. Habit and experience are not likely to leave one's vision totally unaffected. Second, even if it is assumed that the ocular *structure* is the same, the question remains whether that alone determines the qualities of its *functioning*. Does the "naked eye" see at all? Or is it the "clothed eye" that sees? Do not memory, attention, and expectation enter into one's act of seeing? Someone who is born blind and then acquires vision as the result of some operation cannot see, order, and organize the objects as we do in the first few days. With the same ocular structure, one might say, "He does not see what we see." Bearing in mind the factors involved in the act of seeing it seems advisable to use some such expressions as "somebody sees" rather than "eyes, naked or clothed, see." Eyes are used by us in various ways, actively and attentively, passively and indifferently, to express or communicate some idea or emotion, to impress someone or other, and so on. In a way the whole personality of a man *orients* his act of seeing. Third, the dialectical relation between the seer and the seen has its level difference, which seems to me very instructive. Sometimes the seer "dominates" the "show" and the physical identity of the seen is "distorted" almost beyond recognition. I say "almost" because if the "distortion" is total then the term *recognition* makes little sense. Besides, the term *distortion* itself begs elucidation. Sometimes distortion is deliberate and intended for some or another creative purpose, such as, an artistic one. The seer's deep-rooted desire,intense dislike or hatred, obsession or complex, of which the seer himself is not ordinarily conscious also colours the identity of the seen as borne out by others' observations of the latter. An element of distortion is perhaps inherent in the situation, in the very act of seeing. The seen-in-itself cannot be perceived in its entirety by the seer, however passive his posture might be. The limits are set not only by the psychophysiological background and abilities of the seer but also partly by the geometricophysical properties of the seen. The seen can hold out (so to say) its identity and unity even in the face of a very active and dominant posture of the seer. The latter cannot wish the former out of existence without deluding himself or, stated differently, except in bad faith. In its dialectical relation to the seer, I feel like saying, the seen has a life of its own that may be changed but cannot be totally destroyed by the former.

Finally, the seer-seen dialectic has a very important bearing on the relation between the cultural *objects* and the way they are understood. If the wiseman of CS(T3), whether he is an anthropologist or a historian of science, wants to understand the science and culture of PS(T1) directly and in terms of his own conceptual framework, that is, totally or partially disregarding the way the wiseman of PS(T1) understands the objects of science and culture from within his own society, he is bound to have serious difficulties. His descriptive account of what he has heard and seen appears incoherent, bizarre, or even meaningless and absurd. If the second-level intelligibility of S of CS(T3) does not take *due* cognizance of the first-level intelligibility of M of PS(T1), the S(Scientific)-account of PS(T1) would be somewhat like the description of his surroundings given by the man who was born blind and has recently gained vision through surgery. The description of the seen ("objects") does not necessarily make sense. For description itself is concept-mediated and not pure. Without being *physiologically blind* a person may well be *culturally blind*. A man who has right cultural vision of CS(T3) may be unable to "see" the cultural objects of PS(T1) or of MS(T2), that is, may fail to grasp the intended meanings and relations intended by the people involved in what he sees. Even then the main factors that explain intercultural communication, meaningful interaction and mutually intelligible translation of their languages are (1) the *continuity* of different societies and (2) the *identity* of the world (of objects) we all, in a sense, commonly share. Besides, (3) interpretation brings different cultural worlds together and gives rise to a new world within which the *postulated* distinction between "the physical" and "the cultural" makes little sense.

Physical objects—"table," "chair," "tree," and so on—are obviously different from cultural objects—"marriage," "market," "solving a problem," and so on. This, however, is not to deny that the latter have some perceptible features that are not essential to the understanding of their meanings. From the other end, one may point out, the physical objects are not bare given either. The line of distinction drawn between them can be neither permanent nor straightforward. For instance, one may always argue that, in spite of its *physical* features a chair or a table is an object of *culture*. The same can be said of a tree as well if it happens to be a hybrid variety cultivated by some known or unknown people. If providential teleology is allowed to have its say in defining an all-encompassing whole of objects, even mountains and rivers may be declared culture-objects at bottom. Though extreme, it is an easily conceivable position; and history abounds in examples of variety.

What is the correct way of understanding an alien society, say, PS(T1)? may be represented by another question, What is the correct way of translating the language of an alien society, say PS(T1), into that of our language, CS(T3)? As we are aware, language is used for different purposes: to make a statement, to express a belief, to deny what is ascribed to or associated with some body, to request, to evaluate, and so on. The diverse purposes that a language serves and the ways it serves are closely interrelated and indefinite. A language that otherwise lies idle or almost dead and is good only for the limited purposes of recording or preserving some past states of affairs, ideas, or practices can by acts of mouth or body be brought back to life and put to uses of different sorts. Because of the interwoven character of language and society and also because of the innumerable ways in which each society uses its language, the task of the culture-translator. often proves extremely difficult and delicate, except in the limited cases of description of one's bodily states and of perceptually identifiable medium-sized physical objects. Translation is inarticulately interpretative in effect.

When we speak of the interwoven character of language and society we imply, among other things, that the nature of culture-objects is very much influenced by the language through which these objects are designated. Expressions of culture-concepts are understandably even less rigid. "Marriage" as a *name* of a culture-object is certainly more rigid than its *description*, "a form of union between a male and a female." But contextual analysis of their meanings will show that none of these designators is absolutely rigid. All over the world "marriage" obviously does not mean an identical group of observables or stimuli: overlapping is unavoidable. Nor are the relations responsible for the grouping together of the said observables or stimuli the same. The "forms of union between" that could be truly predicated of "marriage" are, on all ethnological accounts, numerous and widely different. "Chair" is certainly a more rigid designator than "marriage," although it occupies, in our context, a borderline position between physical objects and culture-objects. For an interculture translator or interpreter, therefore, "chair" is likely to pose fewer problems than "marriage." A description of "chair" is certifiable by stimulus-similarity. The scope of stimulus-certificate in the former case is comparatively limited. But the difference continues to be one of degree. However, to the culture-translator the most serious difficulties are posed by the objects of belief, worship, praise and blame. We can well imagine of a PS(T1) in which gods, angels, demons, and so on, are all objects of "true" belief and worship, and the concerned people have their *own accepted ways of justifying* those beliefs and acts of worship. We can also imagine a PS(T1) or a MS(T2) in which gods, angels, and demons are all objects of belief but, whereas gods and angels are loved and worshipped, demons are feared and propitiated in different exotic ways, and they too have their conventional ways of justifying their beliefs and acts accordingly.

When from the area of knowledge we move to that of evaluation, the elements of indeterminacy and therewith the difficulties for the culture-translator increase. One possible way of circumventing the difficulties has been to draw and highlight a questionable distinction between the meaning of a term and the ways in which its reference is given. The description of marriage by which the reference of "marriage" is given in a PS(T1) may not apply to the intended referent of the term in (other possible worlds), say, MS(T2). By postulating a meaning of "marriage" that is equally neutral to all languages and societies we may think of a logically possible way out of the culture-translator's difficulties. But that proposed solution has its own difficulties. In abstract theoretical contexts postulation of intentional objects is permissible or perhaps even necessary primarily for "constructionist" purposes, but in the cognitive sociological context it seems unnecessary, if not misleading. Whichever society is taken to be the "basic" locus of the meaning of "marriage," its languages and other associations are bound to enter into the very ways of its being given (as an object of understanding). To deny this entails an indefensible form of essentialism. It is difficult to imagine the identity of a culture-object totally disregarding the ways in which it is determined. If the object is conceived as a purely ontic entity and in a strictly nonepistemic context, one finds no harm in it. But one wonders whether there is any interesting point in taking culture-objects within the scope of a modal operator to indicate their nonepistemic status of rigidity or flexibility. For to the culture-translator or the historian of science perhaps the more interesting question would be to study *how* it is determined: who speak(s) of it; where, when, how, and in which language it is spoken of. In other words, his main concern is the social character of meaning, that is, *how* a particular sense is attached to an expression by the group of people who use the language in which the said expression figures. And this important point, relatively neglected by Frege and Russell, fortunately has been brought to the focus of our attention by the later Wittgenstein and Quine.[1]

Whether science and philosophy can be satisfactorily *demarcated* remains a controversial question. Carnap and other positivists at one stage argued that philosophy is a metatheoretical activity and that it does not add to our knowledge of facts obtained otherwise from science. The main aim of philosophy is to make use of logical language for the purpose of constructing a worldview accepted by the scientific community. Proper use of logic in that case can enable the philosopher to keep science pure or purge it of the pernicious effects of the pseudo problems resulting from metaphysical speculations. It is well-known that Carnap later extensively revised this view of the relation between philosophy and science. But, given this view, the right aim of the historian of science would be to relate the story of how scientists in the course of time, step by step, relying on observations, devising suitable experiments, and using more and more "powerful" formal languages, have succeeded in freeing the "essence" of science from its speculative trappings.

One very basic question is left unanswered by this approach: why it is that the "essence" of science itself has persistently exhibited a historical character. Is it not a fact that what are called philosophical *speculations* have often favourably influenced the course of science by enabling scientists to frame testable hypotheses for the purpose of organizing available experiences and anticipating possible ones? Have not scientific discoveries often sparked different speculative hypotheses for the purpose of rationally organising available as well as possible experiences? Disregard of these basic questions and the underlying *dialectic* between the speculative elements and the empirical ones in man's cognitive enterprise explains to a great extent the unfortunate but instructive fact that during the heydays of logical positivism although we all heard much admiration for science no significant history of science was produced by any leading spokesman of the movement. Exclusive preoccupation with the formal language of science, forgetting its parentage, that is, ordinary language and its social context, made many a positivist somewhat blind to both the roots and the fruits of science.

In recent years Popper and his followers, on the one hand, and Quine and his followers, on the other, have done most to undo the effect of this fancied cleavage between science and philosophy. For Popper philosophy is basically scientific, consisting of framing bold and problem-oriented conjectures that mature into scientific or other empirical theories through criticism and testing. This process of maturation is uneven and unending.

Popper is prepared to accept only to a limited extent Wittgenstein's stricture against philosophy that it has no problem of its own. But that does not mean that philosophical problems are not genuine. Maybe their roots are elsewhere, in science, politics, religion, or some practical needs. It is misleading to distinguish "studies" or "disciplines" by the subject matter which they investigate. The same subject matter may be studied and used to solve different problems. Popper speaks of three sorts of reasons defining the scope of different disciplines: (1) historical, (2) administrative, and (3) theoretical, theories designed to solve problems. For a proper understanding of the relation between science and philosophy, and that between society or history, on the one hand, and philosophy or science, on the other, one has to look mainly into (1) historical reasons, and (2) theoretical reasons. According to Popper, the philosopher does not merely "talk about philosophy": he tries to solve problems both theoretical and practical, linguistic and factual. Since philosophy does not generate the problems generally known as philosophical but those that result from the interaction between philosophy and other disciplines, their *degenerative development* is contingent upon the character of the interaction between the philosopher and, for example, the sociologist, the theologist, the scientist, and the mathematician. And this is evident from the histories of philosophy and science, taken both separately and jointly.

One of the main reasons used by the earlier positivists for the exclusion of philosophy from the domain of science is that so-called philosophical statements are neither factual (synthetic a posteriori) nor logical (analytic a priori). That the analytic/synthetic issue cannot be easily decided., à la the positivist, has been persuasively argued by many contemporary philosophers: Heinemann,[2] Quine,[3] Watkins,[4] and Putnam.[5] One and the same statement or set of statements may be interpreted as both factual and analytic. Popper refers to Newton's theory, which, though generally recognised as factual, has been interpreted by Poincaré and Eddington as implicit definitions. Unless a language is sufficiently formalised and its rules of interpretations or bridging principles are clearly formulated and illustrated, we cannot logically and satisfactorily decide which statements are synthetic and which ones are not. Popper and Watkins speak of some speculative statements, which are nonanalytic, criticisable (but *not* testable), and establish their factual bonafides by influencing science.

To illustrate the point Popper refers to ancient Greek thought: how the crisis in Pythagoreanism and early Greek atomism led Plato to lay the foundation of Euclidean geometry.[6] The point, however, was noted earlier, by Singer and Sarton, among others. Plato's philosophical or speculative theory of Forms owes its origin to the then problem-situation in Greek science, especially Democritus' atomism, which followed the discovery of the irrationality of the square root of 2. Pythagoras thought that all things of the world, including even the qualitative ones, are, in essence, numbers or ratios of numbers. The Pythagoreans, Aristotle writes in his *Metaphysics*, thought that mathematical principles are "the bases of all things" and that almost all things are numerically expressible. But, then, they also developed a conception of irrational quantities not expressible by ordinary numbers. Singer has rightly pointed out: "with the imperfect mathematical notation of the time . . . great algebraical advance was impossible, and irrational numbers could not be algebraically represented. Greek mathematics was thus forced to preserve its geometrical bias."[7] However, this theory of number was successfully applied to simple geometrical figures such as squares, rectangulars, and isosceles triangles; to certain simple solids, such as pyramids, and also to abstract ideas, such as Justice, Beauty, Harmony, and Knowledge.

Though the Pythagorean theory of numbers, which can be represented by dot diagrams, contains the rudiments of a "very primitive atomism," Popper's conjecture[8] is that the atomic theory of Democritus was mainly influenced by the *theoretical* controversy on the *problem* of change between Heraclitus, on the one hand, and Parmenides and Zeno, on the other. Heraclitus' theory is simple: nothing is, everything flows; identity is illusion, change is reality. Equally simple and attractive is Parmenides' theory: the world is one and full; it knows no void, has no parts, and, therefore, is motionless. Democritus rejects Parmenides' conclusion and having done that questions the premises as well. His view is that the world consists of parts, is not full – the void is there – and, therefore, motion is possible. Motion is external to atoms and not within them. For Democritus' atoms are full, that is, know no void within, and invisible, somewhat like miniature replica of Parmenides' big world. Movement in the world is due to different possible arrangements of atoms. Democritus' theory of atoms has been credited with the power of explaining such empirically known properties as degrees of hardness and resilience, rarefaction and condensation, compressibility, coherence, and disintegration. It also anticipated the calculus of integration. "But perhaps," Popper says, "the most fascinating elements in Democritus' theory is his doctrine of the quantisation of space and time." The proof of the irrationality of the square root of 2, $\sqrt{2}$, was unknown to both Pythagoras and Democritus and its implication shook the very foundations of their theories, for both of them thought that every measurement is reducible to pure numbers. This proof "destroyed the hope of deriving cosmology, or even geometry, from the arithmetic of natural numbers." To save the Greek science of that period from this crisis Plato developed his theory of Forms, an autonomous geometrical method, freeing mathematics from the "arithmetical" assumption of commensurability or rationality, and anticipating the elements of Euclid.

Of course Plato's theory of Forms was speculative or, as a radical positivist might like to characterise it, fanciful. If a theory has to establish its "scientific" credentials in terms of its "being based on sense-experience," both the Pythagorean theory of Numbers and the Platonic theory of Forms are bound to be expelled from the arena of science and criticized as fanciful. Singer has very rightly observed that "fancies of this type have been repeatedly of value in the history of science."[9] The radical positivist fails to formulate the relation between the role of theoretical speculation and that of experiment and observation correctly. "(T)he formation of general ideas on theoretical grounds has [often] preceded and not followed practical (experiment and) observation."[10] The mystical Pythagorean view that the sphere is the perfect figure led most of the astronomers of the later ages to think that the earth as well as the planets are spheres. Tycho Brahe's (1546-1601) hypothesis of the Universe as according to the ideal form of the circle is one of the last great reminders of the Pythagorean spirit. Kepler's (1571-1630) idea of Universe was also essentially Platonic and Pythagorean. Right from the beginning he was persuaded that the order of the Universe and its parts is in accord with some abstract ideal of the beautiful and the harmonious, and that it must be expressible in numerical and geometrical form. However, it was left to Descartes' genius to bring about the long-awaited union between the Pythagorean theory of Number and the Platonic theory of Form in 1627. His analytic Geometry was the point of convergence of Hindu algebra and Arab geometry, and its application proved to be the greatest single step of the seventeenth century in the progress of the exact sciences. And this is evident from the scientific works of Pascal, Galileo, Torricelli, Huygens and several other eminent scientists of the time.

Interaction between science, the observational-experimental quest for knowledge, and philosophy, the speculative quest for the same, is not peculiar to Greek or European thought. The same theme with local variation can be illustrated by a rational reconstruction of Hindu thought of the ancient period and the Middle Ages. George Sarton's view on this point is noteworthy: "Many Greek ideas in science and philosophy are duplicated in India. It is very interesting to compare those duplications. . . . The duplication helps to prove the essential identity of the human mind. Given definite problems that admit of only a few solutions, it is not astonishing that wisemen of Greece, India, China, etc. hit independently upon the same solution."[11]

Necessity, practical as well as theoretical, is rightly said to be the mother of invention. Necessities are of different sorts: cooking food, irrigating and cultivating land, measuring space (plots of land) and time (hours, months, years, and so on). Over the years and in the light of organised experience necessities change and so do the forms of meeting those necessities. This is true for both the growing individual and the changing society. Our actions are in the nature of a response to external stimuli or internal urges: stimuli or urges may invite efforts to understand or attempts to solve problems or both. Annual floods in the Nile Valley washing away the boundary lines between the plots of land and renewing the disputes between the owners of those plots proved to be a pressing practical problem to the geometricians (literally "measurers of land") of ancient Egypt. The *Elements* of Euclid was in the main a theoretical response of far-reaching consequence to the practical needs of the time.

The origin of *Śulba-Vijñāna* (literally "science of measurement") in India is connected with the construction of the altars of the Vedic sacrifices. Baudhāyana and Āpstamba, the two most outstanding geometers of ancient India, are said to have flourished well before 500 B.C. *Śulba* meant not only "measuring" but also "the unit of measure" or "an instrument of measurement," which was a rope or chord (*rajju*) at that time. The ancient geometers of India spoke of three kinds of measure—linear, surfacial and voluminal—and five types of specialists in mathematics—expert in the *śulba* or geometer, inquirer (*pariprechaka*) into the *śulba*, and uniform-ropestretcher (*sama-sūtra-nirancaka*). Democritus (470-500 B.C.) is also said to have used the term *harpedonaptae*, the Greek equivalent of rope-stretcher. Satya Prakash surmises that the geometrical ideas of India influenced Greek sciences.[12] The ancient Indian geometers such as Baudhāyan and Āpastamba did recognise the irrationality of the square root of two, $\sqrt{2}$). They had their proof of it as well.[13] Some scholars like Schroeder and Burk think that the credit for the first discovery of irrationals goes to the ancient Aryans of India. However, other equally competent scholars like Zenthen, Cantor and Vogt have expressed their doubt over the matter.

The *Nyāya-Vaiśeṣika* theory of atom embodies another bold speculative attempt to solve the problems of unity and multiplicity, of identity and change. And the problems have to be studied against the background of controversy between the *Mādhyamika Buddhist*, emphasising the principle of *dynamics* or flux, and the Vedāntin, emphasising the principle of *status* or identity. Against the Nihilist school of the Buddhist, which holds that void (śūnya) is the only real entity, Kaṇāda, the propounder of the atomic theory, says that atoms (*paramāṇu*) are partless and eternal "reals". Motion (*karma*) is external to atoms and all the noneternal objects are ultimately reducible to various atoms through motion. Atoms are brought together by two forms of motion for the formation of composite wholes:

(1) desert (*adṛṣṭa*) of the human beings or creatures who are to make use of their body or object concerned, and (2) shock (*samkṣobha*) entailing impact *saṁskāra* and velocity (*vega*). Both desert and shock are externally produced on the atoms by some or another conscious agency helped by God. All objects consisting of atoms have space, *ākāśa*, as their locus or substance, an eternal continuum: and the latter, imperceptible in itself, is known inferentially through its quality, sound. To account for the relations of priority and posterity, of simultaneity and succession, and so on, and to measure the units known as moment, minute, day, month, year, and so forth, the atomist feels logically obliged to posit time, *kāla*, another all-pervasive and eternal substance. In itself imperceptible, time is known through its determinations. Time relates the objects of the universe with the movements of the sun, is the instrumental cause of motion and, therefore, also of the production, existence, and destruction of every product of atoms.[14]

It is very difficult to state with definiteness whether Indian atomists influenced their Greek counterparts or the latter influenced the former. Sarton's guess that "the Phoenicians, who were very clever dragomans and middlemen, may have transmitted some Hindu (atomic) theory" to the Greeks may or may not be right. But his antidiffusionist and proparallelist conclusion on the matter appears very rational and accords well with a wider range of independently accepted historical facts: "the Greeks were quite capable of reaching that solution (of the problems of unity and multiplicity, of identity and change, in terms of speculative atomic theories) by themselves, and so were the Hindus."[15]

In the face of the same or similar problems thinking human minds are repeatedly found to have discovered independently the same or similar solutions in the past. The question, Why do thinking human beings face same or similar problems? seems to me very interesting and a part of a larger issue that has to be studied in cooperation with the cultural anthropologist, the sociologist of knowledge, the linguist and the ontologist. Not that science cannot be understood as a secular subject, that is, strictly in terms of its "technical" problems and solutions as viewed by the professionals from within their own community. But my concern here is with the history of science in its sociological perspective, or, to put the same thing somewhat differently, the sociology of science in its historical perspective. Whether it is taken as a corpus of theories or a form of activities, science is undeniably social in several complementary senses. First, basically it is a product of social cooperation and interaction and not of some individual's insight and excellence.

Occasionally "accidents" do contribute to the career of science. Second, the set of symbols or the languages used for *doing* science or for the purpose of construction of its *theories* is also social. The rules of interpretation of scientific language/activities are a part of social life. Thirdly, both the problems and the proposed solutions of science are social or public, that is, open to common understanding and test. Problems result from the perception of inadequacy of an accepted conceptual framework to deal with some or other objectively recognised objects of experience or information ascertainably grounded in nature *and* culture. Fourthly, the very development of science shows its objective and social character. The individual scientists who discover the problems of science and try to solve them are all mortals like ourselves, but what they leave behind, their works outlive them and may be understood without making any specific *reference* to them. Finally, *rationality (from within)* of science and its *intelligibility (from without)* provide yet another proof of the socially and historically continuous character of science. The considerations and proofs I am offering to show clearly the social moorings and implications of science are interrelated, overlapping and convergent. Before I conclude perhaps one point, already mentioned, needs to be stressed. Once the nature/culture dualism, clearly untenable in the light of modern findings of such sciences as biophysics, physiological psychology and biolinguistics, is given up and, in the wake of that, it is duly recognised that rudiments of cultural problems are there in the natural level as well, we would find it easy to understand why historically distanced and geographically scattered groups of people came across similar problems and solved or tried to solve them in more or less similar ways. From this one might hastily infer what Lévi-Strauss describes as "cultural universals"; we should not give the impression that they have a fixed essence in relation to or in opposition to time. Nature is diversely individuated by time. Culture is diverse because of the incurable individuality of historically evolving men and groups. The said two sorts of diversity are admittedly identical at bottom, but too much of emphasis on "bottom" often leads one to metaphysical and sociological *essentialism*, making one avoidably blind to the diverse and refined factors of social life.

CHAPTER THREE

Dialectical Relation Between Science and Philosophy

Related to the needs of men-in-society the growth of science lends itself to clear understanding. Somewhat (but not quite) like science, philosophy too can be understood as a secular discipline. Some people have gone further and claimed sovereignty for it, trying to free philosophy from the "disturbing day-to-day details" of science. One of the upshots of this unwelcome freedom, that is, lack of interaction between science and philosophy, has been this: whereas the history of the problems and solutions of science is found to be primarily progressive and occasionally static or even degenerative, the history of philosophy is marked by the repetition of the same old problems dressed up in new idioms. Let us not forget that this *growthlessness* of philosophy is peculiar only to a particular interpretation of philosophy, namely, that it is *the* sovereign and supreme form of the human wisdom. And one of the unfortunate "consequences" of this ambitious concept of philosophy is that sciences are mere partial expressions and very incoherent fragments of the whole truth embodied in the first principles of philosophy.

One version of this concept of philosophy is found in Aristotle and Hegel and another in Kant. Collingwood's attempt to clarify the relation between science and philosophy or metaphysics in terms of what he calls *absolute presuppositions* is highly ingenious and represents a position in between Kant's and Hegel's drawing upon both. According to Aristotle and Hegel,[1] the endless *details* of science are confusing and meaningless unless these are viewed under higher-level general *principles*, and that the cognitive ascent *ends up* in God or the Absolute Spirit, which lends complete and the best possible intelligibility to both the details and the principles. In the words of J. N. Findlay, "Hegel's view of Nature is, in fact, a carrying to the limit of an immanent, Aristotelian teleology, in which Nature is to be understood as throughout working towards an end which will ultimately carry it beyond itself."

Kant's philosophy is essentially a philosophy of science or a metaphysics of scientific experience. Assuming Newtonian mechanics as the paradigm of science and taking Euclidean geometry for granted, he argues back to the epistemological presuppositions and then to the metaphysical ones that rationally sustain the former. To justify the necessary and unified character of the best form of empirical science Kant refers to the ascending and convergent series of syntheses: in sense, in imagination, in understanding, and finally in the transcendental apperception of the self, calling upon the self to do the double duty of freely uniting the empirically determined elements of experience, that is, to *receive* the materials of object-construction from without, from not-itself. Buchdahl[2] observes, "Kant certainly thought it a vital achievement to have exhibited putative links between the formulations of Newtonian mechanics and the transcendental principles of experience in general; moreover the former historically no doubt conditioned the general construction of the architectonic of the *Critique*". Without an all-designing God to support it from within and behind, the self cannot be expected to do its double duty and philosophically justify the paradigm science of the period. If a little "oversimplification" is allowed, one can say without misleading us, without being unfair to the texts of Aristotle and Kant, that the latter in his definition of the relation between science and philosophy, although liberally resorting to formalistic and dualistic idioms, never departs from the absolute justificatory principles, that is, providential teleological intelligibility, as suggested by the former.

A constructive follower of Hegel and Croce, Collingwood too wanted to "justify" or understand science in terms of some absolute presuppositions, which are metaphysical and nonpropositional in character: neither true nor false. But at the same time to take away the absolutistic overtone of Aristotle and Hegel and the ring of finality associated with Kant's *Critique*, and perhaps primarily to account for the growing character of science, he imparted a historical character to the presuppositions relativising them to the scientific investigations of different periods. Toulmin[3] has rightly pointed out that Collingwood "left it uncertain whether he intended his term, 'absolute presuppositions', to apply to the most fundamental theoretical principles within a science, or to the disciplinary principles constitutive of it." I would like to put the matter somewhat differently. It is not clear from the *Metaphysics* what is it that he wants to relativise to the absolute presuppositions of the period. Is it a set of specific theories of science, such as, the quantum mechanics of Planck and Einstein, or what I would call science as a subculture of the contemporary period, taking all sorts of science – physical, chemical, life, mechanical, formal, political, economic, linguistic, and so forth – within its comprehensive scope?

The presuppositions of the former are different, at least in part, from, and less general than, those of the latter. The pace and character of their change also differ. The experimental fortunes or test-consequences of quantum mechanics or relativistic physics have had considerable feedback impact on the presuppositions of the set of theories concerned. But the same cannot be said of the whole of science as a subculture, for its presuppositions are very broad in scope, highly general and abstract in character; the relation of the latter with the former is "logically weak"; these presuppositions cannot justify science but only help us to understand it. Strictly speaking, science as a subcultural whole has little or no test-consequences in the strict sense and their feedback impact on its abstract and general presuppositions are weak, slow, and, in the short run, almost imperceptible. This, however, is not to deny the subtle and continuous interaction between science and other subcultures, the former influencing and being influenced by the latter. The reflective scientist himself, an Einstein, for example, can tell, in fact has told, us clearly what the presuppositions of his theories are.

But when a historian of culture gives us a synchronous account of science as a subcultural whole and its presuppositions abstractly spread over and silently working through all other subcultures of the concerned society, we need some middlemen, interpreters, especially professional scientists and philosophers or scientists-cum-philosophers (depending mainly upon the period and partly upon the persons), to "show" us the "almost invisible" logical connections between the two. Unfortunately for us, in these days of professional specialisation, generally speaking, neither the philosopher nor the scientist likes this job of middleman, and gradually it is being left to the sociologist of (scientific) knowledge or the philosophically trained historian of science. The problem is that within the range of the modern age, CS(T3), it is perhaps possible through cooperative studies of the concerned professionals to show only a sort of weak logical connection between science as a subculture and its presuppositions, but to trace and show the connections between the sets of presuppositions themselves of the different ages—PS(T1), MS(T2), and CS(T3)—may not prove so easy. Since Collingwood takes these sets of presuppositions as historical, one naturally expects him to show their connections, continuous or discontinuous, or partly continuous and partly discontinuous. If the historian of science or the history-conscious philosopher working at the similar wavelength refuses to undertake and discharge this responsibility, he is likely to fall back upon a sort of adhocism in the matter of reconstructing the abstract and general presuppositions of the sciences as the totality of subculture belonging to the cultural wholes of the different periods of history. If it is claimed that M of PS(T1), for instance, can be made logically intelligible not only by one set of highest-level presuppositions (HLP[1]M) but by several other sets—say, (HLP[2]M), (HLP[3]M)and so on—and if each of them proves, in the words of Collingwood, equally "logically efficacious," the case of objectivity in history is seriously weakened and compromised. And if this claim is conceded, it is very difficult to draw a tenable line of distinction between rational reconstruction and imaginary reconstruction of the past. The same considerations apply to the presuppositions of P of MS(T2) and S of CS(T3), namely, (HLP[1]P), (HLP[2]P), (HLP[3]P), and so forth, and (HLP[1]S), (HLP[2]S), (HLP[3]S), and so on. If we cannot agree upon a rational criterion for drawing a line of distinction between rational reconstruction and imaginary reconstruction and, therefore, are obliged to resort to adhocism, we fail not only to account for objectivity but also continuity of what we term today the history of science or, more plainly and generally speaking, history.

Presuppositions work differently at different levels. The number of levels is indefinite and varies from discourse to discourse, and the explicit reference to the number of levels depends upon the assumed or actual composition of the audience: assumed by the philosopher or the historian of science. Let us call lower-level presuppositions LLP, and commonsense presuppositions CSP. To what extent or how are CSP and LLP related, if at all, to HLP? We will be well advised to bear in mind that these presuppositions of different levels were there in all societies and at all times, corresponding roughly to the different levels of the workings of the human mind, commonsense, scientific, and philosophical. But of the distinction between these levels neither all of us in CS(T3) are nor our predecessors in PS(T1) and MS(T2) were equally conscious. The main reason is perhaps this. The layman or he who operates at the commonsense level can well carry on normally without bothering himself with the scientific presuppositions, LLP, of what he does and says or thinks; and still less is he concerned with HLP. The case, of course, takes a different form if one closely questions his acts and thought and thus almost rationally forces him to reflect and recognise that there *are* certain LLP and HLP behind his acts and thoughts, and that without any implicit reference to the same neither one's questions on his acts and thoughts nor his answers to those questions could be rendered meaningful, intelligible, and communicable between them. At his own level the scientist is also placed in a somewhat similar position, except that his room for manoeuverability (particularly from within) is relatively "restricted" or narrowly defined, for his acts and thoughts are expressive of attempts to answer or solve more precisely and clearly formulated questions or problems. Compared to the acts and thoughts of the commonsense level, those of the scientific level are more clearly marked by question-consciousness and problem-anticipation.

The difficulties with HLP seem to be most intractable. The HLP of the discourse of common sense (DCS) is different from the discourse of natural sciences (DNS) and that of social sciences (DSS). The HLP of the discourse of the formal sciences (DFS) is different from those of the rest. Some theorists firmly believe that different levels and characters must be discerned for HLP, its application, and its interpretation. Related to this issue is the controversy over the competing claims of the methodological monist, of the methodological dualist, and of the methodological pluralist. Discourse of common sense (DCS) seems to be marked (roughly speaking) by three or four levels: question and answer or description of facts, norms, or forms of the concerned social context, and the principles that are cited to justify or to account for or to make intelligible the said norms and forms.

> Level 0: driving a car at 60 kilometres per hour
> Level 1: traffic police note the number of the car and file a case
>   before the appropriate authority
> Level 2: driver or owner of the car punished
> Level 3: safety consideration for the human life

One may like to bracket level 1 and level 2 together. The question may be raised (level 0), Why should he not drive at 60 kilometres per hour? The answer may be, He may be prosecuted for violating traffic laws (level 1), or "driver or owner of the car punished" (level 1 and level 2). The answer may even be a straightforward level 3 – Safety considerations demand observance of the speed limit – assuming level 1 and level 2, and, therefore, leaving them unmentioned. It is clear from this example that HLP of DCS is open to many questions but may be put at level 0 or level 1 in a discourse of social or moral science. In other words, level determination is discourse-relative. Some analysis, however, is necessary to show that level 3 of the preceding example may be related to and presuppose many other level 0 descriptions or questions. For a historian of social or moral science level 3, human safety considerations is more in the nature of a *form* of statements or prescriptions than a specific statement or prescription itself. But the history of the *form* becomes clear only when the specific statements-prescriptions satisfying the *form* are made: when we are told of the specific conditions that are recognised as safety measures in a society at a given time. Recognised safety measures-requirements implicitly presupposed (but not necessarily observed) by the car driver, the traffic police, and the judicial authority obviously change over time in response to technological, administrative, and other factors.

The discourse of natural science is also marked by similar levels:

Level 0: reports of sense-data
Level 1: reports of observations of objects
Level 2: empirical general truths about objects
Level 3: exact and universal mathematical physics

It may be made clear by an example:

Level 0: perception of several colours (in bow shape immediately
before or after rain in the sky)
Level 1: (perception of) a rainbow of the sky with red at one edge
and violet at the other and all other colours arranged between them
Level 2: the white light of the sun refracted through raindrops
shows the dispersed and separate colour corpuscles of
the visible spectrum of the sun
Level 3: all phenomena, including optical ones such as a rainbow,
are (explainable by) the action of forces representing at-

traction or repulsion, depending only upon distance and
acting between unchangeable particles

The (perception of a) rainbow in the preceding example has been
rendered intelligible or explained by, or represented under the presuppositions of Newton's (1643-1727) *corpuscular theory of light* (LLP, Level
2) and the *mechanical view of the universe* as a whole (HLP, level 3).[4]
It is interesting to recall that the same (rainbow) phenomenon was
rendered intelligible by, or represented under, Huygens's (1629-1695)
wave theory of light, a different presupposition (LLP, level 2)—namely,
that the rays of different wave lengths of different colours, though they
have the same velocity in the ether, differ in velocities in raindrops
and are separated. HLP (level 3) of Huygens's work is also mechanical
but not Newtonian. "His" reported understanding of a rainbow (level
1), it is held, presupposes the so-called Huygens's principle of secondary wave fronts, which is claimed to be independent of his mechanical
hypothesis (level 3).[5] If the secondary wave front principle is itself
a level 2 principle and independent of the level 3 mechanical
hypothesis, then certainly their relation begs some explanation. Otherwise the charge of adhocism is inescapable.

Unless the logical relation between a particular statement of object
(level 1) and its explanatory theory (level 2) and/or presupposition(s)
(level 3) are established by some crucial arguments and, if possible,
experiment(s), alternative explanatory theory and presupposition(s)
claimed to have equal logical efficacy to explain the same statement
of object or to make it intelligible can, and in fact do, exist simultaneously and enjoy equal recognition. Newton and Huygens were more
or less contemporary, and their theories of optics and principles of
mechanics were propounded at about the same time. Interestingly
enough, both theories of light "peacefully coexisted" for nearly a century and half, but more physicists preferred the corpuscular theory,
which offended the law of parsimony by postulating innumerable
substances, to the wave theory, which assumed the existence of only
one hypothetical existence, the ether. In the absence of a crucial experiment the choice at this point would be "more a matter of taste
than of scientific conviction."[6] However, it must be said to the credit
of Newton's and Huygens's scientific conviction that they both agreed
on a possible crucial experiment, which, if it could be devised, would
clinch the issue this way or that. If it could be experimentally shown
that light, which, according to Newton, travels in straight lines and

when passed through an obstruction casts sharp shadows, is capable of bending, and, if passed through a sufficiently small obstacle, casts no shadow, then that would have meant the refutation of the corpuscular theory and the vindication of the wave theory. The precisely anticipated refutation of the corpuscular theory was brought to the notice of the scientific community by Young and Fresnel in the mid-nineteenth century. They succeeded in demonstrating experimentally that a beam passing through a hole in a screen does cast a shadow on the wall opposite the source of light and that light diffracts or bends, that is, deviates from the rectilinear propagation.

Needless to say, the verdict of the last century in favour of the wave theory was not the end of the story of optics. Many problems remained unsolved or only partially solved. Einstein and Infeld have observed[7]:

> In the attempt to understand the phenomena of nature from the mechanical point of view, throughout the whole development of science up to the twentieth century, it was necessary to introduce artificial substances like electric and magnetic fluids, light corpuscles, or ether. . . . (T)he principal physical ideas (of classical mechanics have left for us) unsolved problems . . . difficulties and obstacles which discouraged the attempts to formulate a uniform and consistent view of all the phenomena of the external world. . . . Modern physics has attacked all these problems and solved them. But in the struggle for these solutions new and deeper problems have been created. Our knowledge is now wide and more profound than that of the physicist of the nineteenth century, but so are our doubts and difficulties.

Problem-solving theories, historically speaking, are found, on scrutiny, to be (1) in accord with hitherto unknown new facts and (2) inconsistent with or prohibitive of many other facts.

Our main concern here is not to trace the history of the problems and solutions of physics but to see how and where philosophy comes into the picture; whether it is a *presupposition* of science or a rational response of man to the findings of science, a sort of *postsupposition* of science, or both, as suggested by Einstein and Popper. According to Popper's "oversimplified schema," P1 yields TT yields EE yields P2, we "start" from some problem P1, then move to a tentative theory TT, a suggested solution, which may be more or less mistaken; then we try to eliminate its error EE by criticisms or experiments; elimination of error puts us into new problem P2 and does *not* mean the end of all problems.[8] Einstein has pointed out very clearly with the help of examples drawn from the history of physics how the solutions of some problems have given rise to "new and deeper problems," how widening and deepening of our knowledge result in wider and deeper "doubts and difficulties."

Presuppositions, we have already noted, are of different sorts. For the sake of simplicity one may refer to and distinguish among three main sorts, (a) logical and mathematical, (b) empirical and scientific, and (c) philosophical or metaphysical.[9] Philosophers are not unanimous on their nature or on their role.

Some philosophers, like Quine, think that the distinction as among logical, empirical, and metaphysical assertions or truths are not "basically" different. In this respect, the positions of Popper and Quine are similar, but not identical. Philosophy and science are continuous with one another, and so are science and common sense.

This view rejects Carnap's account of the difference between science and philosophy. According to Carnap, whereas the scientist *uses* such words as *electron, positron* and *proton*, the philosopher only talks about such words. Spelling out his "strategy of semantic ascent" Quine tries to show that it is not quite correct. For instance, we can both talk about the respective merits of the wave theory and the corpuscular theory and also use the theories if we discuss whether corpuscles and waves exist. Of course, a pro-Carnapian defender of the wave theory can say that the corpuscular theory contained false existentially quantified statements and vacuously true universally quantified ones. And Carnap's advice to the defenders of both the theories would be to operate at the metalinguistic level. But, Quine points out, both of them have to agree that *statements* (or *theories*) exist and provide them a common ground to communicate.[10]

Whatever is relative to a language, well-defined or ill-defined, is, like science, incomplete and improvable. Sense-impressions, objects, laws of nature, and even framework principles or categories are identified and communicated within a socially accepted conceptual schema. Biology, epistemology, physics, and mathematics all sail in the same boat. Quine warns us against seeking "an implicit sub-basement of conceptualisation, or of language." Beneath or behind "our ordinary language of physical things" there is nothing more basic one can rationally hope to get at. One is advised not to treat ordinary language as "sacrosanct" and to remember "its disposition to keep on evolving."

> Neurath has likened science to a boat while, if we are to rebuild
> it, we must rebuild plank by plank while staying afloat in it. The
> philosopher and the scientist are in the same boat. If we improve
> our understanding of ordinary talk of physical things, it will not
> be by reducing that talk to a more familiar idiom; there is none.
> . . . Scientific neologism is itself just linguistic evolution gone self
> conscious, as science is self conscious common sense. And
> philosophy in turn, as an effort to get clearer on things, is not to
> be distinguished in essential points of purpose and method from
> good and bad science. (Quine, *Word and Object*, p. 3).

One cannot think of language outside language. One cannot feel one's
body by getting out of one's own body. It is only after great difficulties
that we can make meanings out of such expressions as "thinking of
language outside language" and "feeling one's body by getting out of
one's own body." One of the main objectives underlying Quine's notion
of *semantic ascent* is to clear up these difficulties. Object-language and
metalanguage are somehow linked within and logically inseparable
parts of one and the same language, whatever that might be.[11] From
the bottom of the sense-data it is practically indeed very difficult, almost
impossible, to have a glimpse of the axiomatic top of mathematics;
the same is true if the ends are exchanged. It is not possible either
from the abstract highest-level principles to derive the details of sense-
data directly or to ascend directly from the latter to the former, although
both the domains logically belong to the same language. It is only at
the middle level of medium-sized objects of the language-pyramid that
the mathematician, the physicist, the psychologist and the layman can
communicate among themselves most successfully. The reason is very
simple: the overlapped area of the conceptual schemes of all these
concerned people is broadest at this level. But the mathematician and
the philosopher (of first principles) should bear in mind that they
cannot indefinitely enjoy the systematic benefit of abstract objects totally
disregarding the perceptible properties of those objects. At one stage
or another they have to make explicit the character of the abstract
objects, give examples, relate the axioms or the first principles to the
objects of the layman's world; otherwise the communication among
them breaks down. The fact that the communication does not break
down is explainable in terms of the pyramidic or conceptual unity
of the different but graded levels of the "objects" that the layman, the
scientist, the mathematician, and the philosopher are using or talking about. Even if the communication "breaks down" or seems to have

broken down, that is also explainable within the language or the conceptual scheme in question. But the most important point to note here is that the latter has no well-demarcated and permanent borderline around it. Do sense-impressions presuppose objects (of the external world)? Do the objects of physics presuppose the laws of physics? Do the laws of physics presuppose certain mathematical formulas (in which these are expressed)? Do mathematical formulas presuppose certain axioms and definitions? Answers to these and similar other questions—yes, no, or cannot say—are intelligible and arguable only within a more or less "definite system" of discourse (or language). The observations of Quine on the point are worth quoting:

> Science, though it seeks traits of reality independent of language, can neither go on without language nor aspire to linguistic neutrality.[12]
>
> The philosopher's task differs from (the scientist's and the mathematician's only) in detail; but in no such drastic way as those suppose who imagine for the philosopher a vantage point outside the conceptual scheme that he takes in charge. There is no such cosmic exile.[13]

Quine does not fail to anticipate the charge of subjectivity or relativity against him. Because of the very nature of his view he does not like to deny the charge totally; on the contrary, he gives a distinct meaning to the charge, highlighting the language-relative and context-bound character of the charge itself and thereby substantially taking away its severity. To vindicate the objectivity of science he proposes to banish what are known as *egocentric particulars* (Russell) or *indicator works* (Goodman): "I," "you," "this," "that," "here," "there," "now," "then," and resort to personal names or descriptions in place of "I" and "you," to dates or equivalent descriptions in place of "now," and to place names or equivalent descriptions in place of "here". Truth-value fluctuations of statements are partly due also to *tense* and *ambiguity* (of their expression). Tense problems may be substantially solved by a four-dimensional treatment of space-time. And ambiguity may be minimised by carefully analysing and distinguishing different logical forms of statements that are apparently alike. To say all these things, however, is not to deny the existence of the problems in commonsense discourse. But continuity of discourse can substantially take care of the problems arising within it.

The best objective basis of truth is language itself within which we all are obliged to operate. Rules and vocabulary of language are essentially social in origin. And the ways of learning the use of words and of following the rules of language are to be gathered from the society. Learning language is an integral part of acculturation. Man knows the world by using primarily the language of his society, but always as a part of it, that is, the world. Language provides him the cues to map the world and the world provides him the more persistent cues to ascertain how and where the previous cognitive mappings of the world have gone wrong. And all these presuppose (1) the persistently existing *world*, (2) the existence of *language*, (3) language-using *man* in it, and (4) intersubjectively sharable (a) *rules* and (b) vocabulary, as well as (c) the cues of *using* or learning the same, (a) and (b). The most important point for us to remember here is that all that we need to know ourselves-in-the world, namely, (1), (2), (3), and (4a), (4b), and (4c), is undergoing change. Elaborating (3) it may be pointed out that (3a), human body, plays a very important role in relating the physical world to language. Stimuli-messages, verbal and nonverbal, of the world are received, processed and interpreted by the body. The body is said to have, like the "innate ideas" of the mind, native capacities and dispositions that enable it to decode the messages received from without. Open to the influences of both heredity and society, the body acquires its capacities and dispositions from both sources. But it is difficult to measure and quantify separately the influences of heredity and society on the body. For society has its own influence on heredity. Language and other symbolic acquisitions of society also shape the body in the process of decoding the messages it receives from the world. Some of the messages are imposed and some entertained. The means and mechanisms of decoding the messages,though socially and biologically standard, are not uniform in respect to all human beings.

One might have had some justification to accuse the Quine of *From the Logical Point of View* of a mild dose of subjectivity, but against the Quine of *World and Object* one cannot justifiably level that charge. Grounding epistemology into biology, sociology, and linguistics and all in turn into physics in a way, he certainly succeeds in making his defense of objectivity very plausible. This sort of objectivity is quite consistent with historical relativity. How could one possibly show, if at all, that the history-relative conceptual frameworks of the scientists of the earlier ages and of the modern age are objectively related and continuous? Before he answers this sort of question Quine takes logical care to point out that the questioner himself will not be able to give clear sense to such crucial words of the question as "show," "history-relative conceptual frameworks," and "earlier ages" unless the questioner implicitly shares certain logical, physical (space-time), and other trivial presuppositions with him. It is in terms of these commonly shared, varyingly implicit, and inarticulate presuppositions that cross-cultural identification and communication of objects and theories are possible. Without these presuppositions interlinguistic or intersystematic translation, a commonly experienced and persistent phenomenon, also is left inexplicable. Better, therefore, we "start" from what is persistently experienced by us irrespective of our cultural affiliation; later on we can try to follow the cues of experience and find out to what extent ideas and the objects of experience can be successfully translated. Making due and ungrudging allowance for the Quinean *indeterminacy*, one has to admit that intercultural translation and communication do not discover a new truth but merely confirm or reassure what is already there. The view will be argued in detail from another standpoint in Chapter 5.

The difficulties of the indeterminacy thesis, though undeniable, need not be exaggerated on speculative grounds. The indeterminacy thesis holds good not only in the case of intercultural translation but, to a lesser extent, also in that of intracultural translation: not only between, say, a speaker of language L(1) of PS(T1) and a speaker of language L(3) of CS(T3) but also between two speakers, one a layman and another a professional scientist of L(3) of CS(T3). If the last test of the correctness of a translation is the assent of the individual concerned, then in fairness to the objective nature of language one should imagine that the concerned individual is social and cannot therefore indefinitely afford to use an idiolect. Dummett's criticism[14] of Quine on the alleged ground that the latter first "recognises the social character of language" and then "jettisons this recognition by pretending that one may shrink the linguistic community as one chooses" seems to me somewhat unjustified. For Quine repeatedly says that language is a social art and that it works in a physical world. Moreover, language users are biologically more or less similar. The indeterminacy thesis puts no undue limit or restriction on intra- or intercultural translation. On the contrary, it tries to reconcile the contextual character of knowledge with its objectivity. However, the Quinean yes—no types of responses fall short of the requirement of communication that I will defend later on.

The limit of translation is the limit of logic. We can have both the common sense and the science of PS(T1) translated in our CS(T3) language, despite the fact that the presuppositions of "common sense" and "science" of PS(T1) and CS(T3) are considerably different. If PS(T1) is really *prelogical* (from within our language), we cannot have its common sense and science translated in our language, even making due *and* extraliberal allowance for the indeterminacy thesis. Rules for translating primitive science into modern science may be found or formed, but the rules for translating prelogic into logic *cannot* be. For we cannot even significantly and coherently talk *about* the logical particles, terms, and rules *of* the so-called prelogic. We can only indicate why we cannot. If the "logic" of the prelogical people is totally unlike ours, we do not know how to translate its unmappable subject matter, and if the translation is ideally perfect, that would mean imposition of our logic on theirs. In either case this unexecutable project of translation is a sort of shadow meeting between a person who is and a person who never was and across a vast uninhabited area in between the two. The executable project is situated in "conversational," not "logical," language.

Fortunately for us, the history of science in primitive society, which we want to reconstruct, does not belong to the area marked "prelogical" by Lévi-Bruhl.[15] In the face of vigorous criticism of Durkheim, Mauss, and Evans-Pritchard, it is true, Lévi-Bruhl partially retreated and revised his theory of the prelogical mentality of the primitive people, trying to rehabilitate it as a form of *mystical group representation* that does not lend itself to what we call logical formulation and treatment. But he never gave it up totally. His revised view that primitive people know by a sort of mystical participation, "knowing by being" as some philosophers put it, is nothing new in the history of ideas. But it would be wrong to conclude on the inadequate basis of this misunderstood thesis that the thought of primitive people had no logical structure in it.

The examples cited to show that their thought had no respect for what we call the fundamental laws of logic—such as those of contradiction, identity, and excluded middle—can well be interpreted otherwise. We all know how many logicians have damaged logic in the modern age because of their alleged failure to respect the laws of contradiction and excluded middle. Mysticism or knowing by participation as such is no enemy of logic. Of course, the question depends partly upon how (narrowly) one wants to define the scope of logic.

The problem one encounters in speaking about the prelogical mind and its ways of knowing and understanding the world has been very strikingly posed, as we all know, by Wittgenstein in the *Tractatus*. Tractarian theory is essentially a possible worlds semantics that can hardly recognise a "prelogical" (and therefore "impossible") world. When one wants to speak the unspeakable Wittgenstein's despair is understandable, but not his stricture against the unspeakables. This point has been highlighted in the writings of many mystics, such as Saṃkara, Eckhart, and Sri Aurobindo, and also in the writings of philosophers, who should not ordinarily be regarded as mystic, such as Vico, Spengler, and Sorokin.[16] "Prelogical mind" is the anti-thesis of "axiomatic set." From the level of indeterminate perception or pure given one cannot logically determine under which set of axioms the concerned sense-contents or the intuited materials could be organised. Antithetically speaking, from the height of pure axioms (that is, without the rules of interpretation) one cannot state what the sense-contents which could be brought and organised under them are. The scientist is free to choose his axioms, but this freedom is not exercised (at least not rationally) without taking the problematic empirical domain into account. It is against this background that one has to understand the significance of Quine's advice that we should begin our inquiry from somewhere near the middle of the pyramid of all that we know and try to organise systematically.

Unless we are very careful about the "things" we propose to discuss or express and about the role of language in the matter, the extreme ends of "pure axiomatic language" and "prelogical language" are bound to create confusion. At one end we fail to recognise the very subject matters that we are called upon to systematise neatly; at the other end we ourselves are immersed or lost in what is to be expressed. Without resorting to abstraction and without forming concepts that do not directly correspond to sense-impressions we cannot climb up the pyramid: "semantic ascent" is impossible. Interestingly enough, to express our sense-impressions clearly and communicably we have to construct language that increasingly disengages itself from those very sense-impressions. In other words and to put the matter a little more paradoxically, to be true of the world, language must be relatively independent of it, must not refer to it in detail but only structurally. At the level of structural reference when language starts functioning logically, ignoring the details of the world of experience and serving argumentative and ratiocinative purposes, Einstein warns us, it tends to become "a dangerous source of error and deception." Cannot we think at a purely conceptual level, that is, not only without any reference whatsoever to the world of experience but also without any inner mental struggle to get at "the right words for the things"? An affirmative answer to the question presupposes that the individual can form concepts "without the verbal guidance of his environment." Although in prin ciple it may be possible, the mental capacity of an individual grown up under such unrealistic conditions is sure to be poor. Einstein observes:

> The mental development of the individual and his way of forming concepts depend to a high degree upon language. This makes us realise to what extent the same language means the same mentality. In this sense thinking and language are linked together.[17]

The language of Euclidean geometry and algebra may be taken as a model of scientific language. It succeeds in perfectly combining the twin objectives of science: to achieve precision and clarity of concepts in this mutual relation and correspondence to sensory data. The model languages consist of a small number of well-defined concepts or symbols (the integral number, the straight line, the point) and some signs designating the fundamental operations (conjunction, disjunction, negation) indicating the relations between the concepts. Acts of counting and measuring according to well-defined rules show the connection between the concepts and statements, on the one hand, and the sensory data, on the other.

Logical unity of conceptual parsimony and perceptual diversity is achieved by stages. Einstein speaks of four stages or layers of unity. In its first stage the unity of science seems to be lost in the diversity of sense experiences. In the second stage unity is partially established by introducing a secondary system that is relatively poor in concepts and relations but from which the concepts and relations of the first layer are derivable. Thereafter in his bid to achieve still higher unity the scientist introduces a tertiary system, still poorer in concepts and relations, from which the second layer and, therefore, by implication, the first layer as well are deducible. The quest for the ideal of highest possible unity marked by greatest "poverty" of concepts and "richest" in content is bound to go on unabated.

Einstein, like Popper, is an anti-inductivist. He does not approve of the inductivist way of treating the layers of concepts and relations as "degrees of abstraction." He does not consider it justifiable to veil "the logical independence of the concept from the sense experience." In the matter of choice of his concepts (or axioms) the scientist is certainly free in a sense. But this freedom has to be exercised, as I have said before, bearing in mind the problem that he is expected to explain or solve in terms of those concepts. His position is like that of a man engaged in solving a "well-designed" word puzzle. He is, of course, free to propose any word to solve it, but in fact there is only *one* word that alone can solve the puzzle in all its aspects. This formulation of Einstein betrays his realistic *faith* that nature is "well-designed" to return a yes verdict only to one proposal and a no to the rest. Here Einstein sounds Kantian. Popper amends this slightly but very significantly.[18] According to him, nature never returns a yes verdict: all its verdicts are either no or not yet no; often we mistakenly interpret not-yet-no as yes. Both Kant and Poincaré took Newton's not-yet-no physics as yes physics forever. Einstein's no physics shook the very foundation of Newton's not-yet-no one to the utter dismay of orthodox Kantians and Poincaréans. To quote Popper:

> The modification of Kant's solution ["our intellect does not draw its laws from nature . . . but imposes them upon nature"] which I propose, in accordance with the Einsteinian revolution, frees us from this compulsion [of belief that "Newton's theory . . . followed inescapably and with logical necessity from the laws of our understanding"]. In this way, theories are seen to be *free* creations of our own minds, the results of an almost poetic intuition, of an attempt to understand intuitively the laws of nature. But we no longer try to force our creations upon nature. On the contrary, we question nature, as Kant taught us to do; and we try to elicit from her *negative* answers concerning the truth of our theories: we do not try to prove or to *verify* them, we test them by trying to disprove or to falsify them, to *refute* them. . . . It is here . . . that scientific rigour and logic enter into empirical science.

However, it would be wrong to suggest that Einstein does not realise the endless revisability of scientific theories. In fact, he explicitly states that the multiple layers of a scientific system are "stages of progress . . . [that have] resulted from the struggle for unity in the course of development"; of the intermediate layers he says that these are only "of temporary nature" and "must eventually disappear as irrelevant." Problems and contradictions at the lower levels necessitate review and revision of the concepts and relations at the upper levels. When not only middle-level theories but also higher-level laws are seriously disturbed by contrary experimental findings, a critical review and revision even of the axiomatic top of the concerned system has to be undertaken, presaging what may be called revolutionary change of the system. Rightly understood, lower-level disturbances may also necessitate serious change at the top. The reason is simple: "The layers," says Einstein, "are not clearly separated."

Consistently with his notion of semantic ascent and distrust of the notion of analyticity, Quine also declines to draw any sharp line of demarcation between categories or the most general principles and ordinary laws of nature. It is on the authority of well-tested theory of physics that we, the laymen, believe that there are electrons. We believe in classes because we have been told that physics needs the theory of real numbers. Our belief in the existence of infinite classes of rational and real numbers also rests on the words of the recognised custodians of science as a subculture, in this case, of the eminent physicists and mathematicians. It is true in a sense that the world would continue to be what it is irrespective of these our beliefs, but the world of the physicist would be quite different if the theories of the authorities, on whose words we entertained these beliefs, were all false. What we accept as a part of our culture, in this case science, on others' authority has been well tested by the concerned authoritative spokesmen of the discipline, and *about* that we have taken care to satisfy ourselves. The layman does not accept or reject the notions of physics and mathematics on the authority of an ornithologist or entomologist, unless of course the latter is known as an established authority also in the field of physics and mathematics. Only a part of our culture is directly known to us; the rest of it is accepted (at least for the time being) by us on others' authority; our disposition to recognise some persons as authorities also in most cases rests on the authority of some other persons.

What we accept at one stage on the authority of other persons cannot and does not remain acceptable or unquestionable at all stages and for all of us equally. What is a presupposition today may be criticised or even tested tomorrow, depending upon the nature of the presupposition in question. Certainly axiomatic, metaphysical, and empirical presuppositions are not all questioned and modified in the same way. Whatever might be the way of questioning the presuppositions and whatever might be the level of the latter, one thing is clear: we cannot question all presuppositions simultaneously. One has to agree with Neurath, Popper, and Quine that to repair or even to rebuild the boat of science made up of different types of planks—perceptions, objects, theories, laws, and axioms—we have to keep it (with ourselves in it) afloat. There is no getting out of it even when it is in need of urgent and extensive repair. And here the analogy of the boat of science with the ordinary one seems to break down. There is no drydock or boat-building yard where we can get out of it and repair it *from outside*. Besides, the boat of science, as is evident from history, never sinks or gets lost at sea, although it is badly tossed and battered by periodic storms of revolutionary changes.

Certain clarifications are called for. The science of today is a unity, especially for the professionals. Except in the matter of interpretation in certain areas, professional scientists all over the world are inclined to agree on the unitary character of science. Of course, one must not minimise the importance of interpretation in science, especially in its higher reaches. What is true for the professionals is not true for the common men. The image of science to the common men is neither very clear nor very unitary. For their views of science are largely shaped by what they read in newspapers, fiction, popular books, TV programmes: on the authority of the persons who should not ordinarily be regarded as professionals. In spite of wide coverage of education and communication, we are simultaneously having two different images of science: one (unitary) image for the professional and the other (multiple) image for the common man. In fact, the multiple image is a cross-section or complexus of many images. If this can happen today, assuming the theory of parallel growth of different civilisations and cultures, we can well imagine how diverse was the image of science and of philosophy not only to the common man but also to the privileged few when the communication system was extremely poor or undeveloped.

I have already said that we must reject the thesis that presuppositions are primarily a matter of choice and can be retained even in the face of questions and corrections of the propositions mapped on them. Though different and at times deviant, the relation between the two is neither ad hoc nor external, that is, not separable or detachable. Since presuppositions in different contexts—mathematical, axiomatic, metaphysical, empirical, down-to-earth common sense, and so forth—serve different purposes change and modification are brought about in different ways. Making intelligible, explaining, relating (weakly or strongly), and making a decision possible regarding the truth-value of the propositions and their assertion are some of the purposes served by presuppositions. Attempts to assimilate all other purposes under truth-value decision making are bound to create confusion in the theoretical context of the history of science and philosophy with which I am primarily concerned here.

To determine whether a particular mathematical or logical theory is true or false what is done is to try to refute it, or, failing that to prove it or to refute its negation. Essentially the same procedure is also followed in the case of empirical sciences. Attempts are made to test them by trying to refute them. In the testing of the latter type of theories empirical arguments and factual considerations play a very important role that is not there, at least not so directly, in the testing of logicomathematical theories. Philosophical theories, including metaphysical ones, are "tested" in a different way: first trying to relate them to the problems they are supposed to solve and then comparing them critically in respect to their problem-solving capacity. The concept of test is evidently different from that of criticism. A philosophical theory may be criticised even though it cannot be shown to be false. A more rational philosophical theory addresses itself to a wider range of problems or the deeper reaches of problems or both and, at the same time, because of this problem-oriented character, lends itself to clear critical scrutiny. It is in terms of the general concept of rationality that all three types of theories—logicomathematical, empirical, and philosophical—can be brought and viewed together as expressive of the kindred efforts of man to adjust himself to the different levels, abstract and concrete, of his environment.

By the general concept of rationality I mean a sort of consistency, direct or indirect, between the end and the means in a problem-solving context of thought or action. There are two different (but related) ways of showing how certain presuppositions are essential to theoretical and practical efforts to solve a problem: (1) The scientist's search for laws of nature by framing hypotheses presupposes that there are uniformities in nature or, as Keynes would have put it, that the variety in nature is limited. The rationality of the search for laws is provided by the presuppositions regarding the structure of nature. (2) the presuppositions which provide rationality to the search for laws are in a sense constitutionally or internally and objectively related to the laws to be discovered. And therefore the presuppositions cannot be contrived or withdrawn and replaced arbitrarily. Given the objective of systematisation—axiomatic, theoretical, or in terms of law—the concerned scientist has to choose his axioms, postulates, and definitions, and frame his hypothesis preparatory to the establishment of law or theory. Besides the objective what influence the choice of axioms, postulates, definitions, and hypotheses are the properties and relations of the objects (of the domain) to be systematised. Axiomatisation is a higher-level systematisation of what has, in a way, already been systematised at a lower level in objects and at the middle level in theories or laws. This, however, does not necessarily mean that objects are *constructs* or that laws and theories are *instruments*. Different levels of system are interlinked and interanimated. If the higher-level animation reaches *all* the lower-level elements and if the newly discovered elements at the lower levels can be adequately accounted for by the higher-level presuppositions (HLP), then the choice of the latter is said to be rational. Rationality is not a static concept. If the new elements of the lower level, for example, objects or experiences, cannot be adequately "covered" by or taken care of in terms of HLPS, that is, theories, laws, or axioms, then the situation rationally necessitates some or another change at the top (HLPs). For otherwise the very purpose of axiomatisation or theorisation is defeated. One should not, however, think that efforts to avoid defeat are desiderata for vindicating rationality, that is, preservation (of HLPS). On the contrary, the genuine test of HLP rationality consists in exposing the concerned HLPs to possible defeat tests; their rationality is established, although provisionally, and can be relied upon the purpose of further research. To resort to such defeat-avoiding strategies as adding new axioms, postulates, assumptions, or auxiliary hypotheses to the existing ones often betrays the weakness of the system and a retreat mentality of the system builder. Rightly understood, the rational scientist has no vested interest in his system or theory, and therefore he is not supposed to try to save his system at prohibitive cost: resorting to the tactics of dodging the attackers, the critics, instead of squarely meeting them. Rationality demands that the theorist face the consequences of his theory or system both in deduction and in the test-cases of its application. Incorporation of only those postulates, assumptions, and so on, within the system that add to its testability, collectively and/or severally, depending to a large extent on the logical structure of the system, is welcome. Unlike in war logistics, in scientific theory-construction and use retreat to "commitments" such as axioms and postulates does not help: for at the appropriate time and level these very "commitments" are questioned and as such not referred to as sacrosanct *reasons* for accepting what follows from them.

This situation calls for another look from a different angle at the rationality of the theoretical picture of the world or a part thereof in science. The problem is how to understand the lower-level statements of insistent sense-impressions and of persistent objects in a theoretical framework. Does their rationality depend upon their *derivability* from HLPs and/or axioms? Or is their being true by virtue of correspondence with certain states of affairs obtained there out in the world? These questions are not basically different. The appearance of difference is due to conflation of two different modes of speech: one in terms of the independent existence of the *extralinguistic* external world with entities such as sense-impressions and objects in it, and another in terms of *intralinguistic* entities like sense-impressions and objects. In the latter case the assumption is that the identities and meanings of the entities are entirely defined and determined within the language used to talk about them. And in the former case the assumption is that the identities and meanings of the entities are entirely defined and determined independently of any language. Both assumptions are naive and prereflective. Neither is the world as it is in itself pictured or described in language nor is the world as it is in language, formal or natural, its only identity. It seems to me that both "the world as it is in itself" and "the world as it is in language" are different (but not necessarily inconsistent) idealised abstractions. In fact we know it both ways. Certainly the world has an independent identity of its own and its structures with many substructures nested in it, as the realist is fond of claiming. Otherwise the unity and intersubjectivity of, and correspondence between, the different pictures or descriptions of the world cannot be correctly accounted for. Even if more or less indeterminateness of the different world-pictures is admitted, that can hardly be construed as an argument against the independent reality of the world. On the contrary, it may be rightly suggested that the elements of indeterminateness themselves are due to the conditions of the world being given as possible objects of knowledge. That is, objects are not unconditionally given. One may even go further and say that the process of objectification involves satisfaction of such trivial conditions as physiological capacities and psychological soundness and such nontrivial conditions as use of appropriate language, use of appropriate concepts, and appropriate use of the space-time framework. However, it cannot be justifiably claimed that the conditions of the object being given are such that they are constitutive of it: objects being independent as they are cannot be conceptually and linguistically completely internalised. One-to-one exact correspondence between the object-in-the-world and the object-in-the-body-mind-complex is an ideal that is never realised, or realisable: the conditions which make partial realisation of the object possible also make correspondence inexact. This is also true in respect to impressions and images as objects: our body is persistently ambivalent—partly in the world *and* partly subjective—irremediably and uniquely. What is an object *for* the body-mind complex can be again an object *within* it but differently, at another level.

What is true of the *horizontal* picture of rationality, one-to-one exact correspondence, is true also of the *vertical* picture of rationality, term-to-term correspondence in deductive (or reverse) relations among the levels (0, 1, 2, and 3) of sense-impressions, objects, theories, laws, and axioms. In both cases the end or the ideal of rationality is such that the available means in relation to it, though necessary, are not sufficient. From the statements of laws or theories alone, that is, without their conjunction with some existential statements describing the concerned circumstances, the detailed features of objects or properties of sense-impressions cannot be derived or anticipated. From the alternative geometries as such the difference in the measurement of spatial properties of medium-sized objects cannot be determined. What difference follows from the different sets of axioms and definitions of alternative geometries becomes understandable in the measurement of large, for example, astronomical, as well as minute, for example, subatomic, distances, areas, magnitudes, and volumes. But to account for the difference the putative parenthood of geometrical entities denoted by the words *straight line, point* and so on, has to be attributed, on the one hand, to (1) the formal-logical system of concepts of axiomatic geometry *and*, on the other, to (2) the coordination of real objects of experience by adding the proposition that solid bodies are related with respect to their possible dispositions. Whenever, for the sake of systematisation of the objects of knowledge, we are obliged to express *many* in terms of *few* the rationality requirement of one-to-one correspondence, horizontal picturing or vertical derivability, cannot be satisfied. In fact, one might point out, the one-to-one correspondence model of rationality and the ideal of systematisation do not go together. Of logical necessity we express many in terms of few. Otherwise we cannot systematise what we have already known and what we can possibly know.

The rationality of system is to be understood in terms of consistency and *not* correspondence between few and many, for example, between objects and sense-impressions or between axioms and theorems. It should be pointed out here perhaps that to insist on *correspondence* to the exclusion of *consistency* is grounded in a confusion about the relation between the formal mode of speech and the material mode of speech or between object-language and metalanguage. Rightly understood, the relation of correspondence of object-language can well be taken care of in terms of the relation of consistency of metalanguage. The statement "S" is true if and only if S (is the state of affairs) or "S" is true if and only if it corresponds to S.[19] Intuitively, that is, in the ordinary prereflective level of language use, one may, perhaps does, think that "S" is *in* language and S stands *outside* language, in the world there, and that there obtains a relation called *correspondence* between the two. Reflection reveals and recursion "proves" that the relation between the two is satisfactorily understandable only in metalanguage, preferably, but not necessarily, in a formalised language.

I have already referred to man's adjustment or adaptation to his environment in the wider sense, including both the physical and the cultural: this adaptation is gradually achieved, step by step, by stored and sorted experiences and information embodied in theories and expectations, expressed in meaningful or purposive responses to the challenges and stimuli provided by the environment. I have spoken also of the general concept of rationality and tried to clarify it in terms of consistency between the end and means of thought or action in a problem-solving context. Now it would be interesting to bring closer the concepts of adaptation and rationality and to note how they work together as the presupposition of our cognitive enquiry. Let me again use an example from the history of science.

Early in this century, 1910-1911, Planck (1858-1947) and Mach (1838-1916), two noted physicists-philosophers, both influenced by Kant's and Helmholtz's philosophical and physiological ideas, found themselves engaged in a lively controversy over the epistemology and ontology of such physical theories as the laws of thermodynamics. The German physicist Rudolf Clasius (1822-1883) stated the first law of thermodynamics in this form: the energy of the universe is constant; that is, whatever transfer or transformation of energy we bring about, we cannot change the total amount. He stated the second law of thermodynamics thus: every time we get something by means of an energy transformation, we reduce by a measurable amount the opportunity to get that something in the future: the entropy of the universe strives always to increase, corresponding to an overall steady increase in the nonavailability of energy for further transformations. We cannot construct a perpetual motion machine. For these occurrences in nature—thermal conduction, diffusion, electrical conduction, emission of light, and heat radiation, atomic decay of radioactive substances—have proved irreversible. Examples of reversible processes are the movements of the planets, free fall in a vacuum, propagation of light and sound waves without absorption or deflection. Clasius's way of defining the irreversibility of a process appears "unduly anthropomorphous" to Max Planck, who is against "too much tailoring (of scientific theories) to the needs of mankind." The answers we solicit from nature in response to our question, according to him, should be formulated from "a more general, and less economic, standpoint." To quote Max Planck:

> It cannot be defined that the system of physics . . . is still adulterated with a strong dose of anthropomorphism. If the definition of irreversibility and entropy reference is made to the feasibility of certain changes in nature, and this really means that the classification of physical events is made dependent on the extent of man's experimental skill, which does not remain constant but is being continually being improved. If the distinction between reversible and irreversible process is really to be of lasting significance for all time, it must be considerably deepened and freed from all reference to human abilities.[20]

It was left to Ludwig Boltzmann (1844-1906) to emancipate the concept of entropy from man's experimental limitations and consequently elevate the second law of thermodynamics to a genuine objective principle. This emancipation consists in relating the concept of entropy to the concept of probability. Nature "prefers" more probable, that is, disorderly, states to less probable, that is, orderly, ones. Objectively speaking, in any naturally occurring process, the tendency is for all systems to move from order to disorder. Since the universe as a whole is subject to this inexorable entropy increase process, it seems that no return or reversion is practically possible. But once it is shown that within this *global* physical picture *local* variations of the contrary sort are statistically probable, the hypothesis of "nature's preference" becomes irrelevant. By introducing atomic theory and the statistical approach Boltzmann succeeds in calculating the variations in the local systems, the precise degree of probability for each condition of a system of bodies. That local decreases in entropy are possible is evident from the manifestation or emergence of living organisms.

The manifestation of a living creatures implies the transformation of disorder into order, transition from a random collection of atoms or oxygen, nitrogen, hydrogen, carbon, and so on, to orderly constitution of the living cell. One may say, "Life consumes entropy." The local consumption of entropy does in no way violate the second law at the global level. Boltzmann's interpretation was furthered and corroborated by the ideas and findings of Maxwell and Gibbs.[21]

Planck thinks that Boltzmann's interpretation of the law of energy conservation shows that it was "valid in nature before any man was able to think about it" or independent of its experimental proof. And he contests Mach's view that "there is no reality apart from our own impressions," that "the dividing line between the physical and the psychical is a purely practical and conventional one," and that "all natural science in the last resort is merely an economical adaptation of our thoughts to our impressions, to which we are driven by the struggle for existence."[22] Mach's positivistic criticisms of atomistic hypotheses and of the theory of electrons on the alleged ground that these are not directly measurable appear "unfounded and untenable" to Planck, for, he points out, there is no system of physical measurement that is totally free of assorted experiences and theoretical abstractions. This is a point of which we have been often reminded in the last three decades by Popper against Bridgman's operationalism. Whereas Planck's demand is for a *constant* world-picture, independent of changing times and peoples, Mach argues that science needs and strives for nothing more than a phenomenally *continuous* world-picture, which, the former concedes, "cannot be proved to contain any inner contradiction," although "its significance is only a formalistic one." The great masters of the exact sciences like Copernicus, Kepler, Newton, Huygens and Faraday had their unshaken faith in the reality of the world-picture and apparently were not interested in drawing what Mach calls "human-economical pictures of reality."

Mach rejects Planck's criticism on the ground that it rests on a false dichotomy between the physical and the physiological. Scientific laws and theories cannot be constructed without reference to the sensations of our body and *via* body of the properties and relations of the objects outside. "Sensations belong to both physical and psychical worlds, representations only to the latter." Mach does not conceal his dislike for what he calls the "hypotheticofictitious physics" of Boltzmann, meaning by that the latter's probabilistic investigations into the second law, based on the kinetic theory of gases. Boltzmann's hypothesis that the concept of entropy is *really* assimilable under the concept of probability, though bold in its bid to present a unified picture of the physical world, is essentially "artificial," noneconomic, extravagant, and unsupported by experience. According to Mach, man can observe man's own sense-impressions and their dependence on the environment, and this enables him to "arrive at a natural interpretation of the world, free of speculative additions." Planck's point is that sense-impressions as such, that is, without speculative aids, cannot picture the physical world. The point is partly conceded by Mach himself when he says, "the world is not as directly given to us as it at first appeared to be."[23] But he defines the "physical" differently, as "that which is directly given only to one, and can only be inferred by others." The physical must not be construed as some self-existent substance; it is an intersubjectively experienceable continuum sustained by "the *permanence of the linking of reactions* described by *physical laws.*" Elsewhere he says, "Experience grows through progressive adaptation of thought to fact" and "ideas gradually adapt to facts by picturing them with sufficient accuracy to meet biological needs."[24]

Planck sounds equally firm in his criticism of Mach's uncritical commitments to "intellectual economy" and "cognitive processes serving biological needs of adaptation." He is for a stable picture of the physical world in science and strongly against "Mach's attempts to weaken the distinction between *stability* and *economy*," "for economy is inseparable from expediency, whereas the concept of stability has nothing to do with expediency," and, what is more, brings the realistic character of scientific knowledge to the fore.

While I gladly endorse Planck's realistic orientation, I find nothing intrinsically wrong with Mach's accent on "economy" and "biological needs" (obviously in the extended sense) for adaptation. In theory-construction we are undeniably guided by the motive of explaining or systematising many in terms of few. In this sense the higher we move up on the pyramid of theories and laws, the more parsimonious we intend to become in the development of concepts. "Be economic in the choice of your concepts, theories and laws" is nothing more than a methodological precept. It does not necessarily imply any retreat from the realistic commitment to the primacy of truth (rather than the paying character) of the theories of science. If the claims of truth and those of "economy" are found to be inconsistent, the latter must give way to the former. Following Popper one may say that the logic of the (theory-building) situation demands that both amoeba and

Einstein eliminate errors in their bid to get to the truth.[25] Quite unlike the amoeba, Einstein knows the soft spots of his theories and also what can possibly eliminate those spots. The scientist knows about his environment by being challenged, not instructed, by it: his responses are evoked by it, and through the *elimination* of the *unsuccessful* responses he adapts himself better to the environment. This is true in respect to both our theoretical environment and our practical environment. Being stable and independent of us as it is, our environment always can and in fact does return a no or not yet verdict to our selected anticipations about it—selected in the light of our background information about it. Whenever one set of our needs, biological, psychological or abstract intellectual, is met, it puts us in touch with another, perhaps more complex and comprehensive, one.

The evolutionary-biological or even the interdependent character of knowledge, one suspects, has an anti-Platonic, if not anti-realist, implication. It seems to me that a correct and an interpretative understanding of science, its laws and theories, does not involve any retreat from realistic commitment. But realism need not be taken as a synonym of platonism.

Obviously the scientist is primarily concerned with laws and theories and not directly perceived objects and constructs in terms of which the former is formulated and tested. The presuppositions on analysis turn out to be different or multilayered. First, science, unlike common sense, presupposes a well-defined language, natural or (preferably) formal, depending upon the social context. Professional scientists forming a homogeneous specialists' group can and do horizontally communicate among themselves using only abstract concepts and formulas almost in an "esoteric" language. What we say "esoteric" they regard "natural." In vertical communication between different sub-cultural groups we are obliged to use ordinary or natural language, utilising its indefinite and rich resources which appear inexact to the professionals but lucid to the interested laymen. The historians of science, although they cannot completely get out of the contemporary theories of science and of history, are required to have some familiarity with the natural or formal language of the society in which his subject-matters were originally expressed. Without knowing Greek logic and mathematics one cannot hope to be a good historian of Greek science. Since the scientific ideas of the time were rooted extensively in the then Greek society or societies, the concerned historian, in addition to the necessary language, must also know the social conditions shaping those ideas directly and indirectly. In fact, the knowledge of a language itself remains highly imperfect unless its social background can be grasped. A good historian is one who works critically and has a double duty to perform: one, to understand the society and language in which lies his subject matter as understood by the people of that time; and, another, to be critically conscious of his own tools of trade, language, social conditions, and the conceptual framework, which he uses for the purpose of understanding the said subject matter. It is true that the language of formal logic or that of mathematics differs from ordinary language in the complexity and at times ambiguity of its different uses under diverse conditions. But every language has its presuppositions, trivial or nontrivial: even the nontrivial ones, because of long and unquestioned use over time, often become an almost self-evident part of a particular professional culture. The validity of logico-mathematical reasoning is, to a great extent, dependent upon its metaphysical presuppositions. The controversy that is now going on over the ontological status of mathematical objects between the constructionists and the Platonists was there in the history of science, under some label or another, over the centuries. Whereas the Platonist thinks that the mathematician, like the astronomer, has to recognise the objects—classes, for instance—which are there independently of being known by him, the intuitionist is of the view that the mathematician enjoys great freedom in devising the concepts he introduces, in defining classes, and in delineating the type or structure to be studied. However, it has been pointed out, even the latter is not free to prove whatever he finds structurally elegant or attractive from his standpoint, reputedly as the result of some real-formal constraints.

Similar disputes exist in other areas of discourse expressed in informal or natural language. History has no language of its own. The historian uses natural language. When he says, to take Russell's well-known example, "The king of France is wise," the truth or falsity of the statement presupposes that there is a king of France. If what he says is expressed in a sentence *S* of the subject-predicate form, then, according to Russell's "theory of definite descriptions," if it is not meaningless, it must be *about* something, must have a referent to be about it. The proposition that *S* expresses, though it appears (*grammatically*) to be of the subject-predicate form, is, *logically* speaking, of a complex *existential* kind, part of which may be said to be "uniquely existential." Strawson criticises Russell, alleging that the latter falsely assumed that if a sentence is logically of the subject-predicate form, "then the very fact of its being significant, having a meaning guarantees that there *is* something referred to by the logical (and grammatical subject)." If S^1 ("One, and only one, person is at present king of France") is a necessary condition of the truth, simply, of S ("The king of France is wise"), then it is "self-contradictory" to conjoin S with the denial of S^1 as the existence of king of France is a necessary condition of the *truth* or *falsity* of S. But it is a different kind of "logical absurdity" to conjoin S with the denial of S^1 in which "king of France" is *mentioned* as a meaningful expression and not used as a part of truth-claiming *assertion*. The relation between S and S^1 in the first case is said to be one of *entailment*. The relation between S and S^1 in the second case may be said to be one of *presupposition*. According to Strawson, Russell's mistake is due to his decision to operate with the "bogus trichotomy," "either true or false or meaningless," based on the confusion between sentences and statements. It is only in respect to the latter that the question of truth or falsity can arise and at times may fail to arise, whereas the meaning of only those sentences that are used for the purpose of making statements is relevant for the determination of truth-conditions of the statements concerned. "The existence of members of the subject-class is to be regarded as presupposed by statements made by the use of . . . sentences" beginning with such phrases as "All," "All the," "None of the," "Some," "Some of the," "At least one," and "At least one of the." But, Strawson argues, to be meaningful a sentence of the statement-making type need not necessarily produce a true or false statement in every use of it, at any place. What is necessary is that it should be possible in suitable circumstances to use it to produce a true or false statement. Similarly, to be meaningful a singular referring expression need not have an *actual* existent thing, person, or place as its referent, but it would suffice that it should be *possible* in suitable circumstances to use it for the purpose of referring to some one thing, person, place, and so on. The linguistic conventions that govern its correct use for referring constitute its meaning. That "the king of France" has meaningful uses can be easily imagined, although there is no king of France at the moment. Such phrases can and in fact do perform a *referring* role although there do not exist objects or persons corresponding to them (in the sense of Russell and Wittgenstein). In brief, Russell confuses, according to Strawson, what is entailed by a statement and what is presupposed by that statement.

This view of Strawson has been criticised by, among others, Sellars,[27] Linsky[28] and Dummett.[29] Linsky points out that the apparent plausibility of Strawson's thesis is derived from his wrong view that there is no important difference between statements, assertions, and propositions. Every proposition is either true or false, but statements can be truth-valueless: therefore, the concept of a statement is different from that of a proposition. Russell can well point out that Strawson has given no argument to show that the proposition that the king of France is wise does not entail the proposition that there is one and only one king of France: and that, instead, the latter has cited *uses* of the statement (*not* proposition) where the question *either* of truth or of falsity does not arise at all. Strawson's notion of presupposition takes "false" in a sense in which it does not mean merely "not true." For him "*S* is false" means "The negation of *S* is true," where the negation of *S* is not to be identified by its truth-conditions, but by its being formed from *S* by the negation operator. The sentential negation-operator is unknown to natural language: strangely enough, Dummett rightly points out, Strawson, primarily interested in the logic of natural language, decides to follow the formal logicians here instead of criticising them.

It is in the following way that the preceding issue is very relevant to historians in general and those of philosophical and scientific ideas in particular. Whereas the realist points out that there is a systematic link between the truth-values of differently tensed statements used or uttered at different times, the antirealist, the empiricist, or even the constructionist, for example, highlights the difficulties associated with the notion of truth of past-tensed statements independently of our means and methods of recognising these statements as true. If Miltiades writes on 21 September 491 B.C., "I have defeated the Persian army under the command of Datis at Marathon," he makes a present-tense statement that is true; let us call it *X*. Now after exactly 2,479 years, let us suppose, someone makes the statement (let us call it *Y*) "2,479 years ago Miltiades defeated the Persian army under the command of Datis at Marathon." If Miltiades' statement, *X*, made on 21 September 491 B.C. is true, then, Dummett argues, "it is a consequence of a truth-value link" that *Y*, a statement made exactly after 2,479 years, is "likewise truth." This realist account of the past-tense statements is undoubtedly very simple and attractive. But the critic may rightly point out that without the existence of certain situations or fulfilment of certain conditions the assertion of such statements as *Y* is unjustifiable. This, however, is not to suggest that truth *is* correct assertability. The conditions that suffice to make an assertion (of *Y*, for instance) correct are by themselves not sufficient to guarantee the truth of the statement (*Y* in this case) asserted. I am not pleading for a reductive thesis, namely, that the conditions for correct assertion of a historical statement are identical with its truth-conditions. The fact that makes a historical statement true is not constituted by the conditions that enable us to recognise that statement to be true. I am for a realistic position in respect to the reality of the past but am not a Platonist. One can always plausibly argue that it is difficult to invoke the notions of truth and falsity independently of our ability to recognise truth or falsity. This is, however, not to deny the reality of the past events with which the historian is concerned. Questions such as, "What really the past events were" can neither be given a coherent sense nor satisfactorily answered unless (1) it is presupposed that past events are real and independent of *how* these are recognised or rediscovered, *and* (2) the pictures or models of the past events are in accord with the evidence and general truths available to the working historian at the time of his work and recognised by his contemporary professionals. Denial of (1) lands one in the position of the sceptic regarding other times and other minds, and denial of (2) implies that the historian has an extraordinary ability to get to the past events without evidence and general truths and, what is more disturbing, that time in respect to the historian is unreal. Truth of both particular evidential and general law statements is revisable. Rationally reconstructed past events or ideas are very much dependent on the revisable truth-values of these statements and their different uses. Consequently there is bound to be a truth-value gap between the statements used to reconstruct past events and the statements of particular evidences and general laws. For the historian, himself a historical creature, cannot form a view of the past that is not influenced by the present, by the conceptual framework and its components with which he is obliged to work. The ever-*open* present, therefore, leaves open many possible ways of reconstruction of the past (events and ideas) and criticism and revision of the same in the light of the criticism. Historical reconstruction is like an open-ended conversation between the historian and his milieu, on the one hand, and the historical agents whose actions he is trying to understand, on the other.

It also follows from what I have said that the history of human culture in general and that of science in particular is bound to be influenced not only by the present but also by the future. Historical consciousness of the historian is contemporaneous, that is, grounded in the present, in a very special sense: this contemporaneity is both receptive of the past and perceptive of the future. While engaged in reconstructing past science, the historian makes use of currently accepted laws and evidence and at the same time is conscious of their historical character: how these have undergone change over the time and that this process *cannot* reach a dead end, a point of time that has *no* future. Since every "present" is physically destined to be "past," the historian in his activities as a historian cannot be unaware of the impact of the future, that is, the *incoming* present, on his professional activities. In the light of new possible laws, techniques, and evidences the historian is professionally obliged, at least in principle, to rewrite-reconstruct the past. Besides, the changing ideology and value-commitment of the historian also enter into his consciousness and influence his activities and conclusions. Both material and nonmaterial (including ideological) conditions of the historian's existence are simultaneously past-determined and future-oriented. But his existence is relatively independent and free, and that, apart from other factors, partially enables him to reconstruct the past and imagine the future *differently*, although the general truths and particular evidence at his disposal are *same*. There is no machine that can effectively suppress man or freeze the flow of time.

CHAPTER FOUR

....

Historism and Structuralism: Sartre and Lévi-Strauss

THE CLASSICAL RATIONALISTS OF EUROPE, BARRING A FEW SUCH AS HEGEL, did not take time seriously. Descartes's and Malebranche's distrust of the historical mode of knowledge is well known. But to all of them *freedom* was very dear. If time is believed to be *real* enough to leave its distinctive imprint on human actions and events, then man as historian cannot be taken as *really* free to reconstruct the past *a priori*, relying only on the structural capacities of his mind and ignoring the diverse and particular details of the past. This point seems to me very relevant to our discussion of the theoretical issues concerning the history of science. Sartre is often credited with the view that history in the form of dialectical reason is the discipline that alone provides a sound method to understand other societies and their intellectual achievements such as science. This privileged access-claim of history to other times and places, that is, societies, has been vigorously challenged by Lévi-Strauss, who, although primarily famous for his *structural* anthropological studies, is, like Sartre, also a first-rate professional philosopher, as is evident from his numerous writings. Besides Descartes's, the other dominant influence on them is Marx's. But they have drawn upon the widely diverse Cartesian and Marxist ideas in their own different ways. I will refer to the Sartre–Lévi-Strauss controversy only to the extent that it touches upon the theoretical problems of the history of science.

The Cartesian cogito, the knowing mind, was equipped with some innate ideas of immense comprehension and consequence in terms of which it could gather not only what happens in other minds but also what happens in other places. To make the passage from mind to matter, from psychology to physics, a possible Cartesian system needed God as the superordinating substance and mediatory functionary. Without a God and without an innate ideal enabling him to move from the self to the *other*, Sartre apparently does not know how to exercise his freedom to know (the acquisitions, including science and technology) of *other* societies. The historian of science as man, facing the contrasts of other societies in history, has to understand the latter dialectically, "initially through human relations." And, according to Sartre, dialectical reason, unlike positivist reason, carries its own intelligibility, is self-supporting "independent of any empirical discovery." Historical process becomes truly intelligible only when it is viewed and critically reviewed from the standpoint of dialectical reason and as a developing process of "totalisation" that includes its reflexive retotalisation essentially through the reflexive experience of individuals. Individual praxis seems to be the model and origin of all praxis. It also sustains the critical character of the scattered totalisation. If history of science continues to be a living and growing history and does not relapse into uncritical cultural borrowing from other societies or, to use Sartre's own phrase, collectives, that is mainly due to the individual praxis, its underlying freedom, responsible and forward-looking character, "project."

Sartre's attempt to graft the dialectical history of Marx on his ontology of "for-itself," the "project," and "freedom" is beset with serious difficulties. Rational assurance of the ultimate realisation of the Sartrean (or for that matter any individual's) project is said to be operative at both the level of totalising historical development and that of the freedom of the historical agents. Certainly there is no guarantee that the freedom of the agents will be exercised toward a convergent goal. On the contrary, if we take other related concepts of Sartre's seriously, it is difficult to escape an opposite conclusion. In a class-ridden society the praxis of the historical agents, both individually and collectively, is primarily marked by alterity, a relation of separation, or a lack of reciprocity, resulting in conflict of goals, whether chosen or imitated. Deepening of consciousness below the "inert-practical" level and touching the true dialectical depth, a suggested Sartrean way out of the difficulty, does not appear to be promising at all. For even at that depth one cannot be assured of a harmony of goals, whether preestablished or praxis-achieved. To resort to the concept of "totalisation without a totaliser," another Sartrean way out, is not plausible either. I do not see how a process of history that is neither guided by God nor conscious of its goal, if any, can be rendered intelligible on the basis of Sartre's ontology, which simultaneously highlights the freedom of and conflict between and within the historical agents, individuals, and groups. His answer to this "real problem of History," though questionable on several grounds, is undoubtedly very audacious and ingenious.

> If History really is to be the totalisation of all practical multiplicities and of all their struggles, the complex products of the conflicts and collaborations of these very diverse multiplicities must themselves be intelligible in their synthetic reality, that is to say, they must be comprehensible as the synthetic products of a totalitarian *praxis*. This means that History is intelligible if the different practices which can be found and located at a given moment of the historical temporalisation finally appear as partially totalising and as connected and merged in their very oppositions and diversities by an intelligible totalisation from which there is no appeal. . . . (T)he regressive movement of the critical investigation has demonstrated the intelligibility of practical structures and the dialectical relation which interconnects the various forms of active multiplicities. But . . . we are still at the level of synchronic totalisation and we have not yet considered the diachronic depth of practical temporalisation; and . . . the regressive movement has ended with a question: . . . it has to be completed by a synthetic progression whose aim will be to rise up to the double synchronic and diachronic movement by which History constantly totalises itself. So far, we have been trying to get back to the elementary formal structures, and, at the same time, we have located the dialectical foundations of a structural anthropology.[1]

Sartre's jargon, as we all know, is the nightmare of the analytic philosopher. And he reminds one of Kant, Hegel, Marx, Dilthey, Max Weber, and, of course, Lévi-Strauss. In his own way he unifies and totalises their ideas in his thought, which itself, if we are to accept Sartre's view of history, is undergoing dialectical change. Whereas Kant's *First Critique* is addressed to the question, "How synthetic a priori judgement is possible," Sartre's Critique is said to be concerned with a more fundamental question, Whether synthetic a priori judgment is possible." *That* synthetic a priori judgment is possible is uncritically accepted by Kant, for his paradigm of knowledge was Newtonian science. Having accepted the paradigm his Critique concerns itself with the limited question of identifying the structural conditions of synthesising and unifying activities of the human mind as a representative of a universal mind or consciousness. To Sartre the model of intelligibility is individual praxis, which itself needs no foundation and, what seems to be more interesting, to which the structural conditions (making science possible) themselves are answerable. At every point of time there is an individual or a group consciousness that so clearly and distinctly represents or totalises all different views, scientific or otherwise, living or dead, "from which there is no appeal." In a very fundamental sense science is required to derive its basic intelligibility from history, and not from its structural conditions. Sartre denies the existence of the universal structure of understanding purported to account for the intersubjectivity of scientific knowledge. By its very nature the dialectic of individual praxis, the continuously future-looking character of being-for-itself, rules out the possibility of universal structure. Rightly understood, structures themselves are said to be historical. Products of history unless recognised as such cannot be rationally expected to make the puzzling and clashing myriad of history intelligible. It is primarily to remove this deficiency in the method for the pursuit of cognitive and other human goals that Sartre proposes to investigate *simultaneously* the synchronic as well as the diachronic movement of history. In other words, he offers to give us a phenomenological description of the dialectical fusion of structural anthropology and freedom-ensuring history.

It is Descartes, first among the French philosophers, whom Heidegger credits with transforming metaphysics into anthropology via the philosophy of the cogito in a dualistic world. Sartre takes the Cartesian cogito very seriously, freeing it from its universal innate capacities supposedly necessary for laying the foundations of physics. Influenced by Marxism he rejects Descartes's antihistorical prejudice, and his *Critique* uncritically assumes "the absolute validity of historical action." Lévi-Strauss is strongly critical of the Sartrean way of deriving his dialectical anthropology from the Cartesian cogito. To quote him on the point:

> He who begins by steeping himself in the allegedly self-evident truths of introspection never emerges from them . . . Sartre in fact becomes the prisoner of his Cogito: Descartes made it possible to attain universality, but conditionally on remaining psychological and individual; by sociologizing the Cogito, Sartre merely exchanges one prison for another. Each subject's group and period now take the place of timeless consciousness. Moreover, Sartre's view of the world and man has the narrowness which has been

traditionally credited to closed societies. His insistence on tracing a distinction between the primitive and the civilised with the aid of gratuitous contrasts reflects, in a scarcely more subtle form, the fundamental opposition he postulates between myself and others. [2]

Sartre's central thesis that is being criticised by Lévi-Strauss seems to rest on four pairs of contrasting concepts : (1) self and other, (2) civilised and primitive, (3) dialectical reason and analytical reason, and (4) history and anthropology.

To take the first pair first: Lévi-Strauss thinks that Sartre's failure to realise properly the significance of history, of science, and also, therefore, of history of science is mainly due to the sharp contrast that the latter draws between self and other, whether that other is a being or a thing, an object of psychosociology or that of physical inquiry. Cartesian dualism between man and history was intended to liberate physics from the ambiguity of body-affected consciousness. Descartes thinks that all physical matters are modes of extension that are both geometrically and durationally measurable. Time is said to be only a mode of thinking. Except God's veracity there is no inherent guarantee in man's mind that the confused beliefs caused by the physical world can, on analysis, be rendered intelligible. History is not amenable to any sort of quantitative treatment. Its propositions are purely conjectural or fanciful. Man's knowledge of the physical world is intelligible to the extent that it can be expressed in the language of mathematics or geometry and, by implication, is free of historical fancies. Sartre is not at all *for* quantitative science and *against* history. On the contrary, he accords primacy to the historical mode of knowledge. But, somewhat like Descartes, he thinks that the model of history is provided by self's history—its consciousness of itself, its lived past and immediate environment—and not others' history or other societies' historical past in which truths and fancies lie inextricably mingled and unrecognisably so.

But to be fair to Sartre in the context of Lévi-Strauss's criticism one should recall that whereas for Descartes time is a mode of thinking and its unity due to its material content, for Sartre time is the very nihilating principle giving to the individual praxis its life and individuality and enabling the self (for-itself) to have its own measure for the duration and self-identity of things. He endorses Leibniz's reaction against Descartes and Bergson's against Kant characterising temporality as "a pure relation of immanence and cohesion" but differs from Bergson and supports Kant in holding that duration is an active and not a given synthesis. Descartes encounters the problem of passage from one instant to another instant because he fails to recognise the active and synthesising nature of the self. To him instants appear juxtaposed and separated. Sartre, by contrast, affirms that "temporality is not solely nor even primarily separation." Time which in a very limited sense *separates* the self from its being-in-the-world, *reunites* it with the latter as its other. Separation and reunion are two moments of time as the structure of the self.

In *Being and Nothingness* Sartre's primary concern is to vindicate the freedom of the self, although he does not fail even at that time to mention the inseparability of the self from the other, of Being-for-itself from Being-in-itself. In his later works, such as *Critique, Search for a Method*, and *Situations*, he shifts his emphasis from *freedom* to *need*. Whereas the primary focus of freedom is aimed at the self, keeping others in the penumbra, need brings both self and others under the focus of freedom. Need both unites self with others and separates it from the latter: freedom acts more as a separative force than as a unifying one. But one must remember that in both his earlier and later writings Sartre, in spite of his avowed Marxist persuasion, never ceases to attach great importance to human freedom. Needs bring people – especially the poor ones – together and provide objective conditions for struggling together to be free from needs. Now whether Lévi-Strauss is justified in characterising the enterprise of collective freedom as a prison house for Sartrean cogito, even if divinised, is open to Sartre's criticism. Sartrean cogito, even if sociologised, is under attack from Lévi-Strauss: for the latter himself is primarily interested in explaining freedom, among other given social phenomena, in terms of an appropriately constructed model or structure and not in drawing up a practical project for broadening the horizon of human freedom. In other words, his approach, unlike Sartre's, is essentially scientific and structurally intended to account for the totality of observed ethnographic particulars across the continents and not to trace the process of historical continuity of individual and group activities developing or totalising over the centuries toward a goal not consciously entertained by anyone.

Lévi-Strauss's second criticism is based on the second pair of contrasting concepts, the contrast between the civilised and the primitive, attributed to Sartre. It has been said against Sartre that he could never get over the basic theoretical handicap or the circumscribing effect of his ontological individualism, although his historical method and accent on dialectical reason are presumably intended to undo that effect, the effect of ethnocentricity, an improved version of egocentricity. Lévi-Strauss makes another complaint against Sartre that to do away with the unfortunate consequence of ontological individualism he moves to the other extreme and overemphasises the role of history and thereby highlights the difference between one society and another, say, between the primitive society and the contemporary one, a variation of the theme of the separation of the self and the other. Sartrean historism has serious implications on the history of science and technology of this (contemporary) society, CS(T3), and that of *other* (primitive) society, PS(T1). And those implications are clearly unacceptable to Lévi-Strauss as is evident from his own words.

> Prevalent attemps to explain alleged differences between the so-called primitive mind and scientific thought have resorted to qualitative difference, between the working processes of the mind in both cases, while assuming that the entities which they were studying remained very much the same. If our (structural) interpretation is correct, we are led toward a completely different view–namely, that the kind of logic in mythical thought is as rigorous as that of modern science, and the difference lies, not in the quality of the intellectual process, but in the nature of things to which it is applied. This is well in agreement with the situation known to prevail in the field of technology: what makes a steel axe superior to a stone axe is not that the first one is better made than the second. They are equally well made, but steel is quite different from stone. In the same way we may be able to show that the same logical processes operate in myth as in science, and that man has always been thinking equally well; the improvement lies, not in an alleged progress of man's mind, but in the discovery of new areas to which it may apply its unchanged and unchanging powers.

If Lévi-Strauss is right, the supposed difference between the primitive thought, PS(T1)M, and scientific thought, CS(T3)S, and also the collateral difference between the underlying mental processes and logical methods are untenable and rest on a positivistic mistake: telescoping our way of thought into theirs, disregarding the difference in the nature of the objects of thought. For a correct cultural understanding of the nature of objects what we need is an adequate theory of signs. Peirce showed the way.[3] According to Lévi-Strauss, *anthropology is a branch of semiology.* The relation between a sign and what it signifies, the object in question, is determined *conventionally* or culturally. For example, there is no *natural* and necessary relation between the expression "stone axe" and the object, stone axe. It is only within a particular cultural context that the relation between the two, sign and significatum, can be determined and that too as a part of a whole system of signs and significata. A particular sign-significatum relation cannot be correctly extrapolated beyond the concerned cultural context, which is like a game-theoretic context.[4] And, therefore, any intercultural or intersystematic comparison of cultural objects such as axe, of steel or of stone; cultural achievement such as magic or science, and technology belonging to different societies is deemed to be misplaced and seriously misleading, completely ruling out the possibility of *qualitative comparison* between them, characterising one as superior and another as inferior. The anthropologist's main task is to discover structural tools or formal devices enabling us primarily to explain the cultural objects and achievements of different societies across the continents and not to pass value judgments on them, committing himself unilaterally to a particular scale or standard peculiar to a society and that too valid for a particular period only. Speaking from within the society using a stone axe one should not say that one's axe is inferior or superior to a steel axe used by others in another society. But the fact that the social anthropologist can *intelligibly* speak about the *meaning* of a stone axe in a primitive society and also that of a steel axe in a modern society is due to his *nature*, that is, *native capacity* to make use of certain "cultural universals," and, one might rightly claim, this nature or native capacity the social anthropologist has in common with all other human beings; although the latter may or may not exercise it, depending on their understanding and objectives, the former must do so in order to escape the prison of the Cogito and explain cultural objects of *different* societies. These "cultural universals" are, or are due to, "unchanged and unchanging powers" of man's mind. The talk of continuous progress of the human mind is an unfortunate expression of an ethnocentric prejudice, namely, that who comes last on the stage of history is wisest because he has at his disposal the cumulative wisdom of all the previous generations. According to Lévi-Strauss, there is no intrinsic difference between myth-logic of PS(T1) and the science-logic of CS(T3). The very transition from nature to culture, the structuralist claims, has been made possible by human natures using its own natural logical powers and drawing on what the natural environment provides. The basic nature-transforming "powers" are "unchanged and unchanging" in the very structure of the human mind. Apparently the stream of history cannot wash or even touch those powers. The structuralist's contextualism, unlike Wittgenstein's, is relativism without tears.

The debate on the issue of superiority-inferiority of cultures, mainly due to the positivistic orientation of such anthropologists as Tylor, Frazer, and Lévi-Bruhl, seems to be a consequence of a misconception about the diversity of cultures. That cultural diversity is a *natural* phenomenon and that it is not inconsistent with the unity of mankind are rarely realised. "Diversity is less a function of the isolation of groups than of the relationships which unite them," observes Lévi-Strauss. Communication and interaction between societies consisting of individuals and groups are always going on at different effective levels. Between societies there is no – as I have called it before – cultural protective belt. What is at the borders of a society to protect it against the (possible or otherwise) influence and invasion of another or many other societies always influences its neighbouring societies silently (at normal times) or loudly (at abnormal times, such as times of war and revolution).

Once we carefully follow the implications of the admitted – admitted by Lévi-Strauss himself – intersocietal dialectics, or what I term intercultural cooperation-conflict situation, antihistorical criticism of the structuralist loses much of its claimed weight. In this connection it is interesting to study Lévi-Strauss's reference to the structural linguistics of Jakobson[5] and the game-theoretic economics of Von Neumann.[6] Jakobson and Neumann are undoubtedly structuralists in the Lévi-Straussian sense, but neither of them is dealing with abstractions as *such* and unaware of the fact that not only *what* they study, cultural objects, but also *how* they study, the structures themselves, are *basically* subject to historical mutation. In other words, structures, whether viewed ontologically or methodologically, are in a nontrivial sense caught up in the dialectic of history. I have argued the point at length elsewhere.[7] This brings me to the third pair of contrasting concepts: dialectical reason and analytical reason.

Lévi-Straussian structuralism is a sort of holism, reminding one of the Durkheimian way of studying ethnographic particulars in terms of strictly "objective" rules and without referring to specific individuals and groups (viewed from within). Lévi-Straussian holism is basically methodological, but his persistent attack on Sartrean ontological individualism might give one an impression that he subscribes to a form of ontological holism. I would say that both Sartre and Lévi-Strauss are methodological holists, but whereas the former, because of his accent on the role of dialectical reason and individual praxis, succeeds in projecting his system as a sustained defence of freedom, the latter's stress on the role of analytic reason and the basic unity of the structures of all cultural objects, myths, totems, and kinship systems; for example, spread over all the continents leads some to think that he is referring (in a non-conventional and realistic sense) to a hidden reality—humanity—that alone can account for the striking structural similarity between the sets of baffling ethnographic data (of widely separate societies) discovered and organised by positivistic analytic reason, and also that he believes in *determinism*. The structuralist takes as his paradigm analytic reason, which defines, makes precise, classifies, and organises much in the fashion of a positivist scientist. And, according to him, what the existentialist calls dialectical reason is only a superstructural product, a product of an ideological-historical consciousness, of analytic reason. In this respect, Lévi-Strauss complains, Sartre forgets the basic aspect of Marx's and Freud's combined lesson, "Man must view himself as meaningful": the superstructural or historical meaning of man, because of its admitted derivative character, is fated to be faulty and abstract. In contrast, the cultural objects studied by analytic reason are intrastructural and closer to nature (but not natural). Analytic reason by its cultural universals is better equipped to take a positivist scientific view and, thus, give a relatively stable (but not exactly ahistorical) and structural picture of subideological characteristics of the social man. "I do not at all mean to suggest," asserts Lévi-Strauss, "that ideological transformations give rise to social ones. Only the reverse is in fact true."

Sartre's distrust of analytical reason and what may be regarded as perhaps its best achievement, the scientific study of man, structural anthropology, is collateral to his distrust of the stability of whatever is ahistorical and falls beyond the ken and enlivening touch of time. He is for analytic reason only as an inert moment of dialectical reason. Ultimate intelligibility both of natural and cultural objects is said to be due basically to synthetic activities of dialectical reason. Sartre says, "The sciences of Nature are analytical with respect to their content, whereas scientific thought is both analytical in its particular procedure and synthetic by virtue of its ultimate aims." Nature in its "raw" form is not the content of science: unless it is subjected to some such analytic procedures as definition, classification, and subsumption under laws, that is, unless it is cooked at least partially, the synthetic function of reason cannot be purposefully employed to do its job: to impart intelligibility to the objects of nature by revealing their structures, relations, meaning, and, above all, changing affiliation to a totalising temporalisation marked by its entertained aims. Sartrean Nature is, thus, not only culturalised in the limited Lévi-Straussian sense but also humanised in the Marxist sense. Even an element of ideology is admissible, almost welcome, in Sartrean-Marxist science.[8] In a sense Sartre's assimilation of analytical reason under dialectical reason reminds one of Marx's emphasis on the dialectical unity of positivism *and* humanism, of how nature makes man possible *and* how man makes nature intelligible and transforms it, using nature's own gift in him, labour, and of the historical necessity of revealing the humanistic orientation of science and the scientific presupposition of humanism. However, Sartre's ontological individualism, highlighting the *validating* or *authenticating* role of the individual praxis, though tempered by the necessity grounded in materiality, practical-inert, and group praxis, is not likely to be endorsed by Marx, not even by the young Marx. Notwithstanding his ontological individualism, Sartre ascribes primary intelligibility of science as an institution to its own history as a part of a totalising temporalisation comprehended by dialectical reason. Within a totalising temporalisation there are partial moments that can provide only secondary intelligibility to what is achieved by the analytic reason of science. But this secondary intelligibility of scientific theories viewed within the confines of a particular period is grounded in the synthetic activities of dialectical reason, which, on the one hand, sets it against its inert past and, on the other, projects it into the future (possible tests to be undertaken by the individuals and groups in their praxis).[9]

Another consideration Sartre persuasively offers in favour of the superiority claim of dialectical reason is that it critically observes and oversees how and whether the abstract schemes of scientific laws and theories devised by analytical reason are corroborated in and by the experience of the professional as well as the ordinary man. Even within the analytical reason used in scientific research activities, like framing hypotheses and devising experiments, there is a distinct synthetic role of dialectical reason. Experimental techniques and mathematical proofs may also be said to have their own dialectical orientation for these are the ways or methods of establishing or disestablishing certain truths that are not otherwise evident to and acceptable to the human beings concerned. Even machines have a built-in human orientation. To map nature man's mind frames hypothetical pictures or structures of its phenomena and processes, and then to ascertain whether these are true (for him or them) mind turns itself on what it assembles and organises for the purpose of ascertainment. Man's ways of mapping and even of transforming nature, Lévi-Strauss says, are in a sense suggested by and grounded in nature itself. On this point Sartre differs from him. Lévi-Strauss takes the Durkheim-Mauss thesis of "collective representations" very seriously and believes that these "representations" are so naturally grounded in the collective consciousness that the individual's mind is hardly left with any freedom but to receive and record them passively in some or another "encoded" form.[10] Nature in "codes," such as kinship system, is, no doubt, primarily a cultural representation, but being very close to nature it seems to defy temporal change. Influenced by Freud, Lévi-Strauss gives a collectivistic interpretation to the former's concept of unconscious and accords primacy to it. He suggests that nature and culture meet in the collective unconscious. Whereas according to Freud sexual instincts determine the contents of the unconscious that are expressed through symbols in dreams and other forms of consciousness, Lévi-Strauss speaks of delibidinized *structures* of the unconscious that find their way up into the collective consciousness in articulate forms and are thereafter reflectively used by man's mind to understand cultural objects, including scientific truths about nature. The suggested account (and its methodological extensions) of discovering and establishing the laws and theories of science is totally unacceptable to Sartre; for, first, it clearly clashes with his notion of the historical or totalising character of scientific knowledge, which through detotalisation and retotalisation, progresses dialectically; secondly, it is also inconsistent with the proclaimed primacy of the individual praxis. Nature-knowing capacity is *in* man and used consciously by him, and the results of the used capacity, scientific truths, are valid primarily *for* him. "Interiority exteriorises itself in order to interiorise exteriority." Objectivity or the institutional character of science, that is, knowledge that is not answerable and responsive to the individual praxis, though not rejected by Sartre, is always suspect in his eyes. Every historian of science, therefore, is entitled in principle to reopen the question of the truth of the past views that are his subject matter. In that case, Lévi-Strauss complains, he arrogates to himself the final right, at least for the time being, to determine what the scientists of other societies at other times, PS(T1) and MS(T2) for example, really meant. In the name of interiorisation of or living the past can the historian of science rationally deny the interiority or lived truth of the past views of the scientist of *other* societies and thus reduce him to exteriority? Sartre may answer the question in the negative, pointing out that his theory of dialectical reason always keeps open the possibility of every scientific truth's being negated and reopened *otherwise*. But, the critic may say, that only ensures the growing character of science in *future*; the question is, What about the sciences of *past* societies, where our main concern is *their* views— views as *they* understood them—and not how those views will or will not grow? At one stage the questions may be or perhaps are *related*, but their *separation* at another stage is not only possible but also desirable from the standpoint of anthropology or that of sociological history.

Rationality of past science, as I have tried to show before, can be approached by the historian at two different levels or in two different ways, either simultaneously or separately.[11] One: how the people or historians of science of PS(T1) understood the "science as magic" of PS(T1). If the questions are sought to be answered *separately*, separating altogether the past conceptual framework from the present one, as the structuralist proposes to do, then, Sartre says, the former resorts exclusively to analytical reason in the vain expectation that he will be able to give a true historical account of "science as magic" as entertained or believed by the people of PS(T1), and that this true account is to be taken as anthropological and meant to be *true forever* (viewed from outside). In other words, the existentialist's complaint against the structuralist is that he wants to freeze the flow of time to catch the uncatchable, to capture "science as magic," or a "science"-modeled account of "magic" and that too "as entertained or believed by the people of PS(T1)" and "meant to be true forever." Yes, in a sense time can be spatialised, that is, captured and preserved, but not as time. An organism, a human body (Lenin's, for instance) can be preserved in a museum or mausoleum for posterity (not for eternity), but not as an organism or human body, only as an embalmed "human" body or mummy. In its bid to capture the past as such in the concealed or prereflective image-model of the present and to preserve it as such (that is, for all time to come) analytical reason "kills" history and gets "structural anthropology" and reduces culture almost (but not exactly) to nature; for the technique of mummification or of preservation of embalmed organisms is a significant cultural achievement enabling man to save a human body, for example, from its being reduced to (the elements) of nature.

It is the existentialist's claim that dialectical reason alone can consciously and successfully approach the problem of the rationality of past science because it takes up both questions *simultaneously* and without conflating the two, that is, without reducing one into the other. In fact, Sartre's notion of the asymmetry between analytical rationality and dialectical rationality seems to be very relevant to the problem of the working historian. "Analytical rationality can be transcended and integrated by synthetic rationality, but it is also clear that the opposite is not true: a dialectical proposition would lose its meaning and dissolve into relations of exteriority if it were 'projected' into the milieu of logical or mathematical calculations." An important distinction between formula or inert abstract schema, and thought or practical knowledge that is "expressed" in it, is recognised by Sartre. Analytic reason may almost mechanically "follow" a formula without comprehending the thought it "expresses," but practical knowledge can only be partially "suppressed" by abstract formulas. Conscious of the signifying tension of this "suppression," dialectical reason succeeds in discovering the underlying practical knowledge. If Sartre is right, that is, if the superiority claim of dialectical reason is right, even formula-following mental acts cannot be completely mechanical: thought sustains and stimulates it all the time. The two distinct structural levels of thought "do not constitute an unintelligibility or a split in thought, since dialectical reason sustains, controls, and justifies all other forms of thought, because it explains them, puts them in their proper place and integrates them as non-dialectical (i.e. analytical) moments which, in it, regain a dialectical value." In other words, level distinction is more structural (viewed from without) than functional: in its analytical function reason assumes and projects an autonomous appearance, and this appearance of autonomy is due to the "deliberate" unconcern with its formative, if not originative, and sustaining stimulus. The analyticity of logicomathematical propositions is apparent and alloyed. Semantics and philosophy of formal language, existentially-dialectically interpreted, make the point abundantly clear.

This argument about the asymmetry between dialectical reason and analytical reason and the superiority of the former over the latter is further pressed by Sartre to reaffirm his two favourite points. One: the structures of Straussian anthropology are in fact mere analytical constructs of dialectical reason in its nondialectical plane of functioning to which the structuralist attributes an autonomy and universality that are not borne out by the relevant facts of their proposed fields of application. Two: in and through the application these analytical constructs are found to be inadequate, inappropriate, or incongruent; making one conscious of the necessity of changing them over time reveals their dialectical character in a round about way. Related to this point is my argument given previously that PS(T1) and MS(T2)T, though ideal types or analytical constructs, to use Weberian terms, are meant to be applied to, and indirectly questioned by, the facts of a particular sort of *social* space-time region scattered over different *natural* space-time regions. Modifications of analytical constructs necessitated by the facts of the field of application and, at intervals, replacement of one construct by another and the partial overlapping characters of the two all point to their hidden historical nature and trend.

The preceding method suggested for showing the historical nature of structures themselves is seriously objected to by Lévi-Strauss, and his objection is justified by a *reductio argument* that if in the matters of constitution and selection of historical facts the historian is free in the Sartrean (*individual praxis*) sense, any analytical constructs could be indefinitely and unilaterally confirmed and retained: history in that case could not be regarded as either critical or dialectical. Given the primacy of the individual praxis or even the group praxis, the aim of totalisation, universal history, is doomed to remain unrealisable. One Sartrean way out of this problem might be to enlarge the historian's "I" to the " We" of his society, hoping to ensure, at least partially, objectivity in the matter of selection of historical facts or ethnographic data. Lévi-Strauss critically reminds Sartre that mere exchange of one prison (that is, psychological cogito) for another (sociological cogito) will not do. Another Sartrean solution, supplementary to the one just mentioned, is to point out that all constituent dialectics influenced by the constituted dialectics and determined by the practico-inert, is bound to converge on the end of totalisation. Here again, Lévi-Strauss suspects, analytical reason is being smuggled in to do this odd job of drawing a neat picture – too neat to be true – of convergent totalisation without any totalising end-conscious mind. His own approach to constructing genuine "universal history" is analytical and structural. To make history meaningful, with or without a totaliser, the historian is bound to be historian *for* a period, or *for* a group, and so on. "History is therefore never (universal) history, but (only) history-for, that is, partial or incomplete." Extending this argument, Lévi-Strauss says, all histories – partial totalisations or different societies – are equally, *not* identically, meaningful within their frontiers: their *continuity* is a myth invented by dialectical reason, but their *unity* as evident in structural anthropology is achieved by analytical reason through what he calls "cultural universals."

Now over to the fourth and final pair of contrasting concepts, history and anthropology. If the last argument of Lévi-Strauss is accepted, there remains no asymmetry between dialectical reason and analytical reason. He has respect for history but hardly finds any reason for according it a special value. To him it is a study complementary to his own. For *comprehension* he relies on anthropology and for *information* on history. To quote Lévi-Strauss on the point:

> [T]he historian strives to reconstruct the picture of vanished societies as they were at the points which for them correspond to the present, while the ethnographer does his best to reconstruct the historical stages which temporarily preceded their existing form. This symmetry between history and anthropology seems to be rejected by philosophers who implicitly or explicitly deny that distribution in space and succession in time afford equivalent perspectives. In their eyes some special prestige seems to attach to the temporal dimension, as if diachrony were to establish a kind of intelligibility not merely superior to that provided by synchrony, but above all more specifically human.[12]

The structural approach in the Lévi-Straussian sense is not peculiar to anthropology. In a less articulate form it is the resort of the historian as well. For historical reconstruction one or several previous constructions (Sartrean practicalinert) have to be taken into account. Both construction and reconstruction involve selection and, therefore, elimination. If this point is conceded, Lévi-Strauss presses his symmetry thesis further and argues that the superiority claim of history, which rests on the questionable assumption that the historian does comprehend time as a continuum, falls through. The historian too has to resort to abstractionist strategy, selecting and eliminating facts from among a (metaphysically) assumed plenum of objects. Whereas the anthropologist uses higher-level "cultural universals," the historian uses the relatively lower-level ones. The difference is one of degree only. History too has to tolerate gaps in it, a result of its unavoidable methodological abstractionism. Whether he takes, spatially speaking, the world, a country in it, or a locality as his unit of study, the historian cannot help using what Lévi-Strauss calls code: temporally speaking, an epoch, a year, or even a date is also a "code," a structural unit, standing for but not expressing countless details or "messages." Epoch, year, date, and so on. are codes not individually but as classes of other homologous units. To make historical "messages" intelligible these are to be represented in and through "codes." Lévi-Strauss reminds one of Walsh's notion of historical "colligation," organisation of historical details under appropriate concepts for the purpose of making the details intelligible.[13] "History does not . . . escape the common obligation of all knowledge, to employ a code to analyse its object." Analytical reason constructs objects by using codes. The only peculiarity of history is that its code consists in chronology, forms a sequence (and not a continuum). The facts colligated or aggregated under appropriate cultural universals are said to "have approximately the same significance for a contingent of individuals who have not necessarily experienced the events and may even consider them at an interval of several centuries." Consequently, the Sartrean idea of history as a totalisation of the set of partial totalisations has to be given up. And, according to the structuralist, the partial totalisations have to be recognised as such and not as constituents of an all-comprehensive totalisation. Only at a later stage, on a different abstract plane, the partial totalisations recognised as constituent—*informations*—are analytically *restructured* for the purpose of clearer comprehension. Information itself is structured, but at the primary plane, that is, the historical plane, and marked by lower-level discontinuities. History is more informative and less comprehensive, anthropology more comprehensive and less informative. The information-comprehension relation is inverse, says Lévi-Strauss. However, there is symmetry between the two: information means lower-level comprehension and comprehension higher-level, or restructured, information.

Relying as he does on the primacy of dialectical reason, Sartre finds the foundation of structural anthropology in the partial totalisations of history. If the Sartrean notion of history that is ideology-loaded is admitted as the foundation of anthropology, then it cannot be a positive science, a product of analytical reason. Lévi-Strauss doubts whether Sartre is clear about the right way of invoking facts for having historical knowledge and anthropological knowledge, and to it the former attributes the latter's alleged failure to draw a sufficiently clear distinction between (1) history made by men unconsciously, (2) history of men made by historians consciously, (3) the philosopher's interpretation of the history of men, and (4) the philosopher's interpretation of the history of historians. History is certainly made by men but all that they make cannot be made in full consciousness: elements of unconsciousness are bound to be there. Not only the facts of history that the historian uses in analytical constructs to make these intelligible but also the historian's acts of making history are more or less un-consciously shaped. Besides, the end product of intended acts has in it some unintended effects and to that extent the actors are not con-scious of the same. Even the historian himself both in his history-making and history-interpreting acts is, to an extent, unconscious: for he cannot possibly know all the factors shaping his standpoint and objective. To a lesser extent this point is valid also in respect to the philosopher's interpretation of the history of historians. I do not think that Sartre is unaware of the distinctions referred to by Lévi-Strauss. Sartre's accent on totalisation with an ideological élan underly-ing it is perhaps mainly responsible for the structural positivist's com-plaint against his view. If the symmetry thesis of the latter is to be taken seriously, his notion of the *science* of man, structural anthropology, in spite of its pronaturalistic leaning, can hardly deny the existence of a humanistic core in it.

Whereas scientific research in the field of "hard" (that is, natural) science postulates a dualism between the researcher and his object, contemporary physics and biology appear to have shown that this dualism is not very sharp. Attempts to sharpen it further indirectly demand of the researcher that he forget what he is when he is engaged in studying the objects of hard science. In the field of social and human sciences the said dualism is shifted within man himself: "the cut-off line passes between the man who observes and the man or men who are observed." Lévi-Strauss is aware of the difficulty of this internal dualism: the attending "awareness appears as the secret enemy of the sciences of man in the double form of a spontaneous awareness (in-herent to the object of the observation) and of a reflective awareness—an awareness of awareness—in the scientist." The method of structural positivism appears to him a very promising way out, bringing the social sciences closer to the natural ones. The structuralist does not deny the genuineness of the problem posed by phenomenological layers of consciousness, but he rejects the existentialist's dubious solution and proposes to follow the method of hard or natural sciences to the extent that it is fruitful for the purpose of tackling the peculiarities of social and human sciences. The suggested methodological unity rests on an implicit denial of the proclaimed asymmetry between the human sciences and the natural sciences.

> Even the biologist and the physicist are becoming more and more aware of the social implications of their discoveries, or, better still,

of their anthropological meaning. Man is no longer satisfied with knowing; as he knows more, he sees himself knowing, and the true object of his research becomes more and more, every day, this indivisible coupling of humanity transforming the world and transforming itself in the process. (*Structural Anthropology*, vol. 2, Penguin, p. 303)

Lévi-Strauss draws a further distinction between human sciences, such as ethnography and history, and social sciences, such as anthropology and sociology. Whereas the former are primarily concerned with gathering facts, the latter with constructing models or structures for intelligible organisation of facts. Ethnography resorts to *complex* (but lower-level) mechanical model-constructions, social anthropology to *simple* (and greater comprehension-content) ones. History uses statistical models of larger information-content or lower comprehension-content, and social anthropology's statistical models are of lower information-content and higher comprehension-content. The relations among these four disciplines have been reduced by Lévi-Strauss to two oppositions, one between empirical observation and model construction, characterising the initial stage of research, and the other between the statistical and mechanical natures of models, constituting the end-products of research. Assigning the sign + (plus) to the first term of each opposition and the sign − (minus) to the second, the following chart is obtained (*Structural Anthropology*, vol. 2, Penguin, p. 298)

	History	Sociology	Ethnography	Social Anthropology
Empirical observation/ model construction	+	−	+	−
Mechanical models/ statistical models	−	−	+	+

One gathers from this chart why the social sciences deal with what Lévi-Strauss terms "two categories of time." Time used by the anthropologist is "mechanical," reversible and noncumulative. A model of a partilineal kinship structure, for instance, shows only its *static* time-frame; from it as such one cannot gather whether it has been preceded by a matrilineal structure or the converse. Historical time, on the contrary, is "statistical," marked by discontinuity and irreversibility. Lévi-Strauss endorses the antievolutionist approach of Franz Boas and his followers: for, concerned as they are with mechanical models from their point of view evolution in a historical sense has no operational value. Like Durkheim, the structuralist is in favour of treating cultural *types* or mechanical models as *if* these are lifted above and untouched by historical time, and, therefore, also uninfluenced by the individuals and the groups who are very much *in* time. True, for analytical and methodological purposes one is entitled, almost obliged, to draw a cut-off line between *models* or *ideal types*, on the one hand, and what underlies them or are used for studying them, on the other. It seems to me that, ontologically speaking, the relation between models and the facts that are studied, organised, and compared in terms of models is more or less *dialectical*, depending on the level of abstraction at which a particular study, anthropological or historical, is planned and carried on; and it is not of one *unilateral application*, that is, models to facts. One is advised to bear in mind that the plausibility of the methodological cut-off line between models of anthropology and facts or details of (even statistical) history is contingent upon the adequacy or inadequacy of Lévi-Strauss's notion of analytical reason, which is itself under fire from Sartre.

I for one am not opposed in the least to the introduction of the abstractionist and in a sense a priori method of model construction in social sciences such as anthropology or even in human sciences such as history. That abstraction is unavoidable or, we recognise, necessary is evident from the structuralist's reference to *statistical* history rather than time-*continuum*. In order to use historical information for supporting analytically constructed models the structuralist may certainly ignore the physical time-continuum and should rely on what I call *times as microstructured* or coded (time-unit-wise, big, small, or medium-sized) events. Broadly speaking, there are two different uses of models: *justificatory* and *critical*. The very construction of models is a legitimate recognition of the problem of "understanding social relations," of ordering many in terms of few or one. But the question is, Is information meant only for comprehension or also for *critical* ascertainment of the correctness and adequacy of comprehension? Is history there only to provide *supporting* evidence for anthropological models or also to provide a test for the latter? Cannot *statistical history be used for the purpose of criticism for statistical testing of mechanical models?*

In fact, Lévi-Strauss's use of the word *model* is somewhat confusing and ambiguous. First, sometimes one gets the impression that he means by it the structural linguistic model used by Jakobson and his associates for organising phonetic information in terms of binary oppositions. Second, sometimes he gives the impression that he is resurrecting Weber-Pareto typologies for a general theorising purpose without being lost in the specifics of this society or that. But, then, often he highlights the *mechanical* character of the model. For example, an engineer may make a model aircraft *before* an actual one is produced and tested in flight and also another model *after* it is produced and tested for the purposes of display and sale promotion. Fourth, some, like Runciman, are reminded of Wittgenstein's (Tractatarian) isomorphism of thought and the world. "The role of logic in the epistemology of the early Wittgenstein is not unlike the role of myth in the epistemology of Lévi-Strauss" (*Sociology In Its Place*, Cambridge University Press, 1970, p. 57). Finally, he also speaks of game-theoretic or mathematical models and rightly laments social scientists' general lack of interest in the rigorous quantitative approach made possible by recent developments in such fields as mathematical logic, set theory, group theory, and topology. His reference to *Theory of Games and Economic Behaviour* by J. Von Neumann and O. Morgenstern (1944), *Cybernetics* by N. Wiener (1948), and *The Mathematical Theory of Communication* by C. Shannon and W. Weaver (1950) is interesting and suggestive in this connection. Further investigation and analysis reveal that there are other variations of the preceding meanings comprising such concepts as analogy, metaphor, and heuristic mechanism.

For the specific purpose of clarifying the disputed relation between history and anthropology, I think, the fundamental question to be borne in mind first is whether the relation between mechanical and ethnographic materials is to be approached only from the standpoint of intelligibility or both from the standpoint of intelligibility and also that of truth or falsity. Consistently with his pronaturalistic methodological attitude, Lévi-Strauss is strongly in favour of treating ethnographic materials as natural facts, without (or with the least) distortion and mutilation caused by the preservative chemicals and conditions of the anthropological museum. In other words, being a neo-Cartesian of a sort, he refuses to accept any material as raw. I think Lévi-Strauss is right on this score. The uses of models are not only explanatory, comparative, combinatorial, ordering, classificatory, and systematising. One of their very important uses is pledged to be truth-seeking and *critical*. Otherwise Lévi-Strauss's symmetry thesis, symmetry between history and anthropology, as opposed to the asymmetry thesis ascribed to Sartre, becomes very trivial and indefensible. I accept his arguments for taking anthropology as "order of orders," considering "the whole social fabric as a network of different types of orders." I am also in sympathy with his characterisation of it as "code of codes," substructures nested in structures, taking idealised (discontinuous) segments of times and (separated) slices of space as lower-order materials for meaningful or intelligible organisation in terms of models. I appreciate this formalistic truth-seeking "bias" of Lévi-Strauss's method.

But my uneasiness remains because from his arguments, example, and references I get a distinct feeling that he is being almost carried away by the elegance and simplicity of the formalistic method, often perhaps forgetting that marshaling of ethnographic materials by itself does not prove the *critical* character of models, a character that is expected of all the models of human and social sciences irrespective of the concerned scientists' chosen level of abstract formal operation. It is in this context that one has to understand the criticism heard at times against Lévi-Strauss that in a way he is carrying on the Tylor-Frazer tradition of using only (a hypothesis or model) supporting (ethnographic-historical) facts. This criticism is partly unfair because he is clearly conscious of the futility of trying "to reach a valid definition of social structure on an inductive basis." The very notion of structure is said to have a noninductive structure of its own. "Social structure," says Lévi-Strauss, "has nothing to do with reality but with models which are built up after it." To clarify the difference between these two concepts he refers to the difference between *social structure* and *social relations*, which often proves confusing. "Social relations consist of the raw materials out of which the models making up the social structure are built, while social structure can, by no means, be reduced to the ensemble of the social relations to be described in a given society." In spite of his preference for mechanical models, Lévi-Strauss admits that there is no necessary connection between *measure* and *structure*. Structures are models of a sort having a dual character. From one end structural properties appear autonomous; from another end one finds that the formal properties of the constructed models of one level can be compared with, and explained by, the same properties as in models corresponding to other "strategic" levels. If this proclaimed isomorphism of the models of natural, social, and human sciences can be plausibly demonstrated, then not only are interdisciplinary studies are promoted but the research programme of unity between the hard sciences and cultural sciences gets a much needed boost.

I wish this methodological programmatic unity envisaged by the structuralist could be worked out to a critically successful end. But having heard him, especially in his response to the existentialist's pro-dialectical criticism, my doubt persists. Is not Lévi-Strauss's statistical history a *dummy* partner of his structural anthropology, or is it a *critical* collaborator of the latter in the quest for truth? Dismissing Sartre's "progressive-regressive" method somewhat lightly as "the very (one) anthropologists have been practising for many years" and that too at its "preliminary step," when he confidently claims "our method is progressive-regressive not once but twice over," frankly speaking, I feel disturbed and askant. To quote Lévi-Strauss:

> In the first stage, we observe the datum of experience, analyse it in the present, try to grasp its historical antecedents as far as we can delve into the past, and bring all these facts back to the light of the day to incorporate them into a meaningful totality. The second stage, which repeats the first on a different plane and at a different level, then begin. (*Savage Mind*, pp.252-53)

The first stage is historical and the second one anthropological. One might say, the former is substructural, the latter structural, and, to extend the analogy horizontally, the possibility and use of superstructural studies cannot be ruled out at all. Comparable level-distinct studies are also well-known in such other disciplines as economics (micro-economics and macroeconomics), linguistics (surface-structural and deep-structural), psychology, biology, and physics. Logical and methodological investigations of the last ninety years or so have opened up the vast possibilities of numerous level-distinct studies and, at the same time, discovered the hidden dangers involved in negotiating these fertile and highly uneven terrains. Lévi-Strauss's claim, in plain language, seems to be this: (1) (a) to incorporate the historical details in lower-level substructures and (b) to see whether the other details *conjectured* to be incorporable within those substructures are *in fact* incorporated; and, (2) (a) to make models of structures purported to incorporate the substructured historical details within them and (b) to see whether other similarly substructured details *conjectured* to be incorporable within those models are *in fact* incorporated. Like the "semantic ascent" referred to previously, this structural ascent, if I may use the expression, may be extended further upward, making the models of "superstructures" and of "supersuperstructures" extensionally more and more comprehensive.[14] In the current literature on induction and probability, especially that centering round the Popper-Carnap controversy on confirmation, one comes across a very similar problem. For inductive generalisation Wittgenstein suggested (and Keynes accepted) confirmation function *cf*, giving an equal a priori probability to each *state-description*, describing completely a domain of possible *individual* cases or states of affairs, each of which is atomic and *independent*. Carnap goes a step upward and speaks of the confirmation function *c* as giving an equal a priori probability to each *structure-description* without mentioning anything about the *independent* individuals of the concerned domain or universe except (statistically) *how many* of them come under the different predicates. Mainly because of Popper's anti-inductive criticism Carnap finds difficulties in the general symmetry principle. That is, what are these symmetrical "possible cases," state-description or structure-description? The *state*-descriptive method does not appear promising to Carnap "because with it," he admits in a Popperian vein, "we could not learn from experience." Hintikka proposes under the name of *constituent description* a broader, more abstract and generalised description. To use his own words, "A constituent does not tell us how many individuals belong to the different predicates . . . only tells us of each predicate whether it is exemplified in the world or not." This combined enumeration-elimination method of description is carried a step further by Carnap in his concept of *constituent structure description* in which one does not say of each predicate whether it is exemplified or not but only how many of them are instantiated in the world and how many are empty. Carnap comments: "This is, so to speak, cleaner still in that it is still further from particular individuals."

Lévi-Strauss's attempts to construct abstract, general, and comprehensive models are unexceptionable in principle. His theoretical motivation to draw a cut-off line between substructural history and structural anthropology is also methodologically called for and, therefore, well taken. But the question is, How does Lévi-Strauss ensure the critical character of the abstract and general models purported to be very comprehensive? On his own admission comprehension and information are inversely related. One suspects that the Lévi-Straussian structural models designed to organise, classify, compare, and explain historical or ethnographical details from different and widely separated (idealised) times and places of the world are twice removed from the reality of down-to-earth details. Their "elegant" and "clean" look is due to their informational poverty or at least inexactitude. To be fair to Lévi-Strauss one has to admit that materials or informational details of anthropology are of necessity once removed from the reality in itself or the given as such, whatever way one puts it. The very name of the discipline, *structural anthropology*, gives a clear indication of the level at which its author proposes to operate and also of the level from which he intends to draw his materials: discontinuous and statistical times and places, ensembles of social relations found there, and so on. Lévi-Strauss seems to have clearly anticipated this criticism and accordingly mentions the necessary methodological caution. The analytical reason, a very potent ability of the human mind, is obliged to define its objects (or materials) of study at an abstract level because it cannot possibly directly encounter and retain the same in memory in an assorted and usable form. Even at this lower level dialectical reason is pressed into operation to ascertain whether the objects in the process of definition have been unnecessarily distorted or mutilated, or distorted for the purpose of facile confirmation of the concerned model-requirements. Having formed the models by analytical reason to explain the same, he says, the mind refers the models to the already defined materials. In this second return journey analytical reason of the mind is again, for the second time, used dialectically for the purpose of critical "verification." Lévi-Strauss writes:

> the procedure would go astray if it were not, at every stage and, above all, when it seemed to have run its course, ready to retrace its steps and to double back on itself to preserve the contact with that experienced totality which serves both as its end and means. The return on itself is in my view a *verification*, rather than, as Sartre regards it, a *demonstration*, for, as I see it, a conscious being aware of itself as such poses a problem to which it provided no solution. (my emphasis). (*Savage Mind*, p. 253).

Lévi-Strauss's *verification* is *conformity* of historical details as substructured at the lower level to models of social structures at the higher level and *confirmation* of the former by the latter. This two way or dialectical functioning of analytical reason, according to him, is to be understood in terms of some cultural universals or near-natural features of the human mind that are objective and not circumscribed by particular times and places, nor conditioned by superstructural ideological considerations. Sartre's *demonstration*, on the contrary, is primarily an achievement of the individual praxis, which, no doubt, is dialectically influenced by the group praxis and ideological considerations. And yet it retains its critical character both by trying to determine the validity and limits of dialectical reason and also by trying to determine its own *developing* analytical role and the limits of its contribution to the dialectical totalisation of the totalities.

Careful perusals of Sartre's arguments to establish the superiority of history over anthropology and Lévi-Strauss's to prove the foundational and scientific character of anthropology are not at all incompatible. Often their difference has been dramatised not so much for scientific methodological reasons as for ideological ones.[15] True to his structural approach, that is, the double movement of the progressive-regressive method, Lévi-Strauss does not recognise the "symmetry" between, and the "complementary" character of, history and anthropology. Because of his relative neglect of the philosophical issues underlying the formalistic tools and techniques, which are otherwise indispensable for higher-level theory construction, he has not paid sufficient attention to the problem of critical use, assessment and improvement of the models. One is justified to think that this is largely due to his acknowledged—acknowledged by Lévi-Strauss himself—Kantian orientation, by which I mean *justificatory* use of the cognitive structure or the categories of understanding. This also partly accounts for his relative indifference to the problem of social dynamics despite his sympathy toward Marxism. From his side Sartre rightly claims that his historical ideological approach and primary use of dialectical reason, recognising analytical reason as a moment of it, have successfully enabled him "to get back to the elementary formal structures" (Lévi-Strauss's historical substructures) and also "to locate the dialectical foundations of a structural anthropology." I am sure that these Sartrean "foundations" of "structural anthropology" will be unacceptable to Lévi-Strauss: for, first, these are *not* foundational but superstructural, and, secondly, these are formulated not for pro-naturalistic scientific inquiry but primarily as ideological tools to overthrow "the oppression of analytical reason" and its material and cultural products. The structuralist's apprehension is that by overideologising history we prevent ourselves from grasping past societies, such as PS(T1) and MS(T2).

To minimise this apprehension the critic might pertinently raise the question, To what extent can the structuralist deideologise anthropology (or for that matter sociology) without seriously diluting, if not giving up altogether, his symmetry thesis. Having recognised that structural anthropology does need the support of history not once but twice at two different but related levels, a consistent Straussian cannot deny the presence of at least a mild dose of ideology in anthropology or for that reason in any synchronic social or human science. The Marxist thesis that history is a superstructural science, to which both the existentialist and the structuralist extend their support, is not of much help to the latter in the matter of purging anthropology all influences of history, for it is well known that the Marxist is never tired of stressing the dialectical relation between the two, that is, history as a human science is not only influenced by but also influences social sciences such as anthropology and hard sciences such as physics. Strictly speaking, the nature-culture dialectic cannot be denied either by Sartre or by Lévi-Strauss. If the latter's pro-Marxist profession is serious, I fail to understand how he can possibly accept such criti cism of his theory as Sanche De Gramount's, "With Lévi-Strauss, the whole humanist tradition goes down the drain. History goes down the drain, too, because it is seen as merely a form of our society's, a collective delusion irrelevant to the scientific study of man.[16] We know that not only the earlier Marx but also the later Marx always spoke of the dialectical unity of naturalism and humanism. May be for some limited theoretical reasons Lévi-Strauss, like many other French intellectuals, thinks himself a Marxist. But his positivistic leanings are unmistakable. He optimistically looks forward to the superscience of FS(T4) in which the gap between the social and human sciences, on the one hand, and the hard sciences, on the other, will be narrowed to the minimum, if not removed altogether. Marx's accent was on the *dialectical unity* of the two, according a special place to history, while Lévi-Strauss's is on *naturalistic programmatic unity*, assuming a graded *structural-ontological unity*, giving a special role to history to investigate it. The ideological implications of the dialectical-historical method did not discourage Marx in the least from applying it to the study of cultural products, including science, of other past societies in sequence, typological or otherwise. True, ideological insemination of history partially affects its *natural* health and subjects it to the falsity of superstructural consciousness.[17] But the Marxist seeks to treat this malady and cure it retaining the materialistic, that is, the natural foundational, character of the historical method mainly through carefully planned group praxis and thus keeping the theory-practice dialectic functionally alive. Unduly worried over the aspect of ideological insemination and the falsity consciousness of history, Lévi-Strauss somewhat berates the role of the historical method, although he occasionally recognises its value-neutral positivistic role in accounting for the diachronic change of social structures themselves over the periods of time. In this respect Sartre, except for his accent on the individual praxis rather than on the group praxis, stands closer to Marx: both are committed to the primacy of dialectical history and the necessity of preserving the creative unity of theory and practice in the pursuit of truth. It is again highlighting other aspects of historical materialism, that is, truth-consciousness embodied in foundational sciences such as productive technology and physics, and "collective representations," as distinguished from the individual praxis, that Lévi-Strauss gives a pro-Marxist push to the naturalists' dream of unity of all cognitive sciences, natural, social, and human.

The Sartre-Lévi-Strauss controversy is not one that can be so easily settled either in favour of the existentialist upholding the superiority claim of dialectical reason and historical method or in favour of the structuralist upholding the superiority claim of analytical reason and anthropological method. The terms of settlement themselves are to be defined with reference to our primary aim in view. If one wants to reconstruct the recorded accounts of science with a definite practical end, say, to construct a theory for emancipation of the proletariat from the bourgeois oppression perpetrated, among other means, by the dominance of analytical reason, one can certainly highlight the way science and technology have been shaped by the productive forces over the ages and the way the ruling class has used the same to its advantage for the purpose of exploitation of the poor. One may also marshal facts and arguments to show how the proletariat can understand and use the existing institutions including science and technology to win its struggle against the bourgeoisie for its emancipation. Undoubtedly to construct such a hypothesis the theorist is obliged, partly consciously and partly perhaps unconsciously, to select facts. This selective approach to facts has often been criticised as *uncritical*. For the sake of imparting a practical character to a theory, however noble might be its aim, should we follow an *unscientific* (or what Collingwood calls scissor-and-paste) method? The propractical theorist does invoke at this stage the inherent dialectical relation between theory and practice to defend the practical and hermeneutic orientation of his theory. Sartre's method presents the sciences of different periods of history as a connected sequence developing to a definite aim that is not fixed a priori and from without but worked out dialectically from within. And this history has to be understood in its intimate relation to what people do in response to the needs or challenges posed by the material and social circumstances. In other words, the existentialist is opposed to treating the history of science as a secular discipline. He brings it close to the human life and formulates it in terms of group praxis and even individual praxis. His totalising, all-inclusive perspective does not leave primitive science or medieval science, whatever name one gives to it, magic or natural philosophy, in its own context, that is, partial totality. When a partial totality, for example PS(T1), is reviewed from another partial totality, such as CS(T3) or FS(T4), the reviewer gets only the secondary identity and intelligibility of the former. It is only as a sort of ideal of practical reason that the reviewer, himself situated in a partial totality, *thinks* of and *wills* an all-inclusive totality in which oppositions and multiplicity of all partial totalities are connected and merged and in terms of which alone the whole process of history becomes intelligible. Intelligible to whom? If the reviewer and his situation in a given (maybe developing) partial totality change, I do not know who can vouchsafe for the intelligibility of the said holistic totality except a totaliser who is not himself subject to the temporalising process of that totality. But that is a notion Sartre rightly rejects. Why then does he hold out an unattainable hope for a totalitarian historical intelligibility in which all practices, individual and group, in spite of their conflict and divergence, will be connected and merged? I hope this ideal of totality is not intended to be a conceptual proxy for an absent ontological totaliser.

From this end I find myself somewhat in sympathy with the structuralist's approach to the matter, allowing every society to speak at least partially for its own science and without allowing any *other* (for instance, the reviewer's) society to have the "final" say in the matter. Primarily it *is* for the "scientists" of PS(T1) to tell us what is their "science," and it is our rational responsibility to try to understand it as faithfully and objectively as possible without trying to impose our theories on his, disregarding the problems and needs in response to which he had developed his views. We must hear *his* "story" first, however mythical or bizarre it may appear to our contemporary mind, working with a different conceptual framework and using an alien language, and, then, we will rationally reconstruct "history." I know exact point-to-point correspondence rules between their "story" of PS(T1) and our "history" of CS(T3) are *not* available, but understanding does not totally founder on that account. We have other coherent means of rationally reconstructing the "sciences" of past societies. We need not invoke the concept of innate idea for the purpose. Suitably redefined "cultural universals" or corrigible hypotheses will do. Popper's notion of *situational logic*, which I have explicated elsewhere, would be of immense value in this context.[18] The situationalist endorses the structuralist's intention to keep the ideological issues separate—as separate as possible—from the methodological ones. Though he is not opposed to diachronic study as such of macrohistorical phenomena, the situationalist thinks that science, whether one takes it as an institution or a set of activities or a corpus of beliefs, should be viewed against its appropriate societal background. This implies, among other things, that the historian of primitive science, for instance, cannot do justice to his job if he does not constantly bear in mind the problems and the societal facts of the concerned time and place, especially those related to his job. Thus in a very important sense the situationalist's approach may work to correct the overgeneralising tendency of the structuralist ignoring the *human* peculiarities of the issue to be explained or compared with similar other issues belonging to other and spatiotemporally unrelated social situations.

As against the situationalist the structuralist may argue that if all human peculiarities of a problem-situation have to be *specifically* attended, then the whole model-making effort will not only be practically tedious but also theoretically unrewarding, for its scope will be very restrictive and its use as a methodological means of comparative study of similar problem-situations negligible or, at best, metaphorical. As a methodological individualist, and even clearly recognising that methodological individualism has no necessary connection with ideological individualism, I have always felt an intellectual uneasiness in my mind over this controversial issue: if to make a past event historically intelligible one has to *narrate* all its details in a connected and *continuous* manner as demanded by such advocates of the continuous series model (CSM) as Croce, Collingwood, Oakeshott, and Geyl, one is saddled with, strictly speaking, a *logically impossible* task; if, on the contrary, to bring the endless human details to manageable proportions or usable sizes one has to resort to substructural clustering or statistical sampling or typifying of the same, then the specific individuals, their intentions, and their praxis are bound to be ignored for the sake of higher-order model making. The structuralist-existentialist controversy has some obvious theoretical and methodological parallelism with the holist-individualist one. Although I do recognise the structuralist's theoretical motivation for accepting and using the Durkheim-Mauss concept of collective representation, disregarding individuals and their praxis, I am afraid this craze for achieving the elegance and simplicity of structural picturing of extremely complex human reality is born out of an orthodox positivistic desire to put sociology on the high and respectable pedestal of natural sciences. As we know, Comte's ideal of sociology was social physics. My uneasiness with the structuralist's lack of concern with individual human beings is not at all ideological: it is both substantive and methodological. One cannot ignore historical details merely to preserve the elegance and the simplicity of structural models. In this connection I recall Wiener's words of balanced caution:

> In the social sciences we have to deal with short statistical runs, nor can we be sure that a considerable part of what we observe is not an artifact of our own creation. . . . whether our investigations in the social sciences be statistical or dynamic – and they should participate in the nature of both – they can never be good to more than a very few decimal places, and, significant information which begins to compare with that which we have learned to expect in the natural sciences. We cannot afford to neglect them; neither should we build exaggerated expectations of their possibilities. There is much which we must leave, whether we like it or not, to the un-"scientific," narrative method of the professional historian. (*The Human Use of Human Beings*)

Our dilemma, in brief, is this: "historical continuum" is *not* available, but then its nearest conceptual approximation, continuous narrative of closely knit series of occurrences (statistical slices), though necessary for correcting the possible abstract gaps of the model-making method, is not a foolproof strategy.

Though constructs of analytical reason, structures are not immune to historical influence, critical or otherwise. Whatever is produced by man is also in a way consumed by man. Structural models, with whatever ingenuity these are produced, cannot defy time or history forever and everywhere. These too are subject to what may be called laws of social entropy, of deliberately devised criticism. Though primarily made to serve methodological purposes, in the process of serving those purposes the same structural models come across or are forced by the design of the investigator to confront some relevant and yet intractable historical facts or ethnographic data and which bring to light the necessity of changing and improving those models. Better that one remember that models are no perpetual motion machine that can defy time and by statistics erase the aggregative effects of individual praxis, the basic dynamic of structural transformations. My words, however, should not be construed as an argument for reduction of social structures to individual personality structures to account for the transformations of the former. The cut-off line drawn between macrostructure and microstructure is, no doubt, methodologically called for, and we know from such diverse disciplines as physics, biology, linguistics, economics, and psychology that structural studies may be autonomously and successfully carried on at different levels without raising (for some specific purposes) the ontological, emergent, or evolutionary, relation of the levels, aggregatively or segregatively, that is, in terms of individual components.

Having expressed my sympathy for the structuralist position in relation to the history of science of past societies and my reservations about the tendency to ideologise history in the name of practico-dialectical necessity, I am qualifying my position with so many ifs and buts for this reason: If to maintain the purity or autonomous character of methodology we keep the ontological issues altogether separate, we land ourselves in serious but avoidable difficulties: we get a sort of calculus without the necessary rules of interpretation, necessary both for its application and its exactitude. Absolutely ontology-neutral methodology is hardly of any practical (in the theoretical sense) use. If, on the contrary, the thesis of (hoped-for) methodological unity is unilaterally, uncritically, and relentlessly pressed forward and accepted by us on the basis of an (implicitly believed in) ontological monism, such as physicalism, we deny ourselves qualitatively rich pictures of the world of complex phenomena.

I would like to add a word here to which one should not attach unnecessary ideological significance. That is about the nature of *needs* as experienced or understood by people of different societies at different periods, such as PS(T1), MS(T2), and CS(T3). The needs of man have, or are expressive of, a biological aspect in a broader sense comprising the needs of adjustment to the environment.[19] It is true, for instance, that in a sense the primitive people who live in the inaccessible forest of Andaman Island, Jarawas, left to themselves do not need any motorboat or telescope, for, one might say, these things and their uses are unknown to them. But when they see that the motorboat is very useful and a faster means of water transport than their canoes, in the course of time or through the process of acculturation, they may develop the need for the same. The case of the "need" for the telescope is somewhat different: unless they are shown that it would help them to see from a distance the approaching motorboat or other vessels of unwanted and alien intruders and thus such appropriate defensive measures as running away and hiding in the deep forest, they do *not* need it. In a way needs are time-place-bound, circumscribed by "social structure." At the same time, as I have said before, human "needs" are in a sense prospective, forward-looking, despite their being otherwise socially circumscribed or time-place-bound. The body-mind complex of man, unlike that of other organisms, is simultaneously tied up with the needs of an environment and also capable of being conscious of or at least vaguely anticipating homologous needs in other or future possible environments. These biologically inset needs of man may (but should not necessarily) be given an ideological-historical interpretation. Would it not sound very odd if, for instance, Radcliffe-Brown tells us about the Jarawas in 1922, "They need a motorboat but unfortunately they do not know that they do?" Similarly how correct would it be for a Radcliffe-Brown to tell a Jarawa that a "motorboat" is a "canoe fitted with a motor engine?" *Externally* speaking, "motorboat" and "canoe fitted with a motor engine" are certainly homologous objects, water transports, but are they semantically, socio-linguistically to be more precise, equivalent signs? Translation of words designating cultural objects raise so many difficult and interesting problems.

Before I consider some of these problems in the next chapter, I would like to reiterate my view of the nature of the human being, which I have argued elsewhere at length and which appears to me very relevant to the issues under discussion, namely, man by his very nature wants to be fair both to his own experiences influenced primarily by his own time and place and, at the same time, to others' experiences influenced primarily by those people's times and places.[20] The historical past, however, is dialectically retained in man's memory, marked partly by its diaphanousness and partly by its opacity, depending on his interest, attention, frequency of remembrance, and so on. This dialectic of history and futurity is contemporaneously operative within him. Complementary to it is the point that the concept of authenticity defined in terms of being fair to one's own *and* others' experiences is as central to the problem under discussion as the concept of truth itself.

CHAPTER FIVE

· · · · · · · · · · · · · ·

Significance and Interpretation

That anthropology could be profitably viewed as a branch of semiology is not an original thesis of Lévi-Strauss's. But certainly the conceptual apparatus of structural linguistics used by him in anthropology, in spite of its being somewhat outdated in the context of the works of Chomsky and his associates, has yielded extremely valuable results, making a confusing and complex mass of ethnographic data incredibly simple and easily intelligible. It is well known that C. S. Peirce, Baudouin de Courtenay, and Ferdinand de Saussure did pioneering work in this era. Structural linguistics as such was initially given definite shape by N. Troubetzkoy, Roman Jakobson, and Jakobson's associates. All of them would perhaps agree to characterise culture as a system of signs. This agreement in itself is not very important unless the nature, formation, function, transformations, and types of signs are adequately clarified. Signs are clearly involved in our, that is, human, thought and action. Scientific thoughts and actions, whether of PS(T1) or of CS(T3), can certainly be expressed or at least indicated by using some or other signs—symbols, indexes, and icons—and their syntactically permissible combinations.

The question that primarily concerns me here is, Can the magic of PS(T1) or the natural philosophy of MS(T2) as a subsystem of semiology be made "correctly" available in the semiological subsystem of the science of CS(T3)? When we talk of "semiology," are we meaning one unified semiology or different semiologies peculiar to different societies consisting of them have a life (or lives) of their own? Or is their life how these are used? Are signs objects or relations?

We have already noted that man stands in a two-way or dialectical relation to the world around him. Although he lives in this world, the latter cannot unilaterally determine how he will understand and act in (and toward) it. This man-world dialectic is in a way enacted within man himself. One might say that it is a semiological microcosm. Man can *partially* understand himself immediately, in what may be called direct encounter. I say "partially" because even this self-encounter is mediated by sensible entities, such as signs or symbols, or some ideal and abstract entities that are relatable, directly or indirectly, to the sensible ones. But to preserve and make inescapable use of these "partial" direct encounters he is obliged to associate or cluster *some* of these, leaving others outside the scope of association or clustering. To achieve even this minimal objective the human mind performs some very related, difficult, and delicate jobs: (1) it makes *itself* what in a sense it is not: *other*, and yet its own *other*, (2) it shows its abstractive ability, ability to disengage itself from itself and, at the same time; (3) keep the memory of this disengagement alive within itself; (4) to make use of an intuitive criterion for clustering *some* of these direct encounters under one structure and differentiating it from other structures, similar or different; and (5) do all these with an end in view, which is partly chosen and partly reflective of the needs of the human life, (6) give some meaningful names or ascribe signs to these structures of direct encounters so that they can be readily and homologously identified, reidentified and distinguished from the analogous and different structures. When we can give names to structures and successfully use the names to denote them, we *objectify* our *subjectivity* and start trying to comprehend ourselves as *other*-than-our*selves*. Self-encounter turns out to be other-encounter and involves *use* of names as signifying or denoting structures. Sign-using and inventing ability is native to human nature, traceable to both its sociological and its biological roots and needs. Whether every "bit" of what is structured along with other "bits" can be individually named and rigidly or fixedly signified is a very well-known disputable issue. In principle the issue does not appear to differ between the *structure* or *forms* or the "mental". and the "social" or even the "physical." The difference seems to be confined to the details and to the methods of successfully tracing and representing them.

Naming is one basic sign-using or signifying activity of man. Whether it is the basic activity is again a disputed issue. Whether the first bridge over the channel (assuming there is one) between the world and language that we cross is at the point of *logical proper name* and what is named, *simple object*, or at the point of *simple proposition* and *atomic fact* is also an unsettled question. These issues and questions, as we know, are being discussed in different idioms according to the concerned authors' preferred philosophical paradigms, for instance, quasi-Platonic ontology expressible in one or another formal language, ordinary realism formulated in terms of unchanging conceptual framework underlying the changing–changing through *uses*–ordinary languages, physicalism represented in a language taken as a whole, and anthropological dialectical realism expressible in a language that, though structurable, is changeable through *uses* over time. Like society, language may be studied synchronically as a static sign-system or diachronically as a changing sign-system.

Even at the very basic level of mental activities, such as feeling and sensing, whatever is structured or formed either is willfully retained in memory for anticipated possible *uses* or leaves behind its unattended mnemonic traces, gradually faded forms. At the relatively higher levels of thought and reasoning these structures or forms are found to be more articulate and relatively free of the "subject matters" that are ordered or "manipulated" by them. In all these activities, from basic-level bodily feeling to high-level mathematical structure designing, from naming to arguing, we perform at least one generic act that (in the absence of a better expression) may be called self-differentiating-cum-self-unifying. What is named, an object, for example, by a name or designated by a designator, and what is stated by a proposition or statement may be construed in two different but related ways or at two different levels. First, name-object and proposition-fact as they are related between themselves; and, second, *how* their relations are understood and used. The distinction between *name* and *object* and that between *proposition* and *fact* are studied in several human disciplines: logic, linguistics, anthropology, and biology. Generally speaking, all these are grounded in man's *need* of understanding himself as placed in some or another social situation and communicating with himself and others. Even subhuman species live under comparable needs and for survival are obliged to signalise them to fellow members of the same species and at times to the members of other species as well. Signifying and signaling activities are in a very important sense biologically founded. Biological (informal) linguistic, (formal) linguistic, or logical competence of sign-using and symbol-inventing are understandable both structurally and historically or evolutionarily. Man has a sign-using structure within himself, enabling him, among other things, to reidentify himself and, at the same time, to adapt himself as one-in-relation-to-others according to his own changing needs and also the latter's (as understood and communicated). Though for abstract and theoretical purposes we, common men, linguists, and logicians, occasionally study *language* as if it has a life of its own quite unrelated to and unaffected by what we do about and with it, how we use and misuse it, for the specific purposes of intercultural communication, for understanding scientific achievements and activities of the people of other societies at other times, such as PS(T1), and MS(T2), we are required to concentrate our attention on the dialectical pragmatics of language: how it is *used* in diverse contexts, both within and over a period of time, short or long. Both psycholinguistics and sociolinguistics or ethnography of speech acts, properly analysed, show that the *man-sign relation is dialectical.* And this is what I have in mind when I say that the man-language relation is marked by at least one generic character, self-differentiating-cum-self-unifying. Self needs to signify something other than itself and also needs to be satisfied that the other signified by the sign used (or invented) by him has indeed been successfully signified. In other words, even at the abstract level of semiology man's decision to stand outside his language cannot be successfully carried out.

Word is a sign. A string of words is a string of signs. But a word as such, *pen*, for example, is a thing and not a sign. Of course, one can think of contexts in which *pen* ceases to be a thing (in itself) and becomes a sign (going beyond itself, signifying something other than itself). In one context *pen* means a quill, in another a fountain pen, in still another a dot pen or ballpoint pen, or pencil. In some parts of India, the pen used to be worshipped as a symbol of the goddess of learning, *Saraswati*. The meaning of *pen* is *not* in itself, that is, in its being a thing unrelated to other things (in a more or less determinable context). To my mind, *significance* and *meaning* are essentially relational, relating a word to an object, a statement to a state of affairs, and the like. In a sense the meaning of the word *pen* is different from the thing named *pen*, and also different from the mental state interpreting the thing (pen) as *quill* or *fountain pen* using the word *pen*, and yet it is the same or at least similar to the interpreter-user of the word and to or for whom it is interpreted or used. Meaning as a relational concept thus does double duty: unites the different and differentiates the unity (of itself). The physical thing-word pen, the English sign-word *pen*, the interpreter's or user's mental state, and the hearer's mental state are simultaneously united and differentiated (or separated) by the *meaning* of pen. Meaning is a sort of interlocutor or prelocutor or intervenor. An element of gap or discrepancy—whatever name one gives to it, interlocution or intervention—is always there between the sign and what is signified or intended to be signified by it; and several factors, physical and psychological, are interfaced and dialectically operative in the semantic field. Negatively speaking, the sign-signified relation is never transparently picturesque and exactly isomorphic.

Semiology is closely linked with some or another theory of thought and mind. In the *De interpretation* Aristotle refers to interpreter and interpretation in his well-known definition of signs. Mind is said to be the interpreter of signs, and thought or concepts *interpretants* that are deemed to be common to all human beings and grounded in the apprehension of objects and their properties by mind. Words are used by the mind to represent concepts directly and corresponding things indirectly. Mind is credited with some freedom to choose words and sounds for the purpose of representing concepts and things. However, the relation between the words and the sounds established by usage and convention cannot be arbitrarily changed; for, in that case, words will not enable us to communicate or deal successfully with the world of objects. In Aristotelian linguistics and rhetoric words are conventional signs of concepts and thought commonly shared by all men. Conventional signs taken as a system are bound to exhibit elements of stability and a sort of rationality resulting from sedimented experience of ages that cannot be arbitrarily disturbed without seriously impairing our communication competence. If we forget about the systematicity of the signs and searchingly consider them individually, taking words or sentences as semantic units, their external look of stability and "picturesque" rationality increasingly appears suspect. The essential merit of the conventional theory of signs is that it admits that the sign-signified relation is *not* so structurally and directly bound up as to defy all historical changes clearly evident from social uses or ethnography of speech acts.

The sign-signified (taking both *sign* and *signified* in a very broad sense) relations may be presented or explicated in three distinct (and, yet, to my mind, very intimately related) ways. The relations between word and object, proposition and fact, and reasoning and what reasoning is about, some related facts or states of affairs, are all included under the label of sign-and-signified. These situations, broadly speaking, may be explicated by a two-term relation: sign directly signifies the signified, for instance, name or designator, on the one hand, and object or designated (whatever may be its ontological status), on the other. These situations may be explicated as a three-term relation: somebody signifies something by using some sign. In the two-term relation sign and signified are directly related: name or referring expression *as sign* properly names or refers to, that is, signifies the object or person or whatever that may be, that is, the signified. Or, it may be put from the other end: this or that object or person or whatever it may be, that is, the signified, is properly named or referred to by (this or that) name or referring expression *as sign*. The claim of directness or logical propriety between sign and signified in any of its forms, say, between name and named, or between proposition and fact, has often been criticised as misleadingly abstract and at variance with the way the sign-signified relation works in a sign (or semiological) system. Besides, this two-term theory, because of its strong directness claim, encounters special difficulties in the cases of reference-failure, oblique reference, and opaque reference. Let us call the two-term version of the sign-signified theory as SS2; Schema I may be taken as its approximate schematic representation.

Schema I

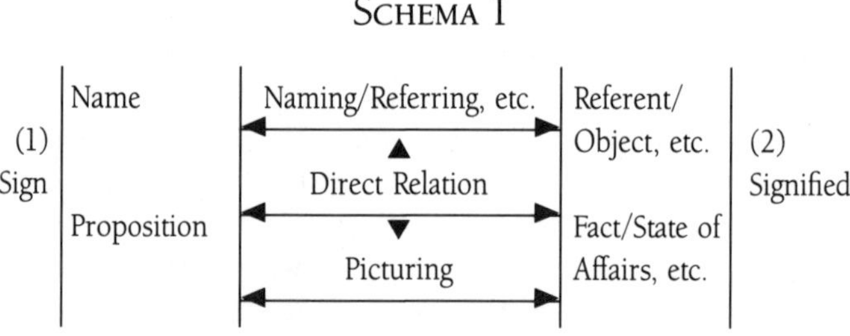

SS2 is reference-paradigm view: it takes the one-to-one direct relation between sign and what is signified as the paradigm between the units of the semiological world and those of the physicocultural. For Frege names and propositions alike have both sense and reference, whereas for Wittgenstein names have reference, a unique relationship to reality, and are "points," but propositions, unlike names, have sense, direction, and are "arrows." Under some interpretations, for instance, Quine's, of proper names, one feels that the logical propriety of proper names, their unique reference claim to reality, is dubious, and that definite descriptions can well be logical surrogates for proper names. And this proempiricist, one might even say proidealist, tilt of the reference theory of name has apparently much disturbed some philosophers such as Kripke. To preserve the logical propriety of proper names they must be freed from the vagaries of the sense-shift of definite descriptions and elevated to the status of what he calls *rigid designators*. A rigid designator, it is claimed, stands for the same object in every possible world in which it has a reference at all. To defend the proclaimed necessary character of the relation between the rigid designators and their designata Kripke draws, one might say misdraws, a distinction between epistemic possibilities and ontic possibilities, for the former being defined with and the latter without reference to our knowledge of how things do behave and might have possibly behaved in the actual and possible worlds. Whether a statement is necessarily or contingently true is said to be ascertained in terms of whether the stated *object's* property is essential or accidental. But can one possibly ascertain it in a correct way without knowing how, for instance, objects are classified in a language, how names are given to them and used? The name or designator is introduced by demonstration, or by means of a definite description fixing its reference, or in some other ways. Later on other speakers use it with the intention of the original introducer(s) to preserve the reference as *rigidly or fixedly* as possible. This process continues and the chain of communication, though changing because of use, does not break down. It is just not practically possible to understand user's sense of the word precisely. Reference-preservation and reference-rigidity unaffected by variations in use-contexts and users' intentions are undoubtedly a necessary and laudable semantic motivation. The recognition of this necessity is, of course, no guarantee against reference-shift, slow or sudden, unwitting or witting, primarily due to diverse uses of names and propositions. Overzealous commitment to a fancied semantic desideratum for exact communication seems at times to make us somewhat blind to the epistemic inseparability of reference and sense and reference-shift.

To be fair to Kripke I must admit that my brief allusion to his insightful view in my SS2 context is merely typologically illustrative and does not give full justice to his detailed arguments.

To remove the inadequacy of SS2 and also to give a better account of reference-shift in actual communicational networks within and between the societies, we perhaps need a three-term sign-signified theory, which in addition to sign (name or proposition) and signified (reference or fact or state of affairs) also recognises a third term, the signifier, by whom the sign is introduced and used. This three-term semiological theory may be called SS3 and schematised in Schema II:

Schema II

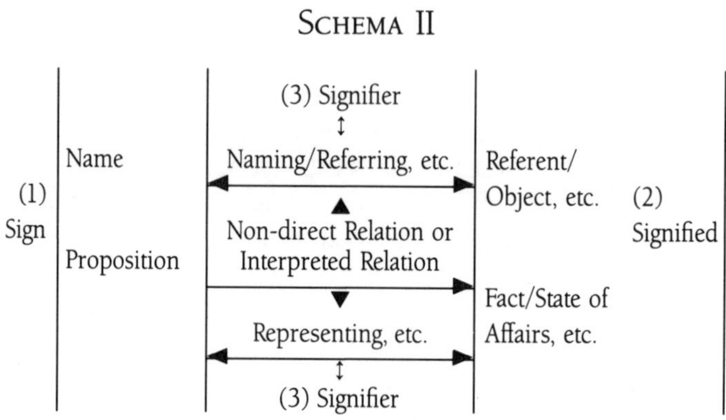

Here the sign-signified relation, that is, the relation between (1) and (2), is shown as nondirect or as interpreted by (3). The relation between name-object, etc., is not necessary and depends upon how name is *used by a signifier* to signify or denote an object. Besides, the relation between proposition-fact is said to be one of representation marked by an element of indefiniteness and *not* picturesque.

The main merit of SS3 is that it recognises the *human situation* of the relation(s) between sign (name or proposition) and signed (object or fact). It is an implicit assumption of the sign-signified relation that there are *signifiers* who act in some way or other in the concerned situation and make it *significant*. What is called sign is not sign if it is not usable in a possible human communication situation; for in that case it is hardly anything other than some physical mark and has no self-transcending and signifying power. *Signifying power* is, as it were, a gift or outflow of human situations. But signifiers alone do not make a situation human, certainly not from the communication point of view. And this seems to me the main deficiency of SS3 and has to be removed. In human situations such expressions as "signifiers," and "signified by" are essentially corelative to such expressions as "signified to," "addressed to," and "meant for." A significant situation or an adequate semiological theory, SS4, has four essential components or terms and may be schematised in the following way:

Schema III

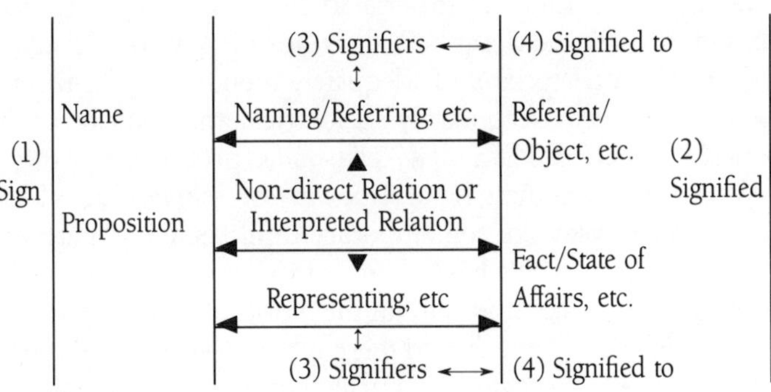

SS4 brings out the fuller human implications of a semiological situation. The proponents of SS2 conceive a *significant* situation as a dyadic relational affair, whereas those of SS3 take it to be a triadic one. In SS2, as I have said before, sign is thought to be *intrinsically invested* or *endowed* with a definite power to signify the signified. And, therefore, the human implication is totally unrecognised in this schema. In this connection one is reminded of the *sphota*-doctrine of the Sanskrit grammarians and of Plato's conception of the **ΟΤΟΙΧΕΙΟΘ**. Is there anything, property or power, *vya* (seed) or *sakti* (power), in a word or group of words (as sign) that can and does generate in one, one's mind, who is familiar with the word, an implicit and appropriate articulation propensity, such as speech acts or writing? If signs qua signs, individually or otherwise, in a phrase or sentence, for instance, were naturally or intrinsically significant—could show their signifying power even to those who are not familiar with their *use*—then we could dispense with SS4 or even SS3 and do as well with SS2. Unfortunately, this does not appear to be the case. Experience of sign-use suggests something else. In response to such questions as, How does this sign or string of signs signify (whatever that may be)? It is hardly convincing to be told "this signifies by virtue of its intrinsic power." The intrinsic signifying power doctrine denies either straightforwardly or by implication the relevance of the rules of use (as to how the signs are to be used and how to prevent and determine their misuse). On the contrary, if this (SS2-like) doctrine is correct, the rules of use themselves are suggested by the said signifying power. In that case, a clue or lead to how in practice, in different contexts, signs are or will be used is given by the so-called natural power of the concerned signs themselves. *Sign* and *signified* are a *necessarily related* ontological pair. Difference of contexts (or worlds) is immaterial to their way(s) of being related. If the signified can be described, the rules or ways of constructing that description correctly and adequately then have to be primarily ontological and only secondarily sociological and context-sensitive. I strongly suspect that Plato, *sabda-sakti-vadis* (proponents of the view that words do have their natural power) or *sphota-vadis* of India, Bolzano, and Kripke-like contemporary thinkers are all harping on the variations of the same basic theme of SS2, and one of their objectives appears to be common: to lift the world of meanings from the vicissitude of social contexts and thereby preserve their definiteness, fixity, and context-insensitive character. I understand the ontological problems underlying "logical proper names" and "propositions." But my question remains: are we, the human beings, concerned with "logical proper names and propositions" as ontological entities, as signs as such, or in their *representative* capacity in one or another language? I find it very difficult to escape the latter alternative without committing myself to an indefensible and perhaps uncalled-for form of Platonism. The fuller human implications of SS4 are badly missing in SS2. The basic fact that we feel, think, and communicate in and through sociolinguistic contexts is not adequately recognised by the defenders of different forms of SS2. The latter fail to see that all "texts" are "contextured," that is, interwoven with the details of the life-world.

My SS3 might remind one of Peirce's well-known notion of logic as semiotic, "the quasi-necessary, or formal, doctrine of signs." A semiotic process of situation, according to him, is a triadic relation among (1) a sign, or *representamen*, (2) that which is created by the sign in the mind of the affected person, or *interpretant*; and (3) that for which the sign stands, or *object*. The *signifier* of SS3 finds no place in the Peircean semiotic schema. Instead he uses the term *interpretant*. But he gives it a narrow meaning: it "creates in the mind of [the concerned] person an equivalent sign [equivalent to the *representation*] or perhaps a more developed sign." If a *representamen* were a "bare given" or passively received by the person as "an actual existent" or "a mere quality," then it could not be transformed into a more developed sign as stated by Peirce, unless one ascribes to the concerned person both *active* involvement in the use of sign and ability to expand it, improve upon it in terms of precision, abstraction, or generalisation. It is this ability of the person that accounts for his role as a *signifier,* his success in imparting an added character to the "originary" sign as recognised not only by him but also by his fellow social beings. Unless we put the *interpreter* in the place of the *interpretant*, that is, transformation or development of one sign into another remains problematic. One possible way out might be to endow the originary sign itself with a self-transforming power. But that hardly accords with Peirce's main philosophical position.

Every sign, according to Peirce, is connected with three things: the *ground*, the *object*, and the *interpretant*. The branch of semiotics concerned with the ground of sign is called by him *pure grammar*, that concerned with its object is *logic proper*; and that which studies the laws governing how one sign gives birth to another has been given the name *pure rhetoric*. The task of pure grammar is said to be determination of what must be true of the signs used by every scientific intelligence so that they may embody any *meaning*. Logic proper is the science of what is quasi-necessarily true of the signs of any scientific intelligence so that they may be true. Or, one might say, it is concerned with the truth-conditions of the signs, simple or complex. It is interesting to note that Peirce does recognise that logic is not primarily concerned with truth-conditions, *not* with construction of an abstract (SS2-type) definition of truth. Equally interesting is to note his emphasis on different (scientific intelligent) types of *uses* of things, from logicomathematical applications to rhetorical ones, from definite uses to suggestive ones. The Peircean theory of sign is fortunately not chained to the immediate reference-paradigm theory of meaning.

Peirce's theory of signs is particularly noteworthy for its richness of suggestion and recognition of the gradual enrichment of language from simplicity to extreme complexity. Following the cues left by Peirce, one can easily see the inadequacy of the two-term relation of signs. Scrutiny reveals that even three-term theory proves inadequate to tackle the problems posed by complex semiotic situations. The more one grasps the complexity of the semiotic situation, the more one sees the closeness of the relation between traditional semiotic and modern semantic. A fully developed and adequate theory of semiotic is hardly distinguishable from a semantic of *natural* language. The transition from *semiotic* to *semantic* has been naturalised by increasingly recognising the fleshing-out effects of speech acts and various other communicative acts.

Peirce reminds us that all forms of thought–"primitive," "modern" and "scientific," are embedded, not imprisoned or encapsulated, in various forms of signs. Even what is known as rigorous scientific thought is subject to such vagaries as theory-ladenness, meaning-shift, context-variance and -sensitivity, despite its proclaimed rigours. Evidently these vagaries have been disturbing the philosophers down the centuries. In order to put a stop to or solve this recalcitrant problem giving rise to various sorts of relativism and scepticism, time and again philosophers, particularly those of realistic persuasions, have been trying to formulate a theory of names purported to show a steady or rigid relation between primitive signs such as logical proper names and what are signified or denoted by them. The search for denotation without connotation undertaken by many logicians such as Mill, the early Wittgenstein, and Kripke, proved more or less futile. The central motivation of the ingenious defenders of logical proper names has been to chase away the ghost of relativism and scepticism and to establish a steady, if not permanent, relation between language and world. One observes these interrelated issues in the Peircean semiotic. From simple iconic and indexical signs Peirce moves to areas of symbolism, indicating the comprehensive scope of this project. It is interesting to note his recognition of the important role of *representamen* in between the *ground*, the *object*, and the *interpretant*. The *ground* that sustains a *representamen*, enabling it to "Stand to somebody for something in some respect or capacity," constitutes *pure grammar.* Grammatical structures ensure the invariance of the meanings of *representamens* used by "every *scientific* intelligence." The relation between *representamen* and objects, "quasi-necessary" in nature, constitutes the subject of *logic proper.* It is said to be "the formal science of the conditions of the truth of representation." The reason why a particular object is represented to a scientific intelligence in a given way and not otherwise is accounted for by *logic proper.* In and through this view of logic one notices how in Peirce's formal logic *human factor* is promisingly introduced. The importance of this factor becomes manifest when he speaks of *pure rhetoric*, spelling out the features of the relation between *representation* and *interpretant*. This branch of semiotic as conceived by Peirce shows how signs give birth to, or generate, new signs, especially how thoughts bring forth new thoughts. In brief, according to Pierce, grammar via logic generates rhetoric. Peircean semiotic is essentially human and dynamic. In it *forms* do not suffocate the *substance* of thought. The latter is sustained and propelled by the former. The former are basically sedimented structures of sociohistorical practices and not at all static in character. The creative and context-sensitive roles of language are clearly brought out by the Peircean logic as semiotic. His observations such as "Man makes the word, the word means nothing which man has not made it mean, and that only to some other men" or "my language is the sum-total of myself" are understandably open to misunderstanding.[1] The structural or societal aspects of meanings are evidently downgraded, if not denied, by Peirce. But, if the Kantian elements in Peirce's writings are adequately borne in mind, one does not have good reason to accuse him of totally disowning transcendentalism or its weaker form, structuralism. His emphasis on *thought*, and frequent identification of it with man, highlighting of the *objective* character of symbols unmistakably indicate his opposition to psychologism and nominalism.

What I am trying to say may or may not be endorsed by Peirce or his modern followers of the pragmatic persuasion. But the basic issue for the reconstruction of a critical history of science demands that we identify the concepts that are simultaneously fair to the flux or the historical character of science and its durable structural or transcendental aspects.

Out in search of the novelty and creativity of scientific achievements, some historians and philosophers of science see in science almost a ceaseless flow of new information, concepts, and their systematisation. To them the paradigm-shift seems to be the life breath of the history of science. There are others who become easily and unusually disturbed over the absence of shift or replacement in the accepted paradigm. There are still others, more conservative historians and philosophers of science, who are tragically anxious to retain the paradigm of science without shift or replacement, even without anomalies and puzzles within it. The names of Kuhn and Feyerabend may be associated with the flux view of science. The moderate view may be ascribed to Popper and Toulmin. And with the conservative view the names that still come first to my mind are those of Plato and Kant. I can easily imagine that Kuhn would not like to sail in the same boat with Feyerabend. I am sure that Popper would refuse to board the boat in which Toulmin was a passenger. I am more than sure that Kant would disown Plato in his reconstruction of history and philosophy of science. Even then the reasons that prompt me to mention these names and in three pairs are only illustrative and typological.

The first view, broadly speaking, is empiricist and works with a notion of man that is essentially social. The empiricist orientation together with its social affiliation is largely responsible for viewing history of science as a series of paradigms interspersed by relatively short or long periods of sterility or lack of creativity or innovation. The defender of the moderate view is opposed to the very idea of downgrading the importance of objectivity of science. Excessive influence of society or social context on science is frowned upon by him. For, he suspects, the alleged context-bound image of science makes it not only unacceptably relativistic but also intolerably subjective. The composition of the defenders of the moderate view is not homogenous. Some of them take a *positive* stand and draw our attention to those features of science that are actually obtained in different social systems or forms of life. Some others are opposed to the idea of accepting sociology of science as legitimisation and affiliation of science. They try to draw our attention to the *normative* needs of science so that its scientific character is not compromised or given up. In a way the extra-contextual or moderately transcendental image of science is projected by this group of thinkers. What baffles genuine transcendentalists such as Kant is the claim, veiled or open, that science even after it reaches its aim of presenting a truly systematic picture of the universe can remain historically open to falsification, modification, and historical change. Antihistorism is the hallmark of the transcendental theory of science.

Underlying the preceding three theories of science are three views of human nature. First, to the radical empiricist the concept of man, except as a psychosomatic complex, is meaningless and confusing. His efforts undertaken at the suggestion of the transcendentalist to identify or discover mind or self have proved futile. To him, self as the core of science of man, as a unifying cognitive principle, is elusive. The personal self is hardly distinguishable from the social self. To the empiricist man is either a machine or an animal or both. His rationality is borrowed from society, tradition, and social experiences.

Second, to the moderate rationalist human self has a structure of its own. Though this structure is not entirely independent of his somatic and social affiliation, it has an identity, a continuity, and a sort of autonomy of its own. According to this view, man, in spite of his social affiliation, can bring about change in the structure of society. In the restructuring of society his enterprise and freedom are important inputs. His somatic exercises are also not entirely imitative. Many of them are genuinely innovative and due to his own initiative. In other words, man is not completely sociologically determined. His psychology of scientific discovery or other forms of innovative work cannot be ascribed to and explained, without residue, by his sociology.

The moderate view is ordinarily opposed to the idea of identification of psychology with sociology of man. It seeks to preserve a demarcation between sociology of knowledge and psychology of knowledge.

Third, the transcendentalist view of science is based on a philosophical anthropology that assumes man in the image of God. The acceptability of the answer to the question, What makes knowledge certain (synthetic a priori and necessarily valid, to use Kant's phraseology) has been made contingent on the nature of man. Only if human nature is endowed with a transcendental and nonhistorical capacity to grasp picturesquely the nature of things or reality, Kant claims, can knowledge assume the dignity of infallible certitude. It is here, in the transcendental foundation as understood by scientific philosophers such as Descartes and Kant, that one has to find out the reason of their antipathy toward history in general and history of science in particular. To the transcendentalist historism is invariably associated with relativism and scepticism. To chase away these twin "evil spirits" from the "respectable" arena of science the transcendentalist views man in the image of God.

It is of interest to recall, in this connection, the transcendental argument of Leibniz, for instance, to vindicate the possible certainty of the cognitive achievement of human nature. The contingency that one finds even in the arena of science is ascribed by him to the free choice of God and, subordinately, to his creatures. To God himself all statements of knowledge are analytically true, that is, certain, and there is no element of contingency in them. In principle the transcendentalist endows human nature with the capacity of the divine: to know reality infallibly and unquestionably. Though God has created the best possible world with the best possible knowing creatures in it, there is room for contingent truths for human beings. The latter cannot see things under the aspect of eternity and *exactly* from God's point of view. Under the aspect of history God's point of view is an ideal that man tries to approximate and use in thought and action. But because of his position as subordinate to God he cannot rise entirely above the realm of contingency. The contingent truths have no place from the transcendental divine point of view. They exist in themselves, apparently isolated from the divine scheme of things comprising both knowing beings and the world at large.

The repeated failures of the scientist as evident from the history of science, the history of scientific paradigm-shifts, make the philosopher seriously reflect on the disturbing question. The question appears in an even more disturbing form to the philosophical anthropologist familiar with the history of science obtained in different, at times isolated, cultures. Reflection leads the philosopher to the conclusion that every concept of "knowing the world" (with different cultures within it) needs critical review. If the world is conceived as something finished and fashioned by God and then given to man as such, the failure of the scientist as knower then, by implication, is to be ascribed to God. Besides, another disturbing implication of this conception is this: the scientist, however gifted he may be, does not have an irrefutable grasp of the world: the spectre of scepticism continues to haunt epistemology and history of science.

One way out of this impasse suggested by Descartes and Kant is to dismiss history as a valid mode of knowledge summarily. This is obviously a negative step born out of their inability to reconcile their foundational (epistemological) structure with the flux (history) of science. The positive part of their attempt to vindicate science consists of two elements: (1) to dehistorise and decontextualise science altogether and (2) to lay bare the "firm" or "unshakable" foundational structure of all sorts of valid knowledge, especially science. To Descartes this firm foundation appears in the form of the cogito principle. And to Kant it is in the apperceptive form of transcendental self. Both these principles are conceived essentially as unificatory and justificatory. All that is given to human senses, imagination, and understanding is sought to be not only unified but also justified by these transcendental principles. It is claimed that these principles, given full play, know no essential distinction between man and man, culture and culture, epoch and epoch. In effect, these principles are called upon to play the role of God as knower on the earth. The transcendental self knows the world not under the aspect of temporality or history.[2]

The cognitive structure associated with the names of Descartes and Kant is God-like in a very important way. The true knower or the scientist is not a passive recipient of the world given in space-time. In the process of knowing it he (in a way) *creates* it. The analogy of divine creation is surreptitiously exploited by the transcendentalist. But in one important respect he departs from the theological analogy of creation. According to the transcendentalist, the scientist creates the world out of something received from "outside," not out of nothing. The *initial* distinction between the "inside" and the "outside," between the material and the formal or the spiritual elements of scientific knowledge, is ultimately blurred by the Cartesian and the Kantian transcendentalists in terms of some telos and sublated by the Hegelians by invocation of the concept of Divine design. Telos or design is purported to unify different cultures and undo the fancied miseffects of cultural diversity and its alleged offshoot, scientific relativism.

It is interesting to note that what the transcendentalist tries to achieve by his foundational structuralism and such allied concepts as telos in epistemology is reiterated with little or no variation in philosophy of language. Cartesian linguistics, in its historical and reconstructed form, aims at laying bare a universal and immutable structure of *all* conceivable languages. Like telos, logos may be conceived both as a firm foundational structure of all logic and language and also as a generator of new logics and languages.

Linguistic structuralism in its pure form assumes a dichotomy between syntactic and semantic structures of language. The purist thinks that syntactic structure of language consists of initial element, phrased structure component, transformation component, morphophonemic component, and phonemic representation of the concerned sentences. A pure syntactic view of language fails to see clearly the striking relation between the structures and the elements of language. The neatness and elegance of structures capture the purist's imagination and make him blind to the specific semantic functions associated with the elements of language. An adequate understanding of language is not possible unless the initial element, phrase component, and transformational component are related collaterally to phonological component and sound, on the one hand, and semantic component and the meaning, on the other. The meaning of complex sentence is to be obtained from its deep structures by means of rules of semantic interpretation, and the phonetic interpretation of each sentence is to be obtained from surface structure by means of phonological rules. By implication a developed form of linguistic structuralism concedes that an understanding of language can hardly be adequate only in terms of its structure: how it is *perceived* is also, perhaps primarily, to be taken into account. Language becomes a *creative* form of life, and in fact it *is* indeed so, not merely because of its structural-foundational fixity but mainly because of its perceptual variability. This variation is largely attributable to the *human use* of language.

It is in this context that one finds Chomsky's transition from his initial phase of thought, marked by an almost exclusive emphasis on the syntactic structure of language, to the second phase of his thought, marked by recognition of the concepts of recursive constructions, semantic creativity, and interpretation. Even more instructive is his second view, which recognises the seeds of creativity not only in the psychology but also in the biology of language-users. It is a long and interesting journey from Bloomfieldian behaviourism via the refutation of the Skinnerian behaviourism to the promising land of linguistic creativity. Linguistic *competence* and *performance* with all their grammaticality are rooted in human nature and cannot be explained in terms of such concepts as stimulus, response, habit, association, conditioning, or reinforcements. But at the same time it has to be pointed out that human nature, which contains the seeds of all forms of language-use, is not impervious to social and biological conditions and variations. To conceive linguistic competence as something innately and immutably given is to fall back upon a sort of unhistorical structuralism. Though often this fall-back position is espoused in the name of vindication of rationalism and avoidance of empiricism, it militates against our deep-rooted commonsense understanding of language. The obsessive fear of physicalism and determinism unfortunately tends to push the structuralist to a sort of linguistic universalism that proves insufficiently powerful for the description of natural languages: how they are actually used by *human* beings.

In self-defence the structuralist tries to point out that his notion of universal grammar is only an ideal and does not propose to offer a *description* of the elements of natural languages. Even its highest aim is nothing more than to give only a *general* description of the *structure* of natural languages. There, too, he hastens to add, his description is not intended to be so general as to apply to other (nonlinguistic) systems of communication. By implication, the structuralist draws a rather sharp line of demarcation between linguistic communication and other (nonlinguistic) forms of communication. The important question that arises here is this, Can the structuralist, without being inconsistent with his view of human mind and body, draw this line of distinction? If what he terms a "highly specific language faculty" is there, why are its spill-over effects, that is, competencies, not evident in man's other forms of communicative activities? Unless it is uncritically assumed that linguistic competence and performance, though seated in body, are separated from such other communicative signs as expression, action, and orientation of our body and that our body itself is sharply separated from its physical environment, I find it difficult to accept why a sharp line of demarcation should be drawn between the communicative function of language and that of other signs of the human body.

A close study of the structuralist view of language discloses a hidden transcendental argument purported to refute linguistic relativism or contextualism. If the concept of competence is kept separated from that of performance, this hypothesis is strengthened. If, on the other hand, the former is brought closer to and presented in terms of the latter, the miseffect of transcendentalism is minimized. But the structuralist fears that this will result in downgrading philosophy of language to sociology or anthropology of language. Some thinkers, such as Hymes, Halliday, and Labov are opposed to the Chomskyan method of studying language. They suspect that in order to preserve the "purity" of structure of language Chomsky overemphasises the importance of competence, underemphasises that of performance, and largely ignores the sociological and *interactive* characteristics of linguistic communication. Sociologists and anthropologists of language are primarily concerned with *communicative competence* or *competence in use*. Too much emphasis on idealisation of language and concentration on its anatomy, ignoring its perceptible body, land the linguists in a sort of relative sterility rooted in transcendentalism. Transcendentalism evident in structuralism and associated with a high degree of formalisation is not necessarily denounced by sociolinguists. What they are basically interested in is regressing to or extracting the structure of language from its uses. "Use" need not mean its narrow idealised sense. Whoever can learn or use language or its communicative equivalents is evidently in command of their underlying *rules*.

Admittedly a set of rules may be deemed or characterised as structure. It is not the word over which we are quarreling. Our basic interest is in how it is formed, how it is used, and how it is transformed through uses. Once the possibility of formation and transformation of a set of rules or structure is recognised, it seems, the historical aspect of language is recognised by implication. But if one insists on the view that all the rules of formation and transformation conform to a foundational or transcendental set of rules, which itself is not historically changeable in character, the insight underlying the interactive theory of language gets lost. Strictly speaking, the interactive theory is more an account of practise than of theory. Failure of interaction is detected in and by follow-up interactions. Misuse of language is identified within the field of uses of the concerned language. The structure or the rules implicitly used for detection or identification of communication failure or misuse of language become clear and discussable *not* in terms of some external or alien criteria but in terms of and within the field of communication itself. Communication throws up and exhibits its own structure.

Once language is recognised as social semiotic or as Halliday characterises it, "social interpretation of meaning," the traditional distinction between *la lingua* (language) and *la prole* (speech), between paradigmatic and syntagmatic, mainly due to Saussure, tends to be systematically blurred.[3] Although one should not be blind to the level of distinction between grammaticality and meaningfulness of language and allied communicative acts, one need not draw a sharp line of demarcation between the two. Although communicative performances are undoubtedly structured, their grammatical structures themselves are also historical in a sense. The characterization that every language has its history does not refer only to its semantics but also to its syntax. The empirical studies of natural languages make it abundantly clear that their grammatical structures, though relatively hidden, are not entirely free of historical change. By using and misusing, both in written and spoken forms, language is changed by human beings. Language has no life of its own. Its life consists in human use and misuse. This is what I call the anthropological foundation of language. It need not be construed as transcendental in the bad or unhistorical sense.[4] This is not to deny that words and their meanings, compared to their relational or grammatical structure, undergo faster historical change. But what needs to be emphasised here is that there is no such grammar, universal or otherwise, that is immune to historical change. The point that is to be driven home is that this change is due to human agency. Sapir rightly observes, "Language exists only in so far as it is actually used – spoken and heard – written and read. What significant changes take place in it must exist . . . as individual variations." Also noteworthy in this connection is the view of Jespersen. "The most notable advance that has been made in the theoretical conception of the nature of language . . . consist(s) in this . . . we no longer . . . conceive language as a self-existing thing or substance, or . . . as a organism, but have learnt to see that language in its essence is a human activity, an effort on the part of one individual to be understood by, or at least come into relation with, another individual."[5]

Once the sociohistorical continuity between the syntactic deep structure and the semantic surface is denied and their dichotomy insisted upon, the *creative* aspect of language is diminished. Besides, the denial of the dialectic between the two entails the revival of dualism between what is changing and what is "changeless" in language. The alleged changelessness or agelessness of syntax gives the incorrect impression that language is a natural, not cultural, phenomenon.

The interesting point which deserves the philosopher's attention here is that Jespersen and Sapir had spoken of the *human* significance of the life of language well before the later Wittgenstein's influence became well known and established. That word and world are not related in a very simple and direct manner, as indicated in Schema I, was clear to anthropologists and sociologists when such philosopher-semanticists as Frege, Russell, and the early Wittgenstein were engaged in getting rid of the Platonic implications of Meinong's theory of language. According to Meinong, whatever is referred to must be an object of some kind or other. An object may be factual (or complete) or fictional (or incomplete) or imaginary. To be an object something need not be a Meinongian object: it need not occupy a particular segment of the physical space-time. Unless this liberal requirement of object is kept in view, it becomes difficult to account for the status, for example, of art object and ethical object. By drawing a distinction between reference and sense (Frege), denotation and description (Russell), and similar other pairs of concepts philosophers have been trying to find a common house in the *world* for both science and arts. But neither Frege nor Russell is primarily interested in explaining the status of art objects or the meaning of literary sentences. Frege's initial interest was in the nature of number. He finds that some object may be differently indicated or identified, referentially and sensewise. A sign, name, or referring expression picks out an object as its reference when some proposition that expresses the sense of sign is true of that object. By implication, Frege admits, a sign cannot signify its object (reference) entirely on its own, in isolation. Only as a part of a sentence, the primary bearer of meaning, can a sign successfully refer to an object. It is simultaneously claimed (1) that a complete symbol or proper name cannot behave properly or rigidly in isolation, and that it can do so only in a *sentential context*, and (2) that in order to be a complete symbol or proper name or referring expression a sign must signify some object *on its own account*. Frege tries to bring (1) and (2) together in terms of his twin concepts of sense and reference. In the back of his mind Frege is always concerned with the question of truth and falsity. Only the senses of sentences that express thoughts (*not* commands, questions, or exclamations) can be true or false. A thought is said to be the sense of a sentence "in which we communicate or assert something." Senses, tied to object(s), are claimed to be objective

Otherwise, it is feared, no plausible distinction can be drawn between communication and communication-failure. It is only because of the proclaimed constancy of thoughts, the senses of sentences, that our affirmations and denials are interpersonally sharable and the claims of their truth or falsity publicly ascertainable. Admittedly thought, unlike chairs and tables, is not a part of the material furniture of the world; yet it can be "presented to people as identical." Frege considers this public character or objectivity of sense a necessary condition of ascertaining the validity of argument and *our* pursuit of truth.

Contemporary philosophers of language are apparently divided into two camps; those who, like Frege, maintain that meaning is to be grasped in terms of *truth-conditions* and those who reject this contention and espouse the view that language is a way or form of *social interaction*. Strawson, for example, speaks of an "apparent conflict . . . between the theorists of communication-intention and the theorists of formal semantics." He mentions Grice, Austin, and the later Wittgenstein as the chief spokesmen of the communication-theory and Frege, the earlier Wittgenstein, and Chomsky as the main defenders of the notion of truth-condition.[6] A good number of philosophers may not be willing to see Frege in the camp of the theorists of formal semantics. His contribution to communication-theory is often cited in this connection. The notion of sense, the main plank of communication-theory, ensures an element of objectivity in communicative acts, despite the fact that it is not a part of the material world. One can easily point out that the material world and its "reliable" and "repeated" perceptions cannot permanently ensure communication-success. Often acts or pieces of fine arts and literary sentences prove communicatively more successful than the scientific statements satisfying the requirement of formal semantics. This shows, among other things, that robust realism or Platonism of the philosophers seeking picturesque truth need not necessarily be taken very seriously. Fictional discourses turn out, not infrequently, to be cognitively more satisfying than the "neat" factual reports of representation of objects.

The distinction between formal semantics and communication theory, which has a significant bearing on the understanding of the nature and variety of science, is due not only to Frege but also to his German contemporary philosopher, Husserl, who too had a mathematical background to his credit. Primarily interested in developing the rigorous science of sciences, he developed phenomenology. Phenomenology is rightly credited with undertaking several laudable aims, namely, to clear up "the Meinongian jungle" consisting of various types of objects – ideal and real, fictional and factual, and so on – to show the unity of the subjectivity and the objectivity, to demonstrate the eidetic unity of the diversity, and to vindicate the history of all forms of science without giving up their structural unity. In his earlier works Husserl emphasises the importance of the meaning-conferring acts of consciousness. He also draws our attention to the fact that words used by us simultaneously refer to and clothe the objects they stand for. However, the fulfillment of meaning is not to be found in the objects themselves but in the way they are constituted, are lived through, and become what they are by the meaning-conferring consciousness of human beings. Right from the beginning one finds in Husserl's works both the use (naming and communicating) and the formal aspects of language.

Ontologically speaking, meanings are understood as ideal unities. Logic and nomological sciences are basically connected with dehistorised essences or ideal unities. That is how Husserl expounds his view of meanings in *Logical Investigations* (1900-1901), for example. All theoretic unity to him is essentially a unity of meaning. The unity of such "things" as proposition, inference, and system is made up of meaning. All theoretical science is claimed to be constituted by one homogeneous stuff, "the ideal fabric of meanings." That fabric is designated as the idea of pure logic and it is construed as a theory of science. After Leibniz, it is also characterised as a *mathesis universalis*. This initial enterprise of the founder of phenomenology is found also in one of his later works, *Formal and Transcendental Logic* (1929).

The main criticism that has been rightly raised against Husserl's initial theory of meaning is that he assumes a yawning gulf between ideal objectivity and real objectivity. It is understandable that the phenomenologist cannot agree to identify the real with the empirical. For, in that case he entraps himself in the basic mistake of the positivist. But, at the same time, his overemphasis on the ideal objectivity makes one think that he is not duly mindful of the diversity of what is empirically given. In order to be fair to the diversity and the changing character of the empirical it is true that one may lose sight of the basic principles, conceptual moorings, which make the former meaningful. But if the phenomenologist is seized by the zeal of unitary meaning of all factual experiences, actual as well as possible, it is very likely that he would be obliged to emasculate or distort the givenness of the facts as available in different historical cultures.

The tension between the two aspects of meaning, structural and historical, theoretical and practical, is evident inarticulately in the earlier works of Husserl and articulately in his later works such as *The Crisis of European Sciences and Transcendental Phenomenology* (1934-37). The crisis has its two roots, one positivistic and the other transcendentalistic (in the bad sense). In this connection, one feels inclined to explore the significance of Husserl's relation with Kant's transcendentalism, on the one hand, and Dilthey's *Lebenswelt*, on the other. First, the crisis of sciences is precipitated by the internal in consistencies of positivistic reductionism. In his dogmatic resolve to cut science off from all transcendental and unifying principles the positivist lands himself either in pure descriptivism as evident from his approach to human sciences or in pure and abstract formalism as evident from his approach to natural sciences. The positivist is driven to either "pure facts" or "pure formulas" by his antitranscendentalism of the dogmatic variety. Huserl's displeasure with these two approaches is understandable. Although he does not regret his commitment to the search for the ideal unity of all sciences, empirical and formal, he remains steadfast in his programme of seeking fulfillment of meaning in the life-world. Cut off from the moorings of the life-world, science is separated from its human roots. And there lies the origin of the crisis of modern *European* science. The ideal of unity lies hidden deep in the structure of human understanding. If the craze for facts and more facts makes the mind's moorings in the deep structure loose and allows its scientific research programmes to drift in the shallow waters of technology, "practical needs," and comfort seeking in the course of time, the mind is bound to feel rootless, aimless, and sick, if not critically ill. The phenomenologist assigns philosophy the task of taking drifting and meaningless science back to its human root and fastening it there again. Once that meaning is captured, philosophy itself will not only return to its meaningful roots but will also take science there. In the depth of unifying consciousness history and science of philosophy may be reunited.

It is interesting to note that while Husserl proposes this otherwise welcome programme he, somewhat like Hegel, takes a Eurocentric view of world history. The form of universal philosophy that is claimed to be essentially scientific in its scope and apodictic in its method seems to be European by its birthright. Though Husserl is not sure whether European humanity has within itself that ideal vision of science and philosophy, he gives the impression that the limited vision of "merely an empirical-anthropological type like 'China' or 'India' " will not do.

In other words, the phenomenologist, like Hegel, suggests that the cradles of world civilisation continue to be preoccupied with the *external* views of history and that the true and internal view of history is for Europe to discover, realise, and present to the world. Husserl's *Crisis* is basically a teleological-historical reflection on the history of science from the standpoint of the crisis-ridden Europe of 1930s.

It has been rightly said that Husserl's reflection on history is essentially philosophical and only marginally historical. For the historiographer who is mainly interested in achieving *universal* acceptability and apodictic *certainty* of his view, it is difficult to be fair to the bewildering, almost irrational, variety, of history: history as an art. The eidetic view of history seems to be committed to making it a science. In spite of his expressed anxiety to be fair to the life-world, because of its very nature, Husserl's dream of *universalis mathesis* and cogito-based certitude appears to be almost unrealisable. This point has been pertinently raised by Heidegger and Paul Ricoeur, among others.

Husserl's research programme to establish the rigorous character of science *together with its history*, though interesting, is bound to be viewed critically by those who take history seriously. In order to make *history* of science as rigorous as philosophy and, following philosophy, science, one feels, Husserl gives us a frozen or a dehistorised image of the discipline. His task undertaken in the *Crisis*, especially "Galileo's Mathematisation of Nature," is likely to remind one of Cartesian foundationalism and Kantian transcendentalism. Given their forms of structuralism, both Descartes and Kant find that if one wants to confer permanent meaning on science, one has to free it from the vagueness and vagaries of history. Descartes's retreat to the cogito and Kant's ascent to (the apperceptive unity of) the transcendental self are conceptually analogous devices to refute relativism and scepticism. In spite of their apparent association with *individual* human beings, both the cogito and the transcendental self are essentially universal in their metaphysical implication and operational scope. It is not difficult to show that when (scientific) understanding is derived from or ascribed to a cogito-like principle, its historical affiliation becomes obscure and invisible, if it is not snapped altogether. "Growth of science," "development of science," "history of science," and other similar expressions are either said to be self-contradictory for their alleged prereflective character or summarily dismissed by the transcendentalist. Growth or development presupposes the *imperfection* of science. Once its "rigorous character" and "solid foundation" can be phenomenologically shown, it is argued, the talk of its history hardly conveys any sense. In other words, it is maintained that sense of history, as ordinarily understood, and sense of science, as rigorously understood, cannot go together. The rigorous sense of history, as explained by the transcendental phenomenologist, freezes history: takes away the refreshing flow of time from it.

The transcendental sense of history may be gathered clearly, for example, from Husserl's account of "Origin of Geometry" or "Galileo's Mathematisation of Nature." Neither geometry nor mathematics is known for its capacity for capturing the sense of flux or change invariably associated with history. These disciplines are primarily known and used for their suitability to systematise and present in structured form the elements that are claimed to be essentially relatable but apparently standing apart. Husserl's basic strategy is to show that the seemingly abstract and elegant structures of geometry and physics are grounded in a prereflective life-world which itself, on scrutiny, is found to be rooted into a unitary foundational principle such as the transcendental self. Whether this relation between abstract scientific world, life-world, and transcendental world (of principle) forms a vicious circle or a virtuous one cannot be easily decided without bringing a living (not dead structural) sense of history to bear upon it. Those who like Kockelmans and Kisiel have taken immense pains to explain Husserl's sense of history have not gone into this very important question with sufficient care and critical attention. That is the impression one forms after going through their otherwise very scholarly works.[7] In this connection one would find the concluding paragraph of Kockelmans's paper "The Mathematisation of Nature" in Husserl's last publication, *Krisis*, very interesting and instructive.

> But even this "ontology of the life" is not an ultimate. Also the life-world itself refers to, and in that sense presupposes, acts of perceptual consciousness through which it is experienced and presents itself as that which it is and as that for which we take it. It is only when we arrive at consciousness as the universal medium of access to whatever exists and has value, including the life-world itself, that our search for foundation reaches its final destination. In other words, our ontology of the life-world itself is the ultimate foundation only in the constitutive analyses of transcendental phenomenology.[8]

The tension between transcendental structuralism and lived historism is clearly evident in this paragraph. If the life-world is not the final tribunal before which the structural world of science is answerable and, what is worse, if the life-world itself is required to appear before a higher tribunal that is both identical with and yet different from itself, it is not clear from which of the said two worlds history would receive its authentic sense. Or are we obliged to fall back on the desperate view that history for its authentic sense might endlessly commute between itself and the transcendental world to which *unknowingly* it is affiliated? If history for its *living* sense is required to be dependent upon or derivable from an unknown or unlived world-structure of the transcendental sort, it appears to me that one of the very basic principles of phenomenology—availability of truth in human experience—is seriously compromised, if not given up. Truth by *postulation*, aligned to transcendental structuralism, is clearly alien to the spirit of phenomenology.

If the attempt to vindicate realism is characterised as scandal of philosophy, it is perhaps even more scandalous to attempt to show its historical character. Both the attempts are uncalled for and rest on grave misunderstanding of the concerned issues. One of the persons who has contributed a lot to the clarification of the essentially *realistic* and *historical* character of science is Heidegger. It has perhaps rightly been pointed out by him that the very undertaking of proving the existence of the external world (in the realistic sense) is misconceived and uncritical. Since the world does not stand apart from man, its independent existence can hardly be proved by him to his fellow human beings. In a very important sense it is a part of, and, therefore, inseparable from, man's own being. The being of man is inextricably bound up with that of the world itself. In other words, man's being is in-the-world. This being the case, Heidegger argues, the independent existence of the world cannot be proved by man. The presupposition of proof cannot itself be a probandum or theorem.

Comparable to the "scandal" of proving the external world is the "scandal" of establishing the historical character of science. The history of science is like that of man himself, being spread out in and inextricably bound up with the life-world. Science is a *thematically* carved-out picture of the world. The themes concerned are obviously man-made. These themes are meant to answer some theoretical and practical *needs* of man. In a sense man encounters himself-as-needed in the world. Science is an abstract being of man's self-encounter (with the world). This image is abstracted not only from the world but also from the history in which man-in-the-world is steeped. Like world, history is an inseparable part of man. In the process of self-objectification or self-presentation man finds himself not only *in* the world but also *against* the backdrop of history. He cannot conceive himself without world and without history. It is impossible for him to conceive himself as a completely *de novo* or a just-born reality. This is due to the fact that in the totality of the meaningfulness of his life man finds, besides himself, world and history or, to put it perhaps more correctly, world-history. History is intelligible only when it is reviewed against the objective background already *otherwise* available. From this point of view, the expression "future history" may appear as a vague metaphor falling outside the ken of meaningfulness. The historian's research is only clarificatory and not constitutive. And this clarification consists in the reduction of the unintelligible to the intelligible. This process is never-ending. This forward-looking character of history keeps it always more or less free of the structural rigidity that one finds in Husserl's account of history, including history of science. In both mathematics and physics man searches for what he already has within him vaguely or indistinctively. His research is calculated to clarify through verification, experimentation, and commonsense experience his themes and projects.

One gets the impression that Heidegger is aware of the paradox or, politely speaking, tension in Husserl's view of history and that he wants to get out of it. This paradox or tension is found in his philosophy itself. This is not surprising in view of the fact that to him history is nothing if it is not *philosophy* of history. That this view of history has almost an incurable infection within it has long been observed by the critics of Hegel, notably Marx. If in the name of discovering the meaning of history the philosopher radically philosophises or rigorously *unifies* the details of events, history becomes *illustrated* philosophy in a *closed* circle. Highlighting the concept of ceaseless human discovery Heidegger tries to extricate himself from the closed circle of philosophical history. The totality of meaningfulness within which he finds human discovery is situated is open-ended and not static. The circle created by *dead* history, unlived past, is sought to be broken up by living history, by doing certain things aimed to answer the needs of life and to confirm certain ideas or projects by living experience. The method of doing away with dead history and that of developing science are identical at bottom and in spirit.

The paradox of Husserl's view of history, as I have remarked earlier, has been insightfully studied and brought out by Ricoeur. That Husserl's history is primarily philosophical with a thin content of historical events has not escaped his critical attention. Husserl's anxiety to articulate the *meaningful unity* of history requires him to emasculate historical facts persistently and tends to make him rather blind to their ragged edges. In this respect his proximity to Hegel and distance from Marx are sure to draw one's attention. Like Hegel and unlike Marx, Husserl fails to see the presence of irrational imponderables in the *unity* of history and "sees" only the past events and *not* advents of history. Understandably this leads one to believe that Husserl is not much interested in the a posteriori sense of history. His preoccupation with the a priori sense of history easily takes him to the transcendental height of the tight eidetic reduction. My uneasiness with this view of history has been discussed elsewhere.[9] It has been rightly pointed out by Ricoeur that Husserl's view of history falls between the two stools, philosophy as philosophy (not as history *of* philosophy) and history as history (not as philosophy *of* history). If in the name of *unity of meaning* philosophy is not shown as a historical enterprise and if in the name of totality of meaning history is denied its intelligibility, despite the gaps and diversity one finds in it, we get the worse of both the worlds.

> The paradox of the notion of history is that it becomes incomprehensible if it is not a unique history unified by a sense; yet it loses its very historicity if it is not an unforseeable adventure. One way, there would be no more philosophy of history; the other way, there would be no more history. . . . [A]lthough the unity of history is forcefully conceived by Husserl, the historicity of history, to the contrary, is understood by him with some difficulty. This weakness appears on several occasions [in his works]. . . . We may come to suspect that history has a paradoxical structure in another way. . . . For the danger of reducing philosophies to the philosophy lies in construing the latter entirely according to the interpretation of the last philosophy which considers the matter.[10]

This is precisely the charge that has also been leveled against Hegel by several critics. Neither Hegel nor Husserl can defensibly claim to have occupied a vantage point in history wherefrom he and he alone can have a *complete* view of history or philosophy of history, because acceptance of the claim amounts to acceptance of the finality of philosophy or the *end* of the journey of history. Besides, when the "vantage point claims" are put forward by many and differently, how can we plausibly understand them without denying the open-endedness or continuity of history?

In fairness to Husserl one has to admit that he has made attempts to overcome the said paradox or tension between the structural *unity* of historical meaning and its *continuity*. What Descartes tries to achieve in his *Meditation* — to get out of the certitude of the cogito and to reach out to the realm of the Other — Husserl attempts to repeat in the *Crisis*. Unless it is assumed that the individual as historical agent can leave the closed circle of transcendental subjectivity or the unity of historical meaning, it is difficult to explain human creativity and responsibility in history. In the *Crisis* Husserl is evidently interested in presenting European society as responsible for the crisis of its science. By implication, he admits that Europeans themselves are responsible for the crisis they are in. At the same time, the true human ego, European or non-European, cannot be held essentially responsible for doing something like precipitating a crisis that is patently against its own interest, both individual and collective. Recognition of a crisis as crisis is bound to be interpreted as inconsistent with the structural unity of the historical meaning. Alternatively, Husserl is obliged to interpret irrational or irresponsible activities of historical agents, human beings, as "the Cunning of Reason," *List der Vernunft*. The tension between the Self and the Other, between immanence and transcendence, between unity and creativity, is unmistakable in Husserl's thought. Unless a historian of science is theoretically equipped to explain not only the progress but also the regress, or even the crises, in the life of science, he cannot be fair or faithful to the recorded events of science. Thinkers like Ricoeur would go further and affirm that a good historian of science must have to his credit a theory of history that might enable him to explain not only the actual events but also the possible advents of science (and technology). Otherwise, in his bid to be objective and faithful to the facts the historian of science would be debasing himself into a dealer with the dead past. Curiously enough, it is neither desirable nor possible. That it is not possible is evident from the fact that the history of science is being written and rewritten and will continue to be endlessly rewritten. That it is not a desirable undertaking may be gathered from the fact that whoever has tried to make the history of science scientific in terms of definitiveness and finality has failed. History of science is reopened time and again not only by the historian of science but also by the scientist himself.

The complete unity or truth of history sought by the historian has always proved elusive. Truth in the sense of picturesque representation or closed and final unity of meaning is elusive by its very nature. Instead, Ricoeur suggests, the truth of history lies in *creating* and successfully *communicating* history, in the process of history making. The truth of history does not lie outside itself to be established by some external criteria. It is within the human beings who are engaged in making history possible. This engagement is primarily a matter of communication, intimate and authentic communication, of man with man, of the Self with the Other. This communication is carried forward in and through both work and word. Work is project-oriented and based on needs. It tends to take men to their intended fulfillment. Word is creative in nature. It does not only capture what is already there but also tries to picture or visualise what is not there. In fact, Ricoeur is more concerned with Husserlian phenomenology of *signification* than with that of *perception*. Man creates more by working and saying than by seeing and receiving. Of course, even in his perceptive and other receptive activities, man is inarticulately interpretative. Creation is more than interpretation. By word and work, literature and science, man moulds and interprets the existing world and, what is more, tries to create a new one.[11] However, one should not reduce work to workfetish. When the worker, whoever he may be, fails to put himself, his ideas and values, into his work, it becomes monotonous to him and its outcome noncreative. In brief, work gradually becomes meaningless. The same point may be made out in the context of word as well. Over use of a word in identical situations gradually erodes its meaningfulness. For example, the words standing for logical constants and operations in propositional contexts are "dead." They cannot be made to perform any "work" that is not well defined and already known. By contrast, the poet, for example, infuses new meaning into words. By putting a word to diverse uses in incommensurable contexts the speaker and the writer invest words with new meanings. This can be shown both synchronically and diachronically. By pressing the point further it may be shown that the fancied dichotomy between scientific language and literary language is false and does not bear the scrutiny either of the philologist or of the historian of science.

Ordinarily, we are told that the essence of literature and other forms of art is *creativity*, generation of something *new*, and that of science is *discovery*. What is hinted at by this sort of distinction is that whereas the scientist is engaged in finding out what is already there—law-governed structure(s) of the world – the artist is involved in making, building, or creating something really new. If this hint is taken to be true, one has to admit that *novelty*, the life breath of art, is not present in science. But this admission is patently inconsistent with the developing or *changing* character of science. The narrowing down of the precritically admitted gap between science and art is due to lack or inadequate realisation of the *human* root of both enterprises. Neither the scientist nor the artist is a creator in the model of God, who is often credited with the ability of creating out of nothing.

All sorts of human creation are necessarily dependent on, or influenced by, or have derived their material from what is already there. The main difference between the said two kinds of enterprises can perhaps best be understood in terms of the varying degrees of the concerned creators' ability to transform what is given, the materials on which they are called upon to work. Neither work nor word can build up, create, or project something new on the basis of nothing. This material basis may be thick or thin, but it is there all the time. The artist, generally speaking, is free to work on a relatively thin material basis. By contrast, the scientist's material basis is somewhat thick. However, this contrast must not be exaggerated. It has to be understood with reference to specific forms of art and science. The freedom of the artist makes him less dependent on the available history of the forms and materials of the area of his creative engagement. He is more a producer than a consumer of history. The scientist even in framing his daring or epoch-making hypothesis is historically obliged to take into account the "hard facts" and problems recognised by the *professional community*. Even this historical "handicap" of the scientist should not be exaggerated. One would be well advised in this connection to remember Einstein's observations to the effect that the great scientist is invariably found to have deep *love* for reality and that his main motive force is a *cosmic feeling* toward the orderliness of the universe.[12] These characteristics of the scientists, rightly understood, are not different from the gifts we find in the creative artist. Both scientific theory and poetry are freely framable, but certain rules are inherent in both freedom and what is framed.

The main point underlying my efforts to show that the works of the scientist and those of the artist are not fundamentally different is to vindicate the anthropological unity, or identical human rootedness, of these two basic modes of self-articulation. The fact that human beings can successfully communicate despite their cultural and historical distance is to be understood primarily in terms of what may be called, in the absence of a better expression, *human universals*. These universals are to be distinguished from linguistic universals or structural universals as ordinarily understood: these are historical, but because of their durational stability they are capable of organising and making meaningful the details of the historical flux. The universals of history, notwithstanding their own histority, are capable of reflecting and working upon the life of history. In brief, one might say, these are self-reflection of history.

The intelligibility of history is due to history itself. The postulation of some metaphysical or innate, that is, ahistorical, universals is not necessary. The general principles or truths that are needed to make the particular details, events and advents, intelligible are themselves subject to historical modification or mutation. As stated earlier, the former are relatively, compared to the latter, stable. But neither is transcendental and immutable in the Platonic or even in the Hegelian sense. Compared to the *explananda*, the details of history to be explained or made intelligible, the *explanans*, the explanatory principles or general truths, are admittedly "transcendental." It is to be noted that here the use of the term *transcendental* is consistent with what is historical or empirical. We propose to do away with the transcendental-empirical or structural-historical dichotomies of all sorts, Platonic, Cartesian, Kantian, and Husserlian.

Even in Hegel and Husserl one notices a tension between the said two tendencies, structuralism and historism. The reason why Hegel does not like to situate the events of contemporary time in history is said to be that being very close, as we are, to them, we, including the historian, are unable to see their *meaningful* perspectives. In other words, according to Hegel, we fail to see the universality of the particular events. It is in this connection that we often recall his famous metaphor, the flight of the owl of Minerva at the fall of the dusk. The gathering darkness of the dusk prevents us from seeing things clearly and in their place. Similarly, the historian, if standing very close to the events to be explained, is unable to explain the same. The gathering darkness of the said metaphor is like the *closure* of history.

A comparable line of reasoning is evident in the works of the early Husserl. As mentioned earlier, in his anxiety to see all phenomena, empirical or historical, clearly and meaningfully, Husserl is constantly engaged in a reflective search for their subjective transcendental foundation. Short of a stable transcendental foundation of history he is not satisfied. His cherished sense of history, like Hegel's, is essentially philosophical. Prior to the *Crisis*, Husserl's works do not provide any genuinely empirical or living sense of history. Only in the *Crisis* one finds Husserl's authentic return to the life-world, a tragic *human* situation. Neither Hegel nor Husserl has any place for the "empirical" (human) factors in his scheme of things. If the crises of European science finds a place of importance in Husserl's last important book, it is first because of its serious crisis character and, second, because of the threat it poses to Husserl's lifelong cherished notion of science. Retreating from the life-world and seeking a "safe" refuge of science in the transcendental world were destined to prove futile from the beginning. But his philosophical refusal to see the *advent* of crisis was responsible for his inability to get to the true or living sense of history. On this point the criticism leveled against him by such thinkers as Gadamer and Ricoeur seems to me very sensible and justifiable.

One of the main reasons why scientific certainty is not easy to reach is a false image of science tagged on to the Cartesian method of doubt. The science that lies beyond the reach of doubt or interrogation and therefore is not available to different forms of interpretation can hardly be doubted. In a sense one might say, following Gadamer, that Descartes's "artificial and hyperbolic doubt" is not of consequence to anybody, neither to the practising scientist nor to the common man of the life-world. *Methodological* doubt systematically, almost religiously, leaves everything *substantive* out of its scope. If Cartesian doubt does not prove of help to clarify the image of science either to the experimental scientist or to the ordinary man of the life-world, it is primarily because of its exclusive concern with the *philosophy* of doubt, a philosophy that has no relation to history born out of the life-world.

Dilthey's distrust of the Cartesian method of getting out of doubt and arriving at scientific certainty is to be understood with reference to his background as a student of theology. To Descartes, Nature is an open book of God clearly and distinctly readable by one who has succeeded in shaking off all doubts due to "external" influences on the cogito. The life-world and its attending uncertainty are the nightmare of the Cartesian. One needs the God-given clarity and distinctness of the cogito to be free of them.

Dilthey is evidently disturbed by the uncertainty of scientific knowledge spoken of by Descartes. Like the latter, he wants to escape it. But the uncertainty as he finds it is of a more serious type, both substantively and historically. Whereas Descartes finds definitive or indubitable science *outside* the process of his methodological doubt, Dilthey wants to find it *within* the historical process of the life-world. The Cartesian image of indubitable science has somehow an unmistakable element of *privacy* in it. For its deprivatisation Descartes himself needs a God-given criterion marked by clarity and distinctness, which is said to be available to *all* rational human beings. This process of deprivatisation of science or disclosure of its public character is not acceptable to Dilthey because of his deep commitment to history and familiarity with different interpretations of identical theological texts. He also wants to get rid of "external" authority. But he tries to derive the needed sense of certainty from the historically changing life-world. The certainty that this life-world can possibly yield is incurably historical. One cannot have it either by standing aloof from it or becoming completely immersed in it. One has to try to get it by *interrogating* the life-world, by *interpreting* and re-interpreting it. This is an endless process. This historical process-world is like a text to be deciphered. Ranke thought that the deciphering of the hieroglyphs was the sacred task of the historian. Considerably influenced by Ranke and Droysen, Dilthey maintains that though meaning is present in history it is not transparent and has to be made so by interpretation. But Dilthey's notion of historical meaning has a rather deep Hegelian mooring. Everything historical is meaningful and intelligible, for everything is textual. Dilthey observes, "Life and history have meaning like the letters of a word." Gadamer adds, "Dilthey ultimately conceives the investigation of the historical past as a deciphering and not as an historical experience."[13]

One of Gadamer's main complaints against Dilthey is that his method is inadequate as the basis of history. His notion of scientific induction is also said to be inadequate. The sort of historical experience Dilthey speaks of is unable to ensure certainty of sciences, human as well as natural. Dilthey has only a vague awareness of the inadequacy of the method of natural sciences in its application to human sciences. This is evident from his criticism of crass empiricism, an *external* view of life-experience. But the hangover of epistemological Cartesianism, a persistent search for certainty, tends to take away the histority of historical experience as understood by Dilthey. Besides, the sense of certainty he is looking for proves elusive, for his understanding of historical experience is rather narrow, one might even say, private. For deprivatisation of historical experience Dilthey, unlike Descartes, has no transcendental or universal principle in his scheme of thought; the nearest analogue to the transcendental principle is "endless openness of interpretation." Unless it is shown that there is something universal in the very structure of the interpreter's understanding, the mere openness of his interpretation by itself does not meet the requirement of the scientific acceptability of his interpretation in *different* cultures. The unity of meaning that people seek in interpretations, successive interpretations, is not brought about, still less guaranteed, by the sort of life-experience that Dilthey has in his mind.

It is in this connection that one has to understand Gadamer's criticism of Dilthey and reference to the "limited intentionality of meaning within the fundamental continuity of the whole." The "whole" or "horizon" of Husserl's "intended meaning" is a moving, not fixed, frontier. In it, one might say, both events and advents are mixed up in an interactive and dynamic relationship. Gadamer speaks of "the unity of the flow of experience." This description of Husserl's position is certainly not true unless one bears his *Crisis* in mind. Gadamer likens Dilthey's "standpoint of life" to Husserl's "conscious life," whereas he is said to have borrowed from Natorp. As pointed out earlier, whereas in Dilthey's *standpoint of life* the experiences of the *individual* figure prominently (without, of course, denying their antiempirical and pro-transcendental implications), in Husserl's *conscious life* the *totality* of the intentionalities of consciousness (regardless of their individual or private sources of origin) appears to be primary. It is clear that Husserl is always concerned with the *production* of transcendental subjectivity. His search is for the *constitution* of universal meaning. Unless radically reinterpreted, Dilthey's "life-world," essentially historical in character, proves antithetical to Husserl's "naturalistic life-world," which stands behind and sustains all experience, historical or otherwise. Dilthey's life-world is essentially antimetaphysical, intended to vindicate the primacy of history, but for the establishment of the intersubjective and intercultural validity of science its contribution seems to be negligible. By contrast, Husserl's "moving horizon of meaning," though notionally encompassing our individual as well as societal or cultural experiences, is like a walking shadow, in effect having no historical heart throb or flesh and blood. The moving horizon of historical meaning is at best the Husserlian cave dweller's perception of *shadow* history and at worst belief in the origin of the historical from the ahistorical.

This tension between the Husserlian and the Diltheyan approaches is the point of departure for Gadamer's notion of hermeneutics. It is essentially historical. Every scientific problem, because of its basic human character, is *textually* identical but interpretationally different. Text has no life of its own unless its meaning is deciphered, disclosed and made available in different historical contexts. From this one must not rush to the conclusion that a particular text and its meaning are destined to lose their meaning-identity in and through changing contexts. If there were no text to be interpreted and understood, interpretation and understanding could be easily credited with the capacity to act entirely on their own without some materials before them to act upon. Besides, this *reductio* form of the argument is intended to indicate the traditional continuity and even break therein of textual interpretation. Both understanding and interpretation are themselves hermeneutic in their nature.

It is always pertinent to raise the question whether understanding or interpretation itself is not subject to historical change. Unless this question is satisfactorily answered, one might plausibly affirm that only the scientific or cognitive interpretation is truly permanent, whereas normative and aesthetic interpretations lend themselves to dynamic and endlessly different interpretations. If this view of hermeneutics is consistently pressed, hermeneutics, like Kant's three *Critiques*, loses its unity and is scattered into divergent approaches. In that case hermeneutics fails to provide a consistent and unified understanding of modern science. The first point to be borne in mind is that hermeneutics is not an abstract discipline. Its life breath is history, historical situatedness. The interpretation or self-understanding of science is essentially like the historical interpretation of a text. In a sense it belongs to a particular age. In another sense it belongs to all ages. In a sense history is of the past. In another sense it is contemporaneous. And that is why it is in need of continuous reinterpretation. By interpretation of a text it is concretised and related to a context. In this process the interpreter presents and represents the author of the text, his meaning, time, and society. Simultaneously, in spite of all his efforts to conceal himself from the work of interpretation he is engaged in, he presents himself in it. The interpreter, willingly or unwillingly, wittingly or unwittingly, is both a critic and a creator. The unity of the critical interpreter with the creative interpreter in one and the same person need not be construed transcendentally in the strong Kantian or Husserlian sense. What sustains history is also historical. What sustains personality is also "personal." Their difference is one of degree: one is more sedimented and stable and the other less so.

History, rightly understood, transcends hermeneutics. The job of the historian takes him ahead of the interpreter. The latter is required to be more or less faithful to the text he is called upon to interpret. This limitation is not imposed upon the historian. He is free to go beyond and behind the text. The historian is free to bring back to life what, strictly speaking, is not in the text but is only hinted at or vaguely implied history of science. The scientific community does not accept the work of one of its members as totally acceptable and acceptable for all time to come. It is reviewed, interpreted, and criticised in different ways and from different points of view. True, there may be a sort of what is called "fusion of the horizons of meanings" represented by the views of the different members of a scientific community. This "fusion" is not an identically repeatable and reviewable idealisation. In a sense it is also historical.

What works as the main input of this ongoing dialectic of scientific experience is interrogation, interrogation of experience by action and new experience. The hermeneutic mode of experience is both self-initiated by the scientist and received by him from the tradition within which he is obliged to work. Transmitted or received tradition is never accepted without interrogation. The questions that intrigue or motivate the scientist as critic are not always the same. The nature of the answer and the interpretation that the scientist offers to himself and to his community is largely influenced by the questions that he has uppermost in his mind. In order to understand a scientific text one has to understand the questions that the concerned scientist tries to answer in his work. The historian of science remains a mere chronicler and fails to be a true historian unless he succeeds in getting to and behind the questions underlying the work of the scientist with which he is concerned as a historian. Gadamer's reference to Collingwood's question-answer method is of considerable consequence to the historian of science. The dialectical character of the historian of science is due to the endlessness of the questions raised by the scientist as critic and consumer of science and the resulting answers and their perceived imperfection. Rejection or negation of the received answer leads not only to the search for new answers, new theories, but also that for new questions, revised and reformulated questions, soliciting new answers.[14]

The dialectical question-answer method may be viewed both synchronically and diachronically. For example, some philosophers such as Vico are interested in following this question-answer method in order to interpret such classics as *Iliad* and *Odyssey*.[15] The epics of India, *Ramayana* and *Mahabharata*, have also been interpreted and reinterpreted in different ways down the centuries. This reinterpretation is needed in view of the new questions raised by different generations belonging to different cultures. If the questions are new, the same old answers cannot be acceptable. The intercultural or interepochal dialogue or conversation is marked by new ideas and values. It is not surprising that the old religious, literary, and legal texts are being reinterpreted time and again. And yet at no point of time the perceptive critic feels that this process can be successfully put to an end by some final and conclusive interpretation. However authoritative an interpretation may be deemed in one period, it is unlikely to preserve its authoritativeness for a long time and to all alike.

The *novelty* of questions and answers brings out the basic historical aspect of hermeneutics. Earlier we have noted how history overtakes hermeneutics in some respects. It is for the historian of science to pay serious attention to these positive aspects of history. Like other historians of different fields of our culture, in a way, he is also prereflectively aware of this need. This awareness is a mark of his professional obligation. But for the historian of science this obligation is of an especially important character because the language of natural sciences is doubly idealised and abstract. Language is idealised by its very nature. The formal and quantitative language of natural sciences is twice removed from the life-world in which the historian of science is obliged to work, decipher and interpret the texts of the scientists of the past, and enter into dialogue with them. Strictly speaking, when we say "history of science" we mean histories of science. Unified text(s) of science are neither possible nor available. Even then we use this expression conventionally and precritically. For reconstruction of history of science what is first needed is a *common language* of interpretation, of the concerned texts. Rightly understood, interpretation of texts involves dialogue, perhaps something more than dialogue – conversation. This conversation is not merely metaphysical or simulative. It is not the *physical* presence of persons that alone can ensure the possibility of conversation. Human beings may be there, yet they may refuse or fail to enter into a meaningful conversation. This sort of breakdown of communication is not infrequent even among the peoples speaking (notionally) the same language. The interlocutors of a historical dialogue or discourse or conversation may be successful in communication even though they may not belong to the same language-speaking group.

Cultural distance that marks both history and anthropology makes it obligatory for the concerned researchers to follow the question-answer method entailing intercultural and interepochal conversation. The complementary character of questions and answers culturally brings the questioners and answerers close to one another. The seminal presence of the answers to the contemporary historian's questions in the texts of the past scientists tends to make them members of one linguistic community. The *basic unity* of language is not legislated or formal. Our idea of *community* is unduly and synchronically narrow. To the historian, the archaeologist, the philologist, and the like, the past is living, almost talking, and not dead. The aim or object of intercultural communication brings the questioners and answerers into a communicative family. And thus is laid the bottomless "foundation" of anthropology and historiography of science.

> Language is not a possession at the disposal of one or the other of the interlocutors. Every conversation presupposes a common language, or, it creates a common language. . . . [A] common language must first be worked out in the conversation. This is not an external matter of simply adjusting our tools, nor is it even right to say that the partners adapt themselves to one another but, rather, in the successful conversation they both come under the influence of the truth of the object and are thus bound to one another in a new community. To reach an understanding with one's partner in a dialogue is not merely a matter of total self-expression and the successful assertion of one's own point of view, but a transformation into a communication, in which we do not remain what we were. [16]

To recapture the past the historian *assumes* the role of a conversationist and interpreter. When he *plays* the role he is not acting as if he has merely assumed his role. The assumed role becomes a played one. To play his role successfully it is not enough for him to have empathy toward the subject and object of his understanding. Neither empathy nor self-projection can be a surrogate for critical dialogue or conversation. Such words as *empathy* and *sympathy* give an impression that the underlying attitude is sufficient to make understanding of distant cultures and events belonging thereto possible. The attitude expressed in and through these words is necessary but not sufficient. The role of self-projecting and sympathetic interpreters and translators, for example, satisfies only the preliminary condition of successful communication with the human beings with whose text the historian is concerned. Because of physically unbridgeable cultural distance between the authors and the interpreters of the text, successful communication between them requires a conversational situation in which the additional condition of *reciprocity* has also to be satisfied.

The concepts of "sympathetic understanding," "free translation," "self-projection," and "rational reconstruction" apparently fail to satisfy this very important condition. In the "operations" referred to by these concepts, there is no *ongoing* conversational element. By contrast, in discourse, or dialogue, or conversation, the interlocutors are engaged in a continuous process in which all the concerned selves are putting across their views and arguments in response to others' views and arguments. If the discourse is to continue unabated the views and arguments of the participants must not be mechanically reiterated or repeated. Repetition without addition or modification tends to kill a dialogue and degrade it into a sort of monologue. Reciprocity and modification are the two requirements for making a conversation successful and infusing life breath into text.

Every text is situated in and expressive of a traditional or social context. Conversation, if successful, discloses not only meanings and new meanings of text, but also related contexts, new contexts. Every word of a text derives a meaning not only from its sentential context but also from its systematic or social or life context. The meaning of language has more than one dimension, both surface and depth. In conventional use, the same words and the same sentences disclose different meanings. Strengthened by the satisfaction of the reciprocity condition the language used by participants in a historical discourse conveys, continues to convey, new meanings in both the depth and the surface dimensions. The occasions of conversation cannot exhaust the possible meanings of text. In other words, there cannot be foreclosure of history. History like conversation by its very nature is a continuous disclosure or an endless ongoing process. Anthropologically speaking, the nature of human beings is such that its ability to mean and interpret never is exhausted. There may be occasional problems and crises in human life, in the life-history of an individual or of a culture, but nothing exhausts the human potentiality of overcoming them.

Unless language is allowed to speak for itself, it proves difficult for the historian of science to understand and reproduce histories of science as available in different and separated cultures. It is to be borne in mind that language is not merely of mediumistic value and that it is pregnant with tradition and culture. The life of language with all its animation and expression is articulated best in discourse and conversation. When I say this, to repeat what has already been said, I want to emphasise the necessity of doing away with the dualism between language and speech. In a different way the emphasis is also an attempt to dispense with the fancied dichotomy between structuralism and historism. It is well known that, in spite of Dilthey's protest, Husserl has tried persistently to defend a sort of structuralism that leaves little room for *ongoing* search for truth. That every worldview with its scientific tradition is not a *finite* structure is not adequately realised or conceded by Husserl. Later on I will show how some scholars, such as Landgrebe and Mohanty, interpret Husserl in a pro-historical way. But in the process, I feel, they identify science with philosophy and in *defining* science substantially disregard the experimental or practising image of the latter.

That the formation of every cultural whole and its scientific system is invariably caught up in a historical process is not openly recognised by the structuralist. From within a structure the seeker of truth cannot reach *out* to it without assuming that it is clearly and exhaustively present or available within the structure itself. One has to realise that every structural formation is open to transformation. Every culture with the truth-seeking search of sciences in its womb cannot be closed. One might go further and add that every culture is a cut-out segment of the process of acculturation. The structuralist view is static, but what is viewed by the structuralist is itself dynamic and open-ended. This openness cannot be done away with by an unfounded fear of scepticism or by a definitional foreclosure of the process.

Derrida, for example, has drawn our attention to the point. According to him, given the structuralism of the early Husserl, one cannot get to scientific truth. In that scheme of thought one has to remain satisfied only with "pretension to truth." The structuralism of Husserl reminds him of Kant's "Idea of truth." The requirement of this idea is "an absolute, infinite, omni-temporality, and universality without limits of any kind." According to him, this notion is not of much consequence to the practising scientist, because his project has both a historical origin and a promised future "funeral" or radical transformation into something else. The weakest part of the structural "description" of science is that it cannot rationally account for its histority or openness, ever or permanent openness to truth. Science, like man, is always open. It is so essentially because of its human roots, ever disclosing nature of the scientist as man. This "opening" is abhorred by the structuralist because he fears that it will frustrate the structuralist project. Derrida, like Husserl, does not like to see "full" frustration of the project. By relating the project to genesis and keeping the concerned genetic structure open Derrida tries to preserve the ongoing character of the project. The structured project is expected to expand like horizon.

His problem is important, but his answer seems to be contaminated by the anxiety to carry out the Husserlian programme of transcendental reduction. Diltheyism seems to him "seductive" and only "a tempting aberration" because of its alleged failure to tie up tidily the endless and unstructured details of the life-world. Historism is to him doubly seductive and misleading. Unless historical "facts" could be transcendentally reduced to some or other totality, he feels, the questions regarding their openness or closure could hardly be meaningfully answered. However, this reduction, being historically based as it is, has to be taken as phenomenological. If it is regarded as a priori, it is only because of its infinite or practical project aspect—an aspect that is not rooted in history but looks forward to create history—to realise value yet unrealised. Derrida tries to resolve the Husserlian dilemma with *genesis* and *structure*. He is convinced that structure has its genesis and is not given a priori. Equally convinced is he of the structured character of genesis. To bring about their unity or, at least, convergence is a historicopractical task. According to Derrida, the unity or totality of structure cannot totally stifle the histority of the phenomena structured within it, and, further, the history or genesis of the phenomena does not mean that they are without any structural unity. The difference between the structural and historical characteristics of phenomena is not absolute. It generates a tension in language and culture, *defers* their unity or closure, and keeps them open. Whatever is signified by signs of any culture and its language has a transcendental element that explains the openness or disclosed nature of every cultural form or structure.

The said tension between, or, one might say, complementarity of, structuralism and historism has been understandably illustrated by Derrida by referring to the works of Lévi-Strauss. The endeavour of finite man to totalise structurally whatever is made available to him can never be *completely* successful. Neither his culture nor his language in its totality is available to him. This is because of his unavoidable finitude. From the other end, it can be shown with equal plausibility that finite man can never be satisfied with what he as finite man can possibly totalise structurally. Because of his awareness of the finitude of what he has for him and within him, he keeps on "playing" with the same and simultaneously seeking what is not possible for him to have at any particular point of history. The significance of what is totalisable is bound to appear phenomenologically incomplete to finite man because of the transcendental reference of all signs available within his structure or system of signs. This also accounts for his historical search for significance, significance elusive because of the transcendental character of the signified. Following Lévi-Strauss, one can try to get rid of this duality between structuralism and historism by resorting to what Derrida calls a formal algebraic method.

Apparently, the latter is not happy with this method. To quote him on the point: "in the work of Lévi-Strauss it must be recognised that the respect for structurality, for the internal originality of the structure, compels a neutralisation of time and history."[17] Since I have already expressed my view on the issue, I do not wish to be detained here to elaborate the point. It is perhaps pertinent to observe briefly that Lévi-Strauss's concession to historism is primarily methodological, not ontological. By contrast, Husserl and Heidegger, with whom Derrida is more concerned, are ontologically oriented in their approach to the understanding of history. To them, as to Derrida himself, both historical understanding and structural understanding are two parts of the same understanding: self-understanding. Consequently, Derrida opts for that interpretation of *interpretation* which tries to bring structuralism and historism close to each other. He does not believe in the ultimate irreducibility of the difference between these two approaches to structuralism, historism, and semiology. He further affirms that this belief is rooted in a historical necessity. For he feels that in the course of time the convergence of these two approaches, though now being repeatedly deferred, is sure to come about. As a result of this deferred convergence the search for commonality of natural sciences and human sciences, of the Self and the Other, will continue in an unabated, if not reinforced, form.

The several forms of tension I have been speaking of are symptomatic of an abiding duality of our human nature. This insistent fact is differently perceived by us at different moments and moods of our life. It has been differently articulated by different artists and scientists in different ages, even in the same age. One form or its articulation is, "The self is elusive." Close on the heels of this disturbing view we hear two other voices: "Know thyself" and "The self is transcendental." One derives the impression from the history of ideas that one is being instructed specially to know oneself mainly because of the difficulty involved in knowing the elusive self. Time and again the self is declared transcendental so that one is not easily led to believe that the self can be made available to anyone, to any point of one's life history, *exhaustively*. By implication this view indicates that the self is abiding and witnessing in its nature. A sort of Parmenideanism or Vedanta view is strongly defended to account for the unitary nature of reality. Because of the inherent tension of human nature expressed in such pairs of concepts as transcendental self−empirical self, inner space-outer space, the structuralist cannot be totally unfair to the phenomenologically insistent experience of continuity or change. The result is endless encounter between the no-changer and the pro-changer, between Parmenides and the Vedantin (Saṃkara), on the one hand, and Heraclitus and Nāgārjuna (the Buddhist), on the other. This self-encounter has been articulated in different forms in different areas of man's self-expression.

In order to correct the excesses of what is called man's *self-expression* or *self-understanding* often we are reminded of how these concepts are corelated to the Other, *other-expression* and *other-understanding*. The whole question of the dialogue or conversation between the past and the present, between the near and the distant, and so on, may be reformulated in terms of encounter between the Self and the Other. The ontological mode or, one might say, mood of these forms of dialogue has received a conciliatory or convergent interpretation in Heidegger's "metaphysics of presence" or "endlessness of being." Lévi-Strauss's claim that he is no less, perhaps more, historist than Sartre and the latter's affirmation that, rightly understood, only his dialectical version of history is truly structural are also illustrative of this convergent trend. A similar spirit is evident in the Hegel-Croce-Collingwood thesis of "contemporaneity of history." All these views aim at, of course in different ways, doing away with the conceptually comparable sorts of opposition, say, between subject and object, word and meaning, language and world, and present and past.

The pairs of concepts mentioned previously are somehow borrowed uncritically and prereflectively from an outdated and unhistorical image of science. In "scientific" discourse the distinction between subject and object is insisted upon. The underlying idea is fear of subjectivism or psychologism. "Knowledge without a subject" and "psychology without a psyche or mind" are the slogans often heard in order to vindicate the so-called objectivity of science. What is prereflectively forgotten is that "I" as subject is not subject of all human beings alike. The distinction between first person and others, second and third persons, is implicitly assumed but its true implication forgotten. What we call well-established scientific theories and laws are believed to be *repeatable* to all persons alike. The satisfaction of "third person" is taken to be the most important thing. If, under some specified conditions, certain theories are not confirmable-infirmable they are hardly regarded as objective. Thus, subjectivity is purged from science or excluded by a sort of methodological decision or stipulation.

Kant's notion of intersubjectivity backed by the notion of the transcendental self is a bold step forward in the direction of vindication of subjectivity in science. But Kantian subjectivity, as we know, is *hardly* human. For he, somewhat like the logicist and the logical empiricist, is unduly scared of subjectivism. Once subjectivism is allowed in science, it is feared, historism with its twin blemishes, relativism and scepticism, will corrupt the character of science.

A comparable anxiety is shown by the scientist and the philosopher of science when they insist on *defining* the meaning of every word to be used by the scientist. Incidentally, that also accounts for the practising scientist's dislike or avoidance of natural language and commitment to artificial and quantitative language. He thinks that meaning-invariance is a prime requisite for making any cognitive discourse truly scientific. It was for such philosophers as Frege, Quine, Sellars, and the later Wittgenstein to point out in persuasive detail that scientificity of science and meaning-variance go well together in scientific discourse.

The prejudice of drawing a sharp line of demarcation between language and world has also not died. In the name of realism or for the sake of vindication of structuralism it is often said that language falls on the human side and that world is out there. The presumption is that *we* and our language are not in the world. It is patently false. Additionally, this sort of formulation conveys a wrong impression that language has in it something that is not worldly and that world keeps itself clear of language. What is forgotten in this sort of formulation is that there is no hard and fast distinction between the world(s) obtained in *myths* (of different cultures), those captured in different metaphysical systems, and those represented in different *scientific* systems. The point has been argued in detail, by, among others, Ernst Cassirer from a neo-Kantian standpoint marked by a sense of history. A comparable point has been persuasively made by Nelson Goodman from a different point of view. The latter has shown that the traditional distinction drawn between *factual discourse* and *fictional discourse* is hardly tenable. The "same" world may be scientifically represented and artistically portrayed. Different forms of representation are available. Different ways of "world making" are possible. What is of interest to note is that alternative ways of describing, depicting and representing "the world" are not inconsistent with realism. This approach, though aligned to historism, is not inconsistent with, still less hostile toward, realism. It is not at all surprising to note that even Putnam, who until recently was very close to the Kripkean variety of realism, has been veering round to this sober and eminently sensible sort of realism. The scientific realist can hardly deny the corrigibility or improvability of the realistic "picture" or theories *of* the world. It is not possible to indicate the cut-off point between "incorrigible" myths, "criticisable" metaphysics, and "corrigible" science. If one claims that it is possible, the claim rests on one's decision, not cognition, and is basically historical in nature. Consequently it is revisable.

Once the reason underlying the untenability of the distinction between *subject* and *object*, *word* and *meaning*, *language* and *world*, and similar other pairs of concepts is deeply realised, our realism starts disclosing its anthropological and historical implications. When Marx says that human individuals are the real and concrete authors of history, he does not compromise his realism in the least. Rightly understood, scientific realism, or even scientific materialism, is not only consistent with but also sustained by historism. It is only by dehumanising science that one can dehistorise it. The gravest error of the Platonic view of science is that in its laudable bid to vindicate realism in epistemology it dehistorises and dehumanises the discipline. In different ways this antihistorical legacy of Plato is evident in the Cartesian and the Kantian views of knowledge, in general, and of science, in particular. They all agree on the fundamental point: true knowledge is "self-enclosed." Besides, their "self" is blind to the future and insulated from the process of history. Hegel, Husserl, and particularly Marx have to be credited for highlighting the "disclosed," *historically disclosed*, character of science. However, as we have noticed, Hegel is not prepared to "see" science or any form of valid knowledge beyond a point of time, in the womb of future, for instance. According to him, not only scientific knowledge but also the highest form of knowledge, that is, *philosophy* (of history), are frozen and become "invisible." The same criticism cannot perhaps in fairness be leveled against Husserl, despite his ambivalence over the basic two concepts of *validation by transcendental reduction* and *validation by life-world*. In this respect Marx's position seems to me more coherent, for it succeeds in preserving the humanist and the historist characters of science.

When we speak of the dialectical character of science, we could speak as well of its dialogic character. Basically this characterisation is intended for the vindication of the historical image of science. There cannot be an image of science or of any form of cognition that is history-neutral or culture-insensitive. Every form of knowledge is embedded in innumerable ways, perceptible as well as imperceptible, in its cultural matrix. We must bear in mind that culture is not an abstract entity and that it consists of individuals, their intentions, dispositions, actions, and societal presuppositions. Neither history nor culture has a life of its own except in a metaphorical sense. It lives in and through the life-histories of its individual members, who, in their turn, are affiliated to the more durable societal structures. To be on the safe side, we must additionally remember that the societal structures themselves are formed and transformed over a period of time by the individuals concerned. The process of formation of different systems of knowledge and values is marked by both conversation or dialogue and action or practice. The authors of the process, its human agents, are not always conscious of it.

For, they are not only its producers but its consumers. However, on reflection, they can be at least partially conscious of this truth.

This process of acculturation is extremely complex. Valuation and cognition overlap in it. Theory and practice interact in it. For the purpose of establishment and disestablishment of validity of both cognitive and evaluative views, *communication* plays a very important role in the process.[18] Whether a particular discourse is cognitive or not cannot be decided by standing outside the discourse, that is, *in vacuo*, or in an abstract and speculative manner. The line of distinction between *inside* and *outside* a discourse is to be "found out" within a given concrete form of life. What is being called finding out is neither clear nor decisively infirmable. It has a curious life of its own. The meanings of such "crucial" words as *subject, object, word, meaning, language*, and *world* are decided differently in different forms of life or, what Wittgenstein calls language-games. Even what is "crucial" and what is not cannot be decided from "outside" the concerned form of life. Even the word *outside* derives its meaning from "inside" the concerned form of life. In brief, the meaning of every discourse, scientific or otherwise, derives its meaning from a particular form of life or culture.

Once the implications of this basic point are grasped, the attempt to understand the undisclosed anthropology and historiography of science becomes relatively easy.

Chapter Six

Anthropology and Historiography
of Science

The two basic points argued in the previous chapters are (1) that distant cultures, in spite of their distance and diversity, are understandable as totalities; and (2) that science as a mode of cultural articulation, or as a part of cultural totality, can be made historically available. In both anthropology and history, broadly speaking, two approaches are discernible: historical and structural. True, both terms have been used in different senses. In the preceding pages some of these senses have been indicated with or without reference to specific authors. My preference for the term *historism* and avoidance of *historicism* is basically due to Popper. One may be, as I am, a historist without being historicist in the Popperian sense. My preference for historism is also closely related to the weaker form of structuralism accepted in the previous chapters.

Structuralism, contrary to popular belief, is not peculiar to anthropology. Of late this view has been gaining currency. Although I have construed structuralism as an antithesis of historism, there is no compelling reason for it. My construal has been mainly influenced by the basic aim of my work. First, structuralism may be interpreted either methodologically or ontologically. But this distinction does not seem to me very satisfactory or exclusive. The Straussian variety of structuralism, for instance, though primarily methodological, is not exclusively so. That this method yields, according to me, good results, is not only because of its own instrumental value but also because of the real or ontological character of the concerned cultures themselves. That widely separated human cultures lend themselves to one or the same structural approach has been explained in terms of the objective – proclaimed objective – nature of the cultures.

Secondly, it is to be borne in mind that after the advent of phenomenology as a method of establishing "rigorous science(s)" ontology has often been put to methodological purposes. Or, one might claim, in the works of such thinkers as Heidegger the distinction among ontology, methodology, and epistemology becomes blurred. This point has of late assumed added historical significance. Without referring to the historical context of an author it is not correct to designate him as an ontologist or as a methodologist. For example, in Heideggerian ontology not only methodology and epistemology but also philology have been almost indistinguishably incorporated or enmeshed.

In philosophy, generally speaking, structuralism appears as an enemy of historism. My frequent reference to Plato, Descartes, Kant, and, occasionally, even Hegel is intended to show that in the name of philosophising, these philosophers and their followers propose to dehistorise the nature of reality and therewith the changing character of human situation(s). It is within a human situation or in a particular cultural context that we are obliged to develop our scientific image of the world – the image that by a sort of consensus becomes acceptable to us. The culture-bound or the historical context-bound image of science may be criticised on the alleged ground that it is distorted by a form of sociological solipsism. If individual solipsism is fallacious, the critic argues, its sociological variant is even more objectionable. In the case of individual solipsism a relatively better, more open, opportunity of correcting its narrowness, is (at least notionally) available.

One's view may be criticised and corrected, at least in principle, by others. In the case of sociological solipsism this opportunity proves rather restricted. Because of the *heterogeneity* of the human composition of a culture, *practical autonomy* available to different individuals belonging to a culture, and *uneven* level and pace of change in the subjective and objective conditions of individuals, it is difficult to believe that about different objects of the world and about the world as a whole, a universally acceptable consensus is likely to emerge.

The answer to the charge of sociological solipsism cannot be found within structuralism. One might go further and affirm that the very concept of structuralism and its meaning cannot be coherently formulated except within a form of life or historical context. The question whether a structure is well formed or ill formed or even formed at all can hardly be meaningfully discussed except within a conversational or communicative context. Just a little probe is enough to disclose the fact that the very dispute or difference underlying the question and answer regarding the character of structure makes no sense unless it is assumed that it is not *literally* available to all the persons involved in the process of communication and that a variety (though limited in number) of interpretations are bound to come forth. In spite of the variety of interpretations available at a particular point of time on a particular subject, we must remember the fact that unless this variety turns out to be limited in number, the concerned persons could not successfully communicate the correctness or incorrectness and relative worth and weight of any interpretation.

A comparable argument is found in Wittgenstein's concept of language-game. It is only within a language-game that we can successfully talk of communication, communication of thought, and identity of objects. Language-games have no external aim to realise. Like cultures they are relatively autonomous. Language is a part of community activity, a form of life and living. By taking part in language-games human beings are connected with (a particular form of) life, with each other. The two-term sign-signified or name-nominatum relation is not as simple as it appears. What a sign actually signifies depends upon its role in the applicable language-game. When we are led to believe by some philosophical structuralists that such words as *term, symbol* and *proposition* stand for ideal entities or unity of meanings, we apparently forget the immense diversity of their uses (meanings). "We remain unconscious of the prodigious diversity of all the everyday language-games because the clothing of our language makes everything alike." Even the rules that "define" a game and demarcate it from "other" games of the like nature cannot be clarified except within the limits of the game itself. From this we must not rush to the conclusion that the rules of a game or grammar are *arbitrary*. The arbitrariness or lack of arbitrariness of the rules could be meaningfully decided if the game *within* which they were of *use* could be shown to have some or another external aim or object. If certain rules prove *unruly*, that "proof" is available only within the concerned game. The "breakdown" of communication is a part of communication. The "futility" or "impossibility" of conversation is a result of conversation itself.

The historian of science is placed in a comparable, but not exactly identical, situation. For he too is engaged in a sort of conversation with other persons, other historians of science, and scientists of his own culture and those of different cultures. Somehow they succeed in communicating with each other; at least that is the perception under which they carry on their work. But the "antiexternalism" that is insisted on by the language-game theoretic approach, is not a precondition for carrying on historical dialogue between the "present" historian of science and the "past" scientists or those of "distant" cultures. What makes this conversation possible has been variously designated as "cultural universals," "family resemblance," and "human universals." None of these expressions need be dubbed as abstract, abstract from one particular cultural context or form of life. This is the least that is expected by a sound historiographer of science who is committed to anthropological rationalism. The very possibility of historiography or philosophy of history is possible because the historian, however culture-bound he may be, can transcend the boundary of his culture and can understand a distant or an alien culture in which he is interested. When cultural distance is construed primarily in terms of time, we solicit the help of the historian. When it is construed primarily in terms of spatial separateness or scatteredness, we ask for the help of the anthropologist. But, as we have noted earlier, the difference between the historian and the anthropologist is only a matter of degree. For both of them are essentially concerned with human intentions, human actions, and their societal or cultural context. Without relating individual human beings to their cultural context, it is not possible to understand the meaning of their actions and whatever follows therefrom. Unless the historian can "see" the logic of the situation of the historical agents of a distantly past epoch or of a quite alien culture, their rites and rituals, customs and conventions, may appear to him very bizarre or grotesque, if not totally meaningless.

What we are trying to highlight by using such expressions as "distantly past epoch" and "quite alien culture" is a relatively simple epistemic point involved in knowing the Other by the Self, every other by every self, irrespective of nearness or distance of their culture(s). The problem that both the historian and the anthropologist are called upon to tackle is to grasp the logic of the Other's situation or cultural context. The problem under discussion is of a substantive, not merely methodological, nature. It is rooted in the real or genuine, that is, not superficial, diversity of cultural presuppositions. The term *presupposition* is to be taken here in an extended sense as discussed earlier (Chapter 3).

The presuppositions of the "subjects" and "objects" of the historical or anthropological investigations we have in view almost invariably belong to and operate under different cultural contexts. Here by "subjects" we mean working anthropologists and historians and by "objects" we mean those human beings whose actions constitute the subject matter of their investigations. Broadly speaking, the cultural presuppositions of PS(T1), MS(T2), CS(T3), and FS(T4) are bound to be *more or less* different. Consequently, the "internal" or "primary" intelligibility of, say, a historian of science of CS(T3) is bound to be different from that of the scientific community in respect to the work of the scientist belonging, say, to PS(T1). In a sense the former's understanding of the latter's work is destined to be "external" or "secondary." In a way this is true of every self's understanding of every other's work. But the said sorts of intelligibility or understanding, that is, primary and secondary, have something in common. Otherwise, history, anthropology, and even epistemology would have become impossible. More generally speaking, if the dialogue between the Self and the Other would not have become a *practical* possibility, the aims of all cognitive, protocognitive, and communicative understanding and exercises would have proved useless. While one writes a book it is difficult, if not impossible, for one to believe that one is engaged in an exercise that is going to be proved futile, that is, not understandable, noncommunicative. Our social life becomes impossible unless we believe, at least to a modest or minimal practical extent, that we understand each other. Even our misunderstanding becomes meaningful within the map of our, the same milieu's, understanding. We form and reform the milieu by work, word, and other signs. In fact, we have between ourselves a communicative familial resemblance. When we talk of "cultural universals" or "human universals" what we have in the back of our mind is this familial resemblance and communicative competence.

The "universals"–cultural, linguistic, or human–may be, in fact have been, interpreted in two different ways, abstractly (as a heuristic device) or concretely. Many thinkers, from the classical rationalist to the contemporary structural linguist, are of the view that we, human beings, have some native capacities or competence, cognitive and linguistic, that know no cultural boundary. At times this argument has been extended beyond epistemology and linguistics and applied to human biology. It is in this connection that one has to relate the works of Lenneberg and those of Chomsky and try to understand the latter's appreciation of the former's findings. Lenneberg speaks of "biological universals."[1] Language is said (in the Cartesian vein) to be species-specific biological propensity not found in subhuman creatures. An impressive corpus of anatomical and physiological evidence has been found to "prove" that human beings are designed for the production and reception of speeches. Human beings are claimed to be biologically disposed (1) to vocalise and (2) to communicate. May be the neurophysiological evidence so far available on the subject is not conclusive. In order to buttress the notions of the preceding sorts of "universals" some thinkers speak, in addition, of another sort of universal, "physical universals." The impression we are given is this: The physical world has in it some invariant structures, despite enormous diversity in its surface features and qualities. This structural uniformity is expressible in the most universal laws and theories of physics. Some writers, both of the structuralist and of the evolutionist persuasion, speak of different levels of universals: physical, biological, psychological or mental, and spiritual. The physical framework is undoubtedly elegant and useful for the purpose of explaining not only human communication but also the possible or proclaimed communication between human and subhuman creatures. However, our available evidence in support of this ambitious view seems to be inadequate. When I say this I do not denigrate the importance of the works, speculative as well as empirical, undertaken in this hitherto largely unexplored area.

The human universals I speak of are intended to explain the actual communication and conversation that we find are regularly taking place between human beings affiliated to, but not really circumscribed by, their different cultural affiliations. Rightly understood, man is both a self-exceeding and a culture-transcending being. In order to exceed himself and transcend his culture man needs the world around him. Strictly speaking, the world which is deemed to be his Other is not quite different from him; he is not separated from it by any unbridgeable gulf. On the contrary, his culture, in which language and history are two all-permeating "forces," integrally and *internally* relates him to and situates him within that world. Metaphorically speaking, history and language work as bridges between man and the world. Strictly speaking, man is always *in* the world. In a way the world is *within* his being. Even if he wants and decides to be a windowless monad, his want cannot be fulfilled and decision effected. To extend the Leibnizian metaphor in a non-Leibnizian context one might say that, notwithstanding the "external" closure of his doors and windows, man remains always disclosed to the world and its forces. To state the relation from the other end, world enters into man's life in very ways. In such statements as "Man is culture embedded," "Man is a semiotic being," and "Man is a tool-using being," the basic truth about the man-world relationship finds its most general expression. Often these statements are offered as *definitions* of man. But I think that there is no single "essence" of man in terms of which an adequate definition of man could at all be constructed. In fact, the preceding statements are *descriptions* of different aspects of the relationship between man and the world. Since all that situates man in the world is changing, or historical in nature, the man-world relationship cannot be correctly grasped in a static framework. For example, the language and the tools that man uses, rather is obliged to use, in understanding his relationship with the world are themselves undergoing historical change. Consequently, the way man is posited or situated in the world by culture is essentially historical. There is no "stark naked" Nature: it is always clothed by culture. From this metaphor one must not infer that there is indeed something like Nature-in-itself or world-in-itself (where the cloth of culture is just not available).

Man's position in the world is immensely complex. When I say, for example, "Man is posited or situated in the world by culture," I fail to convey the immense, almost unfathomable complexity, intricacy and diversity of the cultural forces underlying and sustaining the man-world relationship. My intention in highlighting the importance of the point is twofold. First, I want to dispel the widely prevalent misconception, largely due to the "external" realist, that unless the world is shown as external to man and his mind, the scientific view of the world is bound to collapse. Second, I propose to show (1) that true realism is "internal," (2) that unless the "internal" character of realism is recognised, history of science cannot be meaningfully reconstructed or deconstructed; and (3) that "internal realism" discloses the anthropological or human roots of science.

The external realist postulates a dichotomy between man and his knowledge, on the one hand, and the structured world, on the other. The dichotomy is claimed by the external realist to be a necessary condition for making scientific knowledge really scientific. In support of this view it has been stated that unless the scientist assumes that there is an external world with its own independent structures and substructures to be known perceptually or otherwise by the scientist and other *normal* human beings, it is difficult to imagine how the truth-claims of scientific theories can be tested, established, and disestablished. Even this consideration or argument of the realist, on scrutiny, turns out to be naive or, at any rate, precritical. For example, it is not clear under what constraint or compulsion the scientist is obliged to assume the external existence of the independently structured world. The whole range of issues concerning test, establishment, disestablishment, and truth-values of scientific theories can be plausibly explained differently, that is, internally.

Some of the basic precritical assumptions of the external realist are (1) cause as force (attractive or repulsive), (2) subject-object dichotomy, (3) fact-fiction dichotomy, (4) theory-fact dichotomy, (5) past-present-future trichotomy, and (4) here-there dichotomy. Each of these assumptions may be formulated in more than one way. The misconception regarding science backed up by numerous naive assumptions is basically due to the very *abstract* image or character of science. That science stands very close to our life is largely forgotten because of its artificial and quantitative language and understandably abstract formulation. That scientific activities, their outcome, and their meaningfulness are not altogether different from other forms of human activities does not become easily clear to the layman because the scientist, generally speaking, does not take the trouble of spelling out the intermediate forms of activities connecting science with other forms of his own activities and social activities. At times his professional (and abstract) preoccupation makes it difficult for him to realise for himself the significance of what he is doing. That partly accounts for his lack of awareness of the relation between his activities and others'.

Hitherto we have been told of the dilemma only of two cultures, science and art. Now we are about to enter the area of trilemma of three cultures: science, art, and technology. An unfounded impression is gradually, but very uncritically, gaining ground that *developed* technology is going to carve out an autonomous, if not exclusive, area of its own in the world of culture. Rightly understood, the foundations of *episteme* (valid knowledge), *techne* or *tekhnetos* (art or artificial), and art (skill or its outcome) is identical: human competence and performance. And it must be noted that these foundations are essentially dynamic, open to changing influences of culture and function dialectically.

The concepts that are believed to have separated the domain of science from that of nonscience have been indicated before. The ambiguity that centers around the issue is clearly evident, for example, from the very nature of technology. It is not easy to affirm definitely whether it belongs to the domain of science or that of nonscience. Though the word *technology* often accompanies the word *science*, there is no good reason why it should do so necessarily. In both its etymological and ordinary senses, technology stands close to what we regard as artificial, as distinguished from natural. Viewed thus, technology stands closer to art than to science. But I am not pressing this point because I mention it only to highlight the untenability of the traditional distinction often uncritically drawn between the different domains of art and science.

The images of science are closely associated with, if not defined by, such concepts as cause, object, fact, there, and then. It is found on scrutiny that the meaning of each one of these concepts is not only different from but also, at times, inconsistent with its common sense connotation. The philosopher who has pointedly drawn our attention to the untenability of the commonsense view of philosophy is Kant. Those who, like him, think that the world of science is "empirically real but transcendentally ideal" are not to be taken as idealist (in any ordinary sense). The point has been persuasively argued by Kant himself in his refutation of idealism in *The Critique of Pure Reason*.

The popular belief that the objects studied by science are present in nature to be known perceptually or otherwise does not stand logical scrutiny. The most general form in which Kant makes this point is well known: Understanding makes Nature possible. This dictum seeks to reverse the ordinary scientific or uncritical realist view regarding the relation between Nature and Understanding. The realist tries to impress upon us the "obvious" view that by sending appropriate perceptible signals nature, its structures, and its forces almost coerce us to believe their "unquestionable" existence. This view rests upon many unexamined assumptions. First, I think that I am exposed to or have been receiving some physical signals as effects of the external world. The "deceptive illusoriness" of the claim can be shown in many ways. It is not at all easy to show where I or myself as subject ends and the external world begins. Is there any rational way of drawing a hard and fast line of distinction between I as subject and what is "presented" to me as object? That in terms of *corporeality* of objects one cannot draw this line of distinction may be easily demonstrated. For example, what is ordinarily believed to be my body appears under certain circumstances as not, at least not totally, known to me. Many experiments are available to show that human body has some sensations that are somatically "rootless." For example, a person who has lost his feet may continue to have painful sensations "of feet." Merleau-Ponty has discussed this point at length in some of his works. In the face of this difficulty Kant is obliged to recognise two concepts of self, empirical self and transcendental self. There runs a sort of cut-off line within ourselves. We are simultaneously *affected* selves-subjects and are aware of this affection. We have representations not only of objects but also of our body and mind as objects; that we do have such representations is not a part of the representations themselves. In other words, our transcendental self has to be deemed as a taker or thinker of these representations as thought. In the synthetic original unity of apperception, to use Kant's own language, "I am conscious of myself, not as I appear to myself, nor I am in myself but only that I am."[2] This representation of self to self is a thought and not an intuition. To believe in the *external* world on the ground of its assumed causal efficacy is also untenable. The push-and-pull theory of causality has long been discarded. It cannot explain "causal impact" at vanishing distance. Kant used to speak of cause as an a priori and universal category of understanding. The categorial feature of the world is in a sense ascriptive, ascribed by understanding to representations in order to objectify them. Unless representations are viewed causally, in succession, they do not become intelligible. The concepts of inertia and gravitation play a central role in the contemporary concept of causality. The Kantian notion of successive causality can hardly account for what is called simultaneous causal equilibrium. Belief in causality, successive or simultaneous, does not oblige one to think that the world is *out there in space* and that it is causally impinging on us. Besides, the very notions of "here" and "there" are very relative or perspectival. There is nothing in any "there" that it must be regarded so. What is "there" for me may be someone's "here." From this one must not think that the notion of space is subjective or anthropomorphic. We, all embodied beings and things, are in space. By such expressions as "here" and "there" we only determine or indicate our position *in space*. This view is, of course, inconsistent with Kant's notion of space as "outer sense." We cannot give any credible account of other selves and my relation with them, unless their (embodied) being (out there) is not assumed in a non-Kantian, rather pro-Strawsonian, sense. The same sort of consideration, *mutatis mutandis*, applies to the concept of time. The privileged position accorded by Kant to time as "inner sense" militates against both our common sense and the scientific frame of reference. Kant's antihistorism is largely rooted in his subjective notions of space and time. Our forms of understanding of the world do not allow us to draw a sharp distinction either between ourselves and the world or between our conceptual framework(s) and the world. In the recent past the first point has been persuasively argued by Strawson and the second one by Davidson. With the former I agree that self-ascription (or -identification) without other-ascription (or -identification) is impossible and with the latter I reject the content-conceptual framework distinction, "the third dogma of empiricism." In defence of their moderate forms of empiricism and *truth*-conditions both Strawson and Davidson are obliged to fall back upon the weaker sort of transcendental structure.

The plea for the conceptual framework(s) (that is, plurality of frameworks) is likely to be rejected by the robust transcendentalist. Alternatively, he will interpret them as subordinate to some unique overarching framework(s), which may or may not have space and time within it but surely would not allow space and time to change it. The main problem with the transcendentalist is that he refuses to see the relational roles of space-time. The *individuative* character of space-time (recognised by transcendentalism) should not be confused with its *separative* interpretation. In the world of culture, it is to be remembered, our main concern is cultural interpretation, not physical theorisation, of space-time. Neither "cultural distance" nor "historical gap" is un-bridgeable. From the historical past we are not exiled by time. Similarly, physical distance between two separately situated cultural milieus does not physically prevent them from communicating. Though space and time are "indirectly" in the "massive ahistorical central core" (of Strawson's conceptual framework) their relation with its changeable (at least in principle) periphery is left intriguingly unexplained.

The so-called bodily aspect of myself or my personality relates me to other human beings. This is my enabling condition and com-petence to be in the world of culture. To start with, we are born in the world of culture. The world we first live in is our own cultural world. The physical world is an abstraction from the life-world. The latter is a presupposition of the former. It is only in and through reflec-tion or philosophy that we may be clear about this basic truth. In a sense the life-world becomes disclosed and transparent to us through deliberation. The difficulty with the prereflective scientist is that he is inclined to take the objects of his research and knowledge as unities of sense qualities. Although he believes that he is a *realist*, his modes of conceiving, constructing, and explaining the objects of study give one the distinct impression that he is a *phenomenalist*, because he fails to see the thick "thing" or the persistent character of what he is engaged in studying. This apparent incompatibility of his attitude is due to his unwillingness to think seriously about what he *is* and is doing. It is interesting to note that the scientist who for his methodological constraints fails to supercede the domain of his objects is primarily interested in *ensuring* the correctness of his knowledge. Consequently, he is obliged to follow a method that presents his objects as "complete" or "self-contained" examples or confirmations of some postulated general truths or hypotheses. It is not therefore surprising that the phenomenalist in his search for certainty and avoidance of scepticism is led to an *instrumentalist* position. Instead of looking for the thick "thing" behind its sensible qualities and its larger structural horizon in which it is situated, the scientist remains satisfied with concentrating his attention on the sensible given. But, persuaded of the fleeting and uncertain character of sense representations, he tries desperately to put it in a definite slot of his constructed theory. Again his chosen method of construction makes him feel unsure of its reliability and stability. The constantly changing perspectives of the perceived objects, rightly understood, are relative. This relativity implies their essential lawfulness. In spite of its seemingly arbitrary and discrete mode of being given, every object is regulated by its preceding (historical) and succeeding (future or possible) representations. Disregarding the firm and the "*thing*" character of scientific objects and theories the scientist cannot feel cured of his sceptical illness; even his instrumentalism proves of short-lived consequence. He needs something more real and solid to fall back upon, because theories, themselves being essentially instrumental, are in need of empirical confirmation. Thus we find that most practising scientists are always buffeted between phenomenalism and realism with instrumentalism as a *tertium quid*. In other words, they move between the abstract and constructed world of science, on the one hand, and the life-world of culture, on the other.

The point has been clearly and perhaps rather strongly brought about by Husserl when he says, "The thing is a regulation of possible appearance." The Kantian ring of the statement is unmistakable. Husserl's point has been persuasively presented by Landgrebe.

> Exact scientific determination wants objective truth and this means inter-subjective truth comprehensible for all thinking subjects. The physicist does not speak of sensible qualities but of mathematical determinable wave-lengths. . . . But in the last analysis all these

> determinations are again related back to sensible objects and oc-
> currences appearing in intuition. . . . The objects subject to such
> determinations are already pre-given in perceptual comprehen-
> sion. . . . [This mode of comprehension], whose end is a univer-
> sally communicable determination – is specifically designated by
> Husserl as that of a *theoretical* attitude.[3]

Evidently this theoretical attitude and the underlying scientific method do not appear satisfactory to Husserl. He finds too much of Kantian formalism in it. Given this attitude and method, he feels that the scientist fails to enter into "the metaphysical essence of the matter of the nature." He rejects Kant's notion of passive sensibility. He speaks of the "kinesthetic spontaneity" and subjective causality of the human body enabling it to penetrate the seemingly persistent veil of the material world.[4] The ontology of living human body situates man in the material world as an active and assimilative agent. The corporeality of man interweaves him with the reality both of causal-physical nature and of the soul or freedom. This seminal idea of Husserl had a profound influence on both Heidegger and Merleau-Ponty.

Placed between the ahistorical materiality of things and the historical reality of the soul, the scientist constructs nature more actively than passively. The image of science that is acceptable to Husserl is neither "naturalistic" nor "personalistic." In a way it is constituted by the meaning-conferring competence and acts of the scientist. His competence is partly – only partly – actuated by the causal forces of the physical world. It cannot be completely ignored or brushed aside by the scientist. But these forces are assimilated by him within his competence of meaning-constitution. Man, who is not identifiable without his body, has a capacity that becomes active and efficacious in scientific theory-construction and in determination of meanings of the concepts and theories used in science. This capacity may be indicated by a sort of "I can" principle. It is indicative of the freedom of *human* body – ensouled body. It is bound to remind one of Kant's concept of man in the *Second Critique* and Strawson's concept of person. But a not-so-concealed uneasiness of Kant toward *human body* is not present in Husserl's scheme of things. Husserl's notion of freedom ("I can") is very much worldly; its efficacy is unrealisable without the "whisper," *not* coercion, of the physical world. Neither Kant nor Wittgenstein is prepared to allow "the true human soul" to hear even the whisper of the physical world. Later on, as we know, Sartre has fully exploited Husserl's notion of "I can" as further liberalised by Heidegger.

Science makes little sense to Husserl unless it can be seen as a philosophical science of foundations capable of providing legitimation for human life.[5] The provincialism and the separatism that have been introduced within the scope of science since the early nineteenth century in the name of specialisation are not acceptable to Husserl. Nor he is prepared to endorse the line of division drawn between technology and science. The temper that leads to the fragmentation of the image of science is a theoretical upshot of a naive naturalistic attitude. Neither historically nor conceptually does the world of science precede the world of life.

The natural scientist, like all other human beings, can put his question to the world (of life) only under the (undisclosed) assumption that there is an *unbounded* world to respond, positively or otherwise, to his questions. Husserl's phenomenology takes some of its basic cues from Hume's phenomenalism. The certainty that is associated with science is precritical, inductive, and practical. If it is not considered as probabilistic, it is only because of man's faith in his experience when formulated in elegant and abstract formulas. It is not surprising that empirical or ontic certainty is believed to have ontological respectability. This is partly because of man's intellectual weariness and reluctance to go into the puzzling details and perplexing mosaic of experience. When experience is put into abstract formulas it gives a sort of unrestricted sense of certainty. This literally unfounded optimism of science, science viewed as detached from the life-world, provides us a rather false foundation of science. The scientist leads us down the garden path of facile optimism, keeping us more or less forgetful of the complex and concrete relations in which science stands to real life-world situations.

This is one of the reasons we have discussed earlier why historism was largely discarded in favour of structuralism during the period of the European Enlightenment. Once the historical forces of the life-world are allowed to enter the world of science, the latter's boundary walls begin to crack, the abstract elegance becomes fuzzy, and the lines dividing art, science, and technology start losing their linearity. History imparts a storic character to the proclaimed pure scientific discourse. The method-logic of science becomes bewildered by the rhetoric of story and ordinary language of history. History as art questions the clear-cut models of scientific theory-construction. Though from the scientific point of view *models* are necessary for theory-construction, what is equally important for us to note is that without *metaphors* even a scientist cannot make his discourse intelligible to other persons.

Scientific objectivity is not a gift only of scientific methodology. Its foundation lies elsewhere, in the life-world and its history.[6]

Kant has his own reason to think that the vicissitudes of the life-world are not good for the health and longevity of science. Therefore, one finds that the Kantian foundation of science is basically transcendental, that is, antihistorical. From that point of view Husserl's willingness to make science answerable to the life-world is a constructive step forward. But to what extent this step was intended to be both constructive and *critical* has understandably turned out to be a debatable question. For, as we have noted earlier, even after his departure from Kantian transcendentalism Husserl speaks of the accountability of the life-world to the objective-logical evidence of the transcendental ego, because he fears that without it the *believed* life-world (*doxa*) may claim itself to be valid knowledge (*episteme*) on its own right. If the history and meanings of the pregiven life-world are not made answerable to transcendental interrogation and reduction, we are told, the former might degenerate into the world of faiths and fancies. Husserl's understandable eagerness to preserve the dignity of science leads him to a sort of high-soaring transcendentalism. In effect, Husserl suffers from the tension between his commitment to the life-world and that to the transcendental world. But it does not recognise any sharp division between the two. His realistic inclination obliges him to postulate the transcendental world, and without it the life-world may be unmanageably pulverized into numerous and incommensurable life-worlds. To Husserl the life-world is a matter of belief (*doxa*) and does not enjoy the respectability of scientific knowledge. This lack of the former requires correction in the form of transcendental reduction. If the life-world is deemed to be numerous worlds of belief, the question of their knowability in the scientific sense assumes an added problematic character. In a way this is Putnam's — the internal realist's — difficulty with Kuhn's many worlds (incommensurable paradigms). In a different way this is also Davidson's difficulty with Kuhn and Feyerabend. In fact, it has been rightly pointed out by many philosophers from Whitehead to Landgrebe that two trends, (1) one highlighting the truth of permanent and unchanging being reflected in the lawful regularities of the world and (2) the other highlighting the truth of ceaseless becoming historically represented by endless variety of incommensurable worlds, are distinctly discernible in the history of metaphysics. If (1) is true, we are condemned to be shadow watchers in Plato's cave, and if (2) is true, it is said, we are prevented even from knowing what incommensurable historical worlds really mean.

Some philosophers, such as Nietzsche and Kierkegaard, wanted to do away with this duality of Western metaphysics in all of its varieties. Strictly speaking, this duality is also present in the Indian and other philosophical traditions. Nietzsche wanted to destroy every sort of "world behind the world." In order to get rid of a transcendental God he rejected every kind of permanent "in-itself" behind the ceaseless flux. His plea for a return to the "innocence of becoming" is symbolic of his disgust with the permanent enduring Being. It is absolutely pertinent in this connection for Landgrebe to refer to Heidegger's view to the effect that Nietzsche's philosophy marks the "end" of Western philosophy, vindicating finally the primacy of becoming. Equally central to the theme of becoming is Heidegger's resolve to "return to the ground of metaphysics." Collateral to this movement is Husserl's programme to "return to the naivete of life," but the transcendental reflection through which he wants to rise above this naivete makes it difficult for him to execute his programme.

In spite of its attending difficulty, this programme seems to be executable to Landgrebe. And this view finds substantial confirmation in Mohanty's thought.[7] Landgrebe tries to show that the solution of the basic problem consists in showing the historical or the flux character of meaning-constituting intentional reason. To him, the traditional opposition between the a priori and the empirical and historical has to be, in fact is being, overcome by the intentionality of human experience. Initially one has to see the transcendental implication of the belief that the life-world is self-persisting and self-explanatory. This implication necessitates phenomenological review and return of it (the content of the belief) to what is called the *transcendental world* of subjectivity. If the life-world is the objective truth, the question of presenting it to a higher truth tribunal may appear to make no sense. But Husserl insists that the so-called higher-level truth seeking, to start with, is a mere postulate, a universal science of subjectivity as pregiving the world.

> The natural life, whether it is prescientifically or scientifically, theoretically or practically interested, is life within a universal unthematic horizon. This horizon is, in the natural attitude, precisely the world always pre-given as that which exists. Simply living on in this manner, one does not need "pre-given"; there is no need to point out that the world is constantly actuality for us. All natural questions, all theoretical and practical goals taken as themes — as

existing, as perhaps existing, as probable, as questionable, as valuable, as project, as action and result of action – have to do with something or other within the world horizon.[8]

Given this formulation, the life-world is already present in the transcendental subject in an articulate form. In that case the question of drawing the line of distinction between "higher level" and "lower level" truths is ruled out *ab initio*. *Pari passu*, goes overboard the traditional distinction between science and history. The life-world is not to be left to the scientist as his *exclusive* area of investigation. In fact, Husserl favours the idea of "taking the sciences into consideration only as historical facts":

> We notice . . . that the first step [towards the establishment of the transcendental universal science of subjectivity] which seemed to help at the beginning, that epoche through which we freed ourselves from all objective sciences as grounds of validity, by no means suffices . . . in a certain way, concern with this sort of thing belongs continually even to [one type of] objective investigation, namely, that of the historians, who must, after all, reconstruct the changing, surrounding life-worlds of the peoples and periods with which they deal. . . . Now *HOW CAN* the pre-givenness of the life-world become a universal subject of investigation in its own right? Clearly only through a *total change* of the natural attitude, such that we no longer live, is heretofore, as human beings within natural existence, constantly effecting the validity of the pre-given world; rather, we must constantly deny ourselves this. Only in this way can we arrive at the transformed and novel subject of investigation, "pre-givenness" of the world as such: the world purely and exclusively as – and in respect to *how* – it has meaning and ontic validity, and continually attains this in new forms, in our conscious life. . . . What is required, then, is a *total* transformation of attitude, a *completely unique*, universal epoche.[9]

Evidently he is opposed to the idea of taking philosophical cues from the objective sciences devoted to the study of the empirical world. Rather he accepts them as cultural facts appearing in (and also disappearing from?) history. From the natural world the transcendental philosopher pregrammatically moves to the cultural-historical world. The latter is a moving *historical* horizon. When Husserl speaks of the horizontal character of science what he has in mind is the untenability of the Kantian view of the world as the idea of all conceivable existents. Because of the closed character of his structuralism Kant fails to see horizontal-historical meaning(s) of science. Husserl claims to have succeeded in capturing the histority of the life-world and of its sciences in their transcendental subjectivity and validity. This validity is obviously not static in character. The scientific images of nature are said to be subject to the "Heraclitean flux." However, the transcendentalist hastens to add that the a priori origin of the life-world transcends the configuration of history as a flux. In this connection Husserl introduces the concept of historical a priori. Simultaneously, he interweaves the concept of historical a priori and the life-world (together with its sciences).

> Through what Method do we obtain a universal and also fixed apriori of the historical world which is always originally genuine? . . . [W]e have the capacity of complete freedom to transform, in thought and fantasy, our human historical existence and what is there exposed as its life-world. . . . [A]nd in running through the conceivable possibilities for the life-world, there arises, with apodictic self-evidence, and essentially general [structure or] set of elements going through all the variants. . . . [I]t is now clear that even if we know almost nothing about the historical surrounding world of the first geometers, this much is certain as an invariant, essential structure: that it was a world of "things" (including the human beings themselves as subjects of this world). . . . Only [through the disclosure of this apriori] can there be an apriori science extending beyond all historical facticities, all historical surrounding worlds, peoples, times, civilizations; only in this way can a science as *aeterna veritas* appear. . . . If the usual factual study of history in general, and in particular the history which in most recent times has achieved true universal extension over all humanity, is to have any meaning at all, such a meaning can only be grounded upon what we can here call internal history, and as such upon the foundations of the universal historical apriori. Such a meaning necessarily leads further to the . . . highest question of a universal teleology of reason.[10]

The transcendental subjectivity is then called upon to perform the double duty of *idealisation* of the life-world and *concretisation* of transcendental self-experience in the life-world. It is not like *unilateral* application of the Kantian categories and concepts. The Husserlian a priori is claimed to be in the nature of flux, conceptualising the world of science and yet transcending it all the time. Landgrebe observes:

> This solution to the problem of the a priori of history, it seems to me, already lies in Husserl's concept of intentionality and in the notion that history and its teleology are founded on an empty primal intention from which follows the intentional reaching-out into a still undeterminate, open horizon, a horizon which is first progressively filled out in the process of becoming. This filling out, as itself opening the new horizon of transcendental life, is not the realisation of a fixed, a priori possibility which already subsists "in itself." . . . But rather it becomes a possibility only as envisioned and reached for. If the reduction eliminates the metaphysical interpretation of the a priori as a permanent world of ideas . . . it also does away with the idea of possibilities which subsist "in themselves" and then, in their realisation, become "for themselves." Likewise it eliminates the Hegelian problem of the mediation between the unconditional universality of the a priori and its constitution in factual, transcendental subjectivity. All that is fixed is the direction of the goal prefigured in the primal intention. Yet this goal itself points to an open future.[11]

Landgrebe's suggested way out is admittedly ingenious. First, it wants to avoid the "scandal of philosophy," the controversy centering round realism and idealism. Second, it also skirts the debate between structuralism and historism. Third, in his interpretation of Husserl the distinction between "in themselves" and "for themselves" does not figure at all. Fourth, he also does away with the distinction between the "transcendent" and the "transcendental." Finally, the key concept, in terms of which the said and allied distinctions are smoothed and related, is "primal intention." Even though I recognise the ingenuity of Landgrebe's interpretation, my uneasy feeling over his view on the relation between "fixed primal intention" and "the pre-figured goal of open future in it" persists. Husserl's claim that consciousness by its very intentional nature is capable of solving most of the preceding problems seems to be flawed on several counts. This theoretical strategy of solving simultaneously a number of problems, distinctions, dichotomies, and so forth, has a central difficulty of its own.

It tends to ignore the difference in shade and shape of the said problems. Although their relatability is not being questioned, their difference deserves careful analyses. For example, (1) to say that "the historical" is structured and "the structured" is historical and (2) to say that "the transcendent" is intentional and "the transcendental" also is are not to say the same *sort* of things. If (2), like (1), is sought to be related in terms of intentionality, then the very purpose of positing the concept of "the transcendent" becomes trivial, if not dispensable. If all distinctions, antinomic or otherwise, are claimed to be removable in terms of intentionality of consciousness, I find, in that case they all turn to be *internal* to consciousness. The distinction between what is corporeal and what is not corporeal and that between the noetic and the noematic and so on, lose much of their significance if we are asked to believe that the "constraints" of the corporeal, of the noematic, and the like, are present only to be overcome. In that case "the refutation of realism" by the phenomenologist appears to be a bloodless victory. Unless it is believed that there is something really obdurate in the world—"the material," "*Hyle*," "the corporeal," whatever we call it—that *can* frustrate at least some of our intentional enterprises, our life-world (or cultural) sense of science is seriously offended. That some of our intentions are not fulfilled or even fulfillable is a persistent verdict of the life-world itself. The meaning-bestowing competence and the meaning-constituting performance that are ascribed to man can hardly be construed as *sovereign*, that is, unquestionable from without. If our transcendental subjectivity is claimed to be sovereign in its cognitive legislative enterprises, we face the closed structuralism of the Kantian type. The image of science that emerges in, and is tolerated by, that structure proves either unhistorical or, at best, pseudohistorical, a walking shadow. If, on the other hand, we pin our faith in Husserl's "historical a priori," we are torn between the "Heraclitean flux" and the "Kantian a priori" and ultimately thrown back to the Hegelian square one: his *philosophy* of history, in which history is thoroughly metaphysicalised, or made to walk on its head (as alleged by Marx). I am prepared to believe, with Merleau-Ponty, that history cannot be made to think by feet; that is, the world of thought or knowledge is not dictated or coerced by the raw or uncooked facts of the physical world. Hegel claims that the past is conceptually (or sedimentally) available in the present. Landgrebe, following Husserl, asks us to believe that the future direction of history is prefigured in the primal intention of the transcendental subject. One is bound to feel uneasy when one is told that the futuristic direction of history in the primal intention is "fixed." Fixed where? In transcendental subjectivity? Obviously we cannot do it in a Carnapian way, in a "naturalistic" manner that totally rejects intentionality. Nor can we do it in a "personalistic manner," ignoring our situation in the life-world and being quite oblivious of our cultural background.

Husserl's problem is really symbolic of the historical hangover of the two trends of Western metaphysics. In their conceptual presentations of this history both Hegel and Husserl have kept science as a sidelight. Or, one might say, they have taken "philosophy" as "the science." Science, as ordinarily understood, witnesses rather helplessly this heroic and endless battle between two mighty schools of thought, sometimes being unsure of its own identity in relation to this engaging phenomenon and sometimes deliberately ignoring it. Even while Kant focuses his attention on science (rather on mathematical physics), transcendental metaphysics continues to cast its shadow on it. Whether the influence that metaphysics (qua philosophy) casts on science is always "shadowy" or "brighten*ing*" cannot be pronounced a priori. Metaphysics or philosophy—whatever it is—may be transcendental in an unquestionable sense or in a questionable one. Let me clarify the point.

When Quine says, "Philosophy is science, neither more nor less," one feels askance. Philosophy in some respects—in respect to precisifiability, quantified formulability, falsifiability, and the like, is less "rich" than science. In some other respects—in respect to generality, interrelatability, interpretability, and the like—it is *more* "rich" than science. When a cautious Quine affirms, "philosophy is science self-reflective," he gets closer to the true relation between philosophy and science. If philosophy is identified with science, it has nothing to add to or subtract from the latter. On this point the early Wittgenstein seems to be very relevant. Even when he says that philosophy, strictly speaking, has nothing to call peculiarly its own and that it is a dealer in facts which belong to scientific disciplines, he is making a reflective statement, a philosophical reflection on scientific facts. Besides, rightly understood, his statement is not scientific, certainly not directly. Quine's philosophical reflection, like Wittgenstein's, is extremely austere in its choice of primitive concepts and seeks utmost definiteness and precision. Whereas Wittgenstein stubbornly refuses to discuss all transcendental "things"—self, freedom, value, God, and so on, on the ground that his chosen language cannot express them, Quine ingeniously tries to assimilate them within the world of science or tells us how to talk logically about them. By thinning down his ontology Quine tries to do away with the distinction between the empirical and the transcendental. But apparently he has not succeeded in his difficult undertaking and one feels that this explains, at least partly, his giving up the philosophy-science identity thesis and espousing the *reflective* interpretation of philosophy. That philosophy cannot be assimilated, without residue, into science is explained in different ways by both Wittgenstein and Quine. In this respect one is reminded of Kant's dilemma with God, self, freedom, and so forth, the objects of ethics and religion. If Quine's way out of the dilemma (pertaining to the relation between the empirical and the transcendental) consists in thinning down the entire realm of ontology, Kant seeks the solution in terms of a formal unity or affinity of the two realms.

But those who like Hegel and Marx want to be fair to the natural or the scientific point of view without foreclosing or denying the possibility of dialectical access to the transcendental point of view take upon themselves an added intellectual responsibility. They have to answer, How is this transcendence brought about? What makes this transcendence possible? Hegelian transcendence is rooted in God's design executed, consciously or unconsciously, by human beings by their *self-understanding*. In the Marxist scheme of things, which is Godless or materialist, transcendence is ascribed to human praxis. In different ways both acknowledge that it is by differently and creatively interpreting Nature that science undergoes change and moves ahead. Whereas Hegel's accent is on understanding and *interpretation* from a providentially affiliated human point of view, Marx's is on understanding and *action* "transcendentally" affiliated to a normative goal. By *philosophising* history of science Hegel unifies it, presents it contemporaneously, and forecloses its future (contingencies). A transcendental and *necessarian* unity swallows up historical continuity. Science in its highest transcendental reaches is transformed into philosophy and freed from fallibilism or scepticism attending empirical sciences. Marx's main complaint against this *unitarian* philosophy of science is that it is not only dehistorised but also dehumanised. In order to vindicate the primacy, nay, sovereignty, of Reason all "counterexamples" to scientific theories are either summarily discounted or indulgently recognised as mere "Cunning of Reason." In either case, one feels, human fallibility and freedom are disregarded.

In recent years some interesting attempts have been made to vindicate transcendental philosophy and redefine constructively its relation with science and its history. In this connection I have in mind particularly the view developed by Mohanty.[12] The Kantian variety of transcendental philosophy is purported to vindicate pure physics and mathematics. Mohanty feels, I think rightly, that Kant's transcendentalism suffers both from necessarian, or rigid, unitarianism and indifference to the historical world of praxis. To Kant vindication of science means vindication of the Newtonian paradigm of science as if it is the end-point of the history of science, or culmination of human knowledge of the empirical world sanctified by an unquestionable transcendental synthesis. If to Hegel *future* history of science is invisible, to Kant it is almost nonexistent. Kant's transcendentalism is a clear example of *justificationism*. The very question of Kant, How synthetic judgments a priori in physics and mathematics are possible? betrays his justificationist or precritical attitude toward science. The more radical question, *Whether* a priori synthetic judgments in physics and mathematics are possible? is not raised by him at all. This attitude shows what I have argued elsewhere as a betrayal of his proclaimed Copernican Revolution.[13] Having promised to show the *human* origin of science what Kant in effect does is something quite different. In place of finite and fallible human beings as authors of the scientific paradigm he tries to show that its authorship really belongs to a transcendental self which ensures its objectivity (inter-subjectivity) and universality. Kant's transcendental justification of science entails a sort of infallibilism, ahistorism, and denial of the role of the scientist *qua* human being. Science turns out to be God's reflection on the empirical world as a *totum simul*. To forestall the possibility of falsification of his chosen paradigm Kant theoretically needs God-made, *not* man-made, science. His anthropological presupposition of scientific epistemology is "anthropological" only by courtesy—in fact, it is the God of theology dressed up in secular formal idioms.

Evidently unhappy with the Kantian turn of transcendental philosophy and taking cues from Husserl, Mohanty tries to reconcile science and its history with transcendentalism. In this respect he makes good use of some insights of Hegel and Hume as reviewed by Husserl.

He is impressed by the Hegelian sublative or progressive dialectic. In his *Phenomenology* Hegel goes *formally* deeper and deeper in search of truth of different "shapes of consciousness." This exploration of differently layered *formal* depths is indicative of the inadequacy of the truth as available at the relatively surface levels. Hegel's exploration of the increasing depth of reality shows the "suspicious" character (to use an expression of Ricoeur's) of his phenomenological search. In the light of "the more deep" he seeks to explain "the less deep." Clearly it is a transcendental journey. In the process of this journey Hegel gives the impression that the given is left behind. Mohanty feels that Hegel's transcendental phenomenology of *suspicion* needs to be subordinated to a transcendental phenomenology of *respect*. In the latter the given will be respected and retained, not sublated or left behind on the ground of suspicion. In fact, Mohanty's primary concern seems to be the *sense* of the given, and not the given as such. For, I suppose, he fears that the given may be historically changed or emasculated in a larger horizon or in an altered context. What can be retained *respectfully* is only the *sense* of the given. The *sense* is thus accorded a sort of a priori status, insulated from the contingency of historical modification. This research programme obliges Mohanty to fall back upon the concept of "historical a priori." One feels like asking, Is not the very concept itself hybrid? Do the a priori and the historical go together? The answer we are provided with is clearly affirmative. It is contended that whereas the Hegelian's main concern is with *truth*, the Husserlian's is with the clarification of the *sense* of history. The sense is essential, not factual. Every act of consciousness has its sense: that is, it is oriented to its intended object, regardless of the latter's ontological status, be it real, imaginary, or fictitious. The sense is said to be an ideal objectivity, which is inter-subjectively sharable and to which one can return again and again. This redefined character of "the historical sense" enables the Husserlian to put the "facts" of history in the slot of the a priori and lift them from the washing and changing touch of the "Heraclitean flux."

> In a constant critique, which always regards the total historical complex as a personal one, we are attempting ultimately to discern the historical task which we can acknowledge as the only one which is personally our own. This we seek to discern not from the outside, from facts, as if the temporal becoming in which we ourselves have evolved were merely an external causal series. Rather, we seek to discern it from the *inside* . . . we obtain it . . . only through a critical understanding of the total unity of histori-cal—*our* history . . . this manner of clarifying history by enquir-ing back into the primal establishment of the goals which bind together the chain of future generation, insofar as these goals live on in sedimented forms yet can be reawakened again and again and, in their new vitality, be criticised; this manner of enquiring back into the ways in which surviving goals repeatedly bring with them ever new attempts to reach new goals, whose unsatisfactory character again and again necessitates their clarification, their im-provement, their more or less radical re-shaping—this, I say, is nothing other than the philosopher's genuine self-reflection on what he is *truly seeking* on what is in him as a while coming *from* the will and *as* a will of his spiritual forefathers.[14]

I find that in the transcendentalist theory of history facts are transformed rather "easily" into senses and accommodated within the reductive and self-complete structure of meaningfulness. But "respect" for details is sought to be shown in terms of clarification and interpretation of all that is present in the self-complete structure: The self, the act, and the sense. The self is disengaged from the perception of the "outer" things and beings and turns its attention to the new interpretation of the structured senses. Its understanding of the historical world consists not in revising what are available in the transcendental structure but only in exhibiting their unity of meanings. This unity is brought about by self-interpretation and retained by endless self-reinterpretations. It is in this way that the distinction between "the mundane" and "the transcendental" is sought to be done away with. The hermeneutic competence of consciousness is claimed to be the responsible factor for undoing the distinction between the two seemingly different worlds.

Mohanty's hermeneutic interpretation of Husserlian historical transcendentalism is undoubtedly perceptive and interesting. But time and again one finds in his argument a tendency to highlight the nontemporal dimensions of consciousness at the expense of the temporal ones. Understandably he asks us always to bear in mind the distinction between "the genetic constitution" and the historical construction. He is anxious to see "that a ubiquitous historicity does not threaten to swallow up other modes of constitution."[15] It seems that he is very mindful of Husserl's basic concept of a priori, that is not derived from the structure of human consciousness. For, like Husserl, Mohanty seems to be committed to the view that any attempt to derive the a priori from the structure of human consciousness would entail a sort of relativism and would make the a priori itself contingent. It is to be remembered here that the concept of a priori as reformulated by Husserl in the *Crisis* is marked by a systematic ambivalence.[16] On the one hand, he concedes that the a priori of the life-world is "subjective-relative," and, on the other, he claims, reminding one of his view in *Logical Investigations*, that the a priori of the life-world is not itself relative.[17] In fact, Mohanty takes pains to discern the different meanings of the life-world: (1) the world of scientific objectivity; (2) the world of perceptual objectivity; (3) the worlds of prescientific objectivity, of common sense, mythology, and so on; and (4) the life-world in the strict sense. Predictably he is not interested in reducing all these different life-worlds into "life-world in the strict sense." In this respect, it seems, he has been influenced by phenomenologists such as Merleau-Ponty who believe in the "primacy of perception." At the same time, he wants to preserve the unity of the basic a priori of the life-world in which, he believes, all *other* life-worlds are nested. In order to show the unity of all possible life-worlds one has to presuppose or show the isomorphism of the *nesting* life-world and *nested* life-worlds.

If it is *presupposed*, the basic principle of phenomenology and its constitutive character are seriously compromised. *Per contra*, if it can be shown, that implies that the phenomenological capacity of the self is of such a nature that it can constitute only those worlds that are isomorphic or nestable in principle. To dramatise, not misleadingly, the issue, the critic may point out that transcendental subjectivity of the self is unable to face any world not constituted by it. If the constitutive power of the transcendental subjectivity of the self is construed only in a *uniform* way, constituting only *homogeneous* and *isomorphic* worlds, the scientific world of contingency, imponderables, and counterexamples is either disregarded by (what Lakatos calls) the "monster-barring method" or all "inconvenient" experiences are conveniently interpreted to make them fall in line and be "obedient" constituents of the transcendentally constituted structural unity of senses (of the concerned experiences). Husserl's rigorous science or philosophy, like Hegel's absolute knowledge, though apparently tolerant, really hates to see "the Cunning [elements] of Reason."

It is clear that Heidegger is not happy with Husserl's way of demonstrating the history of science. The unitarianism of the latter is not to the philosophical taste of the former. For, as we know, Heidegger takes human reality—*Dasein*—and temporality very seriously. If Husserl's explanatory principle of the historical life-world is essentially *unificatory*, Heidegger's is *revelatory*. It is through unity of meanings of historical events that Husserl finds history as a whole meaningful. One might say that this meaningfulness is due to the meaning-bestowing acts of transcendental subjectivity. This line of argument can hardly sound convincing to Heidegger. According to him, the meaningfulness of the human's existence consists in his ontic relatedness to the world. Through this relatedness is revealed his knowledge. But this relatedness itself is grounded in the human mode of being—*Dasein*. In a sense *Dasein* is the ground or the source, but not presupposition, of knowledge, ontic and ontological. *Dasein*, though claimed to be basically existential, is clearly called upon to perform a transcendental role. For

Being is never totally available to *Dasein*. To state the matter from the other end, *Dasein's* grasp of Being is never complete. The process of revelation or unconcealment of Being through *Dasein* in the world is destined to be ongoing or endless.

It is to be noted that Heideggerian transcendentalism, compared to the Husserlian type, is limited as well as diluted. In the former scheme of things the possibility of unconcealment is preconceptual and cannot be formulated in predicative judgment. But, at the same time, Heidegger insists that preconceptual apprehension of Being, articulated in and through *Dasein*, is apprehension nonetheless. In other words, *Dasein* embodies and discloses Being in a peculiar way, its primary mode being practical and affective, *not* theoretical and cognitive. This formulation of Heidegger's notion of human reality, it seems, brings him closer to historical reality. In history human reality is represented. And this representation is simultaneously subjective and objective, human and worldly, grounded in consciousness and yet projected in the world. It is in this way that Heidegger tries to do away with the traditional distinction between realism and idealism, idealistic historiography and realistic historiography. The history of the world and the history of human understanding, in the Heideggerian analysis, are identical at bottom. The history of the world and that of understanding are found to be mutually involved. In this connection, Mohanty's observation "What Hegel's critique is to Kant, Heidegger's is to Husserl" seems to me very insightful. Neither could Hegel by his surface dialectic break the Kantian ahistorical unitarianism nor could Heidegger by his temporal existentialism break Husserl's circle of transcendental historism. Mohanty seems to be partly right when he questions the justifiability of Heidegger's claim to have brought about a radical improvement of the Husserlian theory of historical consciousness.

To find the possible way out, understandably, Mohanty, foot-firm in Husserl, turns towards Gadamer's concept of transcendental but continuous self-constitution. Gadamer wants to show that meaning-constituting or interpreting acts that originate in consciousness are *always* addressed to the world "ahead" and "outside."[19] Both the past (history) and the future (reinterpretability) are rooted in consciousness, living presence. According to Gadamer, not only history but also the future are open to different perceptions and interpretations. One can be *disgusted* with one's past; one can also feel *happy* in reminiscing about the "same" past. One can be *anxious* about the future; one can also be *hopeful* about the same future. Difference in interpretations is possible not only in theoretical-cognitive matters but also, perhaps more so, in practical-affective matters. In this respect, predictably, Gadamer is more inclined to Heidegger than to Husserl. It is not at all surprising to note that Gadamer finds the best of Kant in his *Third Critique* and not in the *First Critique*. The history of art is believed to be more authentic than that of science. Man qua artist is more revealed and less concealed in his artistic works, whereas man qua scientist is more concealed and less revealed in his scientific works. In the name of objectivity the scientist tries to be withdrawn from his work and thus make it more acceptable to the Other (first and second persons). By contrast, first-person privileges are never given up or disowned by the artist. Yet he succeeds in communicating himself to others. It is for this reason that works of art lend themselves more easily and widely to different interpretations, without compromising their extensive as well as intensive communicability and intersubjective sharability.

After the hermeneutic approach to philosophy has received wide acceptance, many defenders of transcendental philosophy are expressing their preference for "ontological hermeneutics" (associated with the names of Heidegger and Gadamer) rather than Husserlian "transcendental hermeneutics" (defended by Hans Lipps and others).[20] It is clear that Mohanty's defence of transcendental philosophy wants to be simultaneously fair both to the original Husserlian tradition and to the "derivative" Heidegger-Gadamer tradition. This is partly due to his intimate exposure to Euro-American analytic philosophy. Consequently his version of transcendentalism is partly "suspicious" of, and yet "respectful" toward, histority, corporeality, linguisticality, and other characteristics of the life-world as ordinarily understood. Therefore, his defence of the diluted Husserlian legacy consists (1) in philosophising history (à la Hegel and Husserl), (2) in assimilating corporeality within constitutive consciousness, according the former (what is corporeal) only a shadowy reality (à la the proto-Platonic early Husserl); (3) in trying to show that meaningfulness of language, language of all sorts (poetic to scientific and mathematical), owes its origin to meaning-bestowing or -interpretive acts of transcendental subjectivity. If all the "constraints" or roadblocks on the way to transcendental philosophy could thus be removed or made to disappear by a grand transcendentalist-essentialist strategy, I am afraid, the resulting transcendental philosophy would become not only "free" but also "poverty-stricken," if not empty. What I am saying in the context of Mohanty obviously applies more pointedly to Husserl, his mentor.

Needless to add, in the process of vindicating Husserl with reference to his contemporary criticisms Mohanty has taken the liberty of reinterpreting Husserl, bearing in mind many of the said criticisms and making handsome critical concessions.

Free of the oft-mentioned "constraints," transcendental philosophy, I feel, is once removed from history *in general* and twice removed from history of science. In the *essentialism* of transcendental philosophy both the generalities and the specifics of the histories of science tend to be dissolved. One feels like asking, Is it not reversion in one way back to Kant and in another way back to Hegel? I recall in this connection Kant's reference to "material bodies." "External objects (bodies) . . . are mere appearances . . . nothing but a species of my representations . . . something only through these representations."[21] Equally pertinent is Hegel's view on the issue. "A matter (or content) without its concept is something extra-conceptual, therefore without essence."[22] Notwithstanding his difference from Kant and Hegel, Husserl's view on the subject has been largely shaped by them. To him, matter is an objective ideality, not coercive corporeality. Every material body has innumerable possible perspectives. Even if this formulation is inverted and it is said that every body may be constituted, viewed, or interpreted in very many ways, the basic point of the question is not substantially altered. Different perspectives interpenetrate, shade off into, and fuse with other possible perspectives. Having said this, the Husserlian realises that he is getting dangerously close to a sort of Berkleyan idealism, and consequently he turns back and reminds us that the perspectivality of the matter is inexhaustible and that it is indicative of the transcendental-objective nature of matter.

My basic question to the modern interpreter of Husserl is somewhat like this: Cannot there be a modest transcendental philosophy sans essentialism, essentialism that is afraid and suspicious of, and therefore wants to get rid of, histority, corporeality, and linguisticality of science?

I think (1) that it is possible, nay, necessary; (2) that without these "constraints," transcendental philosophy (a) will be reduced to a sort of *Divine* transcendentalism, (b) will be obliged to deny the *human* roots of transcendentalism, and, what is worse, (c) will be able to accord only a shadowy reality (of cave and for cavemen) to the life-worlds of different cultures and scientific objects. Besides, I am afraid (3) that without these "constraints" transcendental philosophy will ultimately characterise the empirically real as the transcendentally ideal.

It is clear that the demise of positivism is an unmistakable signal for the resurrection of a newly interpreted transcendental philosophy that is scientifically sensible and historically conscious. But if those who are interested in plausibly and constructively interpreting Husserl are not adequately appreciative of the importance of the "constraints," the human and historical significance of phenomenology is likely to be unnecessarily compromised. From this point of view one must be thankful to Mohanty for his effort to take care of the said "constraints" and indicate their rightful place in his scheme of transcendental hermeneutics. Unless the *human* problems posed by these "constraints" are suitably explained, the main purpose of hermeneutics becomes objectively, that is, unintentionally, pointless or otiose. It is the *human* encounter with the so-called constraints that necessitates and also accounts for interpretation, reinterpretation and endless processes of human creativity. All sciences, natural or otherwise, are born out of man's experience of his situation marked by the preceding constraints. God never experiences or encounters any constraint to be overcome or to inquiries into its origin or cause. Consequently, God knows no history or creativity. His "creation" is not creative. For he is credited with the capacity of bringing something out of nothing. By contrast, human creativity essentially consists in acting upon and/or interpreting what is already present or given to him. It is for this reason that man needs science to know what he has been given and what is around him. His search for and research into the things and beings around and within him are boundless. That accounts for the inexhaustible character of human anthropology and the endlessness of human history.

I cannot help feeling that the transcendentalist's fear of "scepticism" is highly exaggerated. When I say this I have in mind particularly Descartes, Kant, and Husserl. Possibly no philosopher or scientist in his *human* capacity can rationally and honestly hope to achieve that sort of knowledge or develop that theory of knowledge that would be able to stand up to all possible known and unknown tests. Yet in the understandable anxiety to have *certain* knowledge when he claims to have achieved that sort of knowledge or developed that form of theory of knowledge, one must look into the underlying considerations.

We are all *practically* historical creatures. But, interestingly enough, called upon to understand history, we develop some theories of history that, some of us claim, are free of the "constraints" of history. This attitude is evident, though in a lesser degree, also in the works of some philosophy-minded "scientists." For instance, philosophers like Hegel, in spite of their readiness to recognise the apparent history of science and its attending "constraints," when seriously engaging in philosophising their professional, that is, theoretical, task, tend to dehistorise the changing practical parameters of what they themselves are doing. They forget—at any rate, their writings give the impression that they do—that their theoretical pursuit or cognitive enterprise is disinterested: unaffected by what has culturally sedimented in their minds and what happens around them. Collateral to the dehistorisation of science is its desociologisation.

If constraints such as history and sociality turn out to be effective, as in fact they do, on human beings, the transcendental phenomenologist's claim to radicalise philosophy, to free it from all presuppositions and thus to transform it into a rigorous science, is bound to be viewed as suspect. Presuppositions, as noted earlier, are of various sorts: natural (ecological), social (culturally ecological), formal (logicomathematical). The intellectual efforts to prove that all presuppositions are calculated in terms of knowledge related to a particular society and a particular period appear to be very misconceived. Besides, the view that these efforts, even if accepted as well conceived, will lead to scepticism, seems to be equally vulnerable. On the contrary, theoretical exercises undertaken and formulated in terms of some or another transcendental arguments are themselves grounded in some or another form of the said presuppositions. Presuppositionless scientific position and proposition are just not logically available to man. Socioculturally constituted man can hardly author anything that is not questionable and corrigible in principle. Of this requirement the transcendentalist himself is vaguely, not adequately, aware. For instance, Kant is very keen to show that his categorial framework is *applicable* to, and necessary for constitution of, objects and making nature possible. Particularly notable in this connection is his analysis of the thesis of schematism. Kant fears that empty and abstract concepts, unaided by appropriate images, yield antinomic results in their worked-out forms. A comparable consideration weighs on Husserl while he insists on the answerability of the transcendentally constituted *formal* world of knowledge to the life-worlds. If the Husserlian had consistently pursued the implication of the *dialectical* relation between the transcendental-formal world and the life-worlds, he could have seen that the latter can, and in fact do, return, at least occasionally, an effective no verdict against what is sought to be constituted by transcendental subjectivity.

The very idea of knowledge as *constituted* raises a grave difficulty. If the *constitutive* competence of transcendental subjectivity is assumed to be unilaterally authentic or valid, the room for question and correction of constituted knowledge is a priori ruled out. The phenomenological method that proclaims its fundamental opposition to the rationalist's a priorism and firm commitment to following the intentional cues of consciousness is not supposed to yield a structure of knowledge that is radically at variance with the practice of the working scientist. Neither in science nor in common sense is the structure of our knowledge taken to be valid solely on the ground of its authorship or constitutive competence. It may be argued here that the transcendentalist is professionally opposed to the naturalist or the positivist standpoint and that he is interested in reviewing and restructuring the knowledge of the naturalist view in a unified and transcendental manner so that it can be free of all "lower-level" presuppositions. In effect, the transcendental phenomenologist's antipresuppositionalism both stems from and aims at an antisceptical and antirelativistic goal of "rigorous science," although it has been historically proved to be ever elusive. Antipresuppositionalism and antihistorism are the two sides of the same coin: changeless Science (Knowledge) of changeless Being (Reality).

In the name of rigorous science the transcendentalist presents us a "secure" science as if in its security-oriented and antifallibilistic character we have developed a vested or permanent interest. Interest in and search for truth are historically divested of the sense of security or permanence and oriented toward genuinely critical research. This insight is unmistakably present in transcendental phenomenology. The requirement of answerability of transcendental knowledge to the life-world is indicative of the possible fallibility of the former. If the life world is structurally preordained to lend support to or to justify, and never to falsify or correct, the unitarian structure of transcendental knowledge, the role of the life-world in the quest of knowledge becomes secondary and ceases to be critical. If the life-world is made always to play a second fiddle to the unitarian structure of knowledge constituted by transcendental subjectivity, the question of obtaining any sort of dialectical relation between the two worlds is ruled out. That the relation, whether it is dialectical or not, between the two worlds is a critical imperative is recognised, at least implicitly, by the Husserlian. This is evident from Husserl's own insistence that rigorous science must somehow be grounded in as well as answerable to the life-world. In the *Crisis* this strain of the phenomenological argument receives pointed emphasis.

The crisis of European science has been ascribed largely to the nonfulfill-ment of this condition: the mutuality of the relation between transcen-dental scientific knowledge and the life-world. Unless the life-world has an independent status capable of modifying, criticising, and thus improving the structure of transcendental science, even if the dialec-tics or the mutuality of relation between the two worlds is recognised in principle, no plausible outcome is methodologically available.

In a sense the transcendentalist's envisaged structure of reason is basically analytic and not dialectic. This is a Kantian legacy taken over by Husserl and many, not all, of his followers. Both Kant and Husserl seriously depart from classical rationalism by recognising the role of the given and recalling its non a priori character. But their deep-rooted fear that if the given is recognised as not only independent but also critical of the constitutive powers of the transcendental sub-jectivity, our knowledge-claim is seriously jeopardized. The spectre of Hume has never ceased to haunt Kant, Hegel, and Husserl. The *fear* of phenomenalism, the fountain of phenomenology, has never allowed the latter to take the given with *respect*.

It is in this context that I find Sartre's critique of *analytic* reason and structuralism or unitarianism very insightful.[23] If the role of dialec-tics in human relationships is not duly recognised, it is found that both the structure of knowledge or consciousness and that of society tend to become stagnant and ossified. The crisis of science is not un-related to the crisis in which a society becomes embroiled. Neither science nor society is an abstraction. It is created or authored, as Marx points out, by concrete human beings. The authors themselves are rooted in history, influenced by the contemporary society, and oriented toward some or another normative (future) goal. But if the primacy of analytic reason makes them forgetful of their history, unaware of their own social roots, blind to the normative goal, and active only in constituting a "secure" structure of knowledge and society, they are in for crisis. Our imperviousness to the causes of crisis does not in any way affect their potency or efficacy. On the contrary, our lack of historical consciousness of the causes allows them to add more to their efficacy and thus to strike or affect us more effectively.

It seems to me that Sartre has rightly pointed out that our un-discharged historical responsibility to be mindful of the causes shap-ing the course of history does not render these *institutional* causes totally inoperative. Institutions have their own dialectical dynamics, sustained by human praxis, which imparts added momentum to the process. In the absence of the active participation of the individual the momentum certainly is slowed but is not totally stopped. The historical fact that the totalities of the structures of our consciousness and society are detotalised and thereafter again retotalised, retaining the dynamic identity of their constituents, is due to the mixture of causes, individual (personal) and societal (institutional). Obviously when the individual authors of history turn out to be highly socially conscious, social structures, including the scientific community substructure undergo faster change. Institutional rigidity is rooted in practical (human) inertia, lack of initiative. But neither a social structure nor a scientific paradigm can be entirely free of puzzles, problems, questions, and quests. These are all incurably human. No amount of institutional rigidity, or even suppression, can remove these "noisy events" from the history of society in general and that of science in particular.

Little analysis is necessary for showing that all these "noisy events" are not only human but also intimately related to the constraints mentioned earlier. First, the naive realist or the externalist may be muddle-headed in asserting that the given has an obdurate self-preserving nature even in the epistemic situation. The point has been well taken care of by many classical thinkers, such as Descartes, Kant, and Hegel, as well as the modern ones, such as Husserl, Heidegger, Popper, Quine, and Sellars. The myth of the *pure* given has convincingly been exploded by them. But the question remains whether the given may be altogether rejected or denied authentically. Even if I agree, as most of us willingly do, that the given is available to us only in some or another judged or interpreted form, it does not negate the existence, almost obdurate existence, of the given. Further, it has to be admitted that the given has a structure of its own—whatever that structure may be like—and that it is *not* blind or amorphous in the Kantian sense. Admittedly, by interpretation its form may be reformed, its structure may be restructured, but its ability to modify and correct our conjecture or hypothesis can hardly be denied. The corporeality of the given only proves that the Other cannot be absorbed or appropriated, without residue, in any epistemic achievement. The world cannot be solipsised by the knowing or even by the affected individual. The existence of other things and beings is a precondition not only of our knowledge but also of our action. Unilaterally we can not ensure the fulfillment of the truth-claim of knowledge nor the fruitfulness of action nor the satisfaction of needs. Rightly understood, we owe our existence to others. One might say, we *are* amidst and with others. Second, our linguisticality is not responsible for any pernicious sort of scepticism. That we are initiated into a language or sign-system and are obliged to make use of it is not a contingent fact. A being that is not semiotic is not human. We are born in some or another language. The fact that we use language, signify in and through signs, does not mean that we cannot put it to a variety of uses and thus change and develop it. In fact, by using language we change it. And this prompts us to deny the Saussarian dualism between *la lingua* and *la parole*. This insight, as we know, has been extensively exploited by the later Wittgenstein and some of his followers, such as Austin, Grice, and Searle. However, one might say that this use-aspect of language does not explain either its origin or our initiation into it. The points to be made clear in this connection are (1) that the "origin" of language cannot be discussed within language and (2) that our initiation into it is not linguistically available to us. We can only *speculate* about our prelinguistic and prepredicative modes of awareness. This speculation is a sort of *reflection* from our linguistic end on our "own" prelinguistic human roots of language acquisition. What we can best achieve in this twilight area of knowledge has been ingeniously spelled out in different ways by thinkers such as Piaget and Quine. Different modes of linguistic apprehension and formulation of reality must not be interpreted as proof of irremediable scepticism.

The radical lesson of the Sapir-Whorf thesis, that every language has a conceptual structure built into it, must not lead one to believe that it entails a sort of linguistic solipsism. Even those who are totally opposed to the thesis, for example, the Cartesian linguists, are obliged to concede that there are different categorial frameworks or conceptual schemes. The transcendentalist's attempt to assimilate all languages (languages-as-used) under one universal syntactic structure has met with innumerable difficulties. For example, the logic of universal syntax can hardly do justice to the immensely varied semantic nuances of rhetoric. The former can hardly generate the latter, unless we define the term *generation* itself in an inexplicably *essentialist* manner. In order to beat off scepticism, allegedly grounded in linguisticality, the transcendentalist often exceeds his brief, ignores the nuances of natural language and richness of its complex uses; and tries to unify all of them in terms of bare formal structures. The subtlety and complexity of the structure-stuff or form-matter relation has not received its due attention and explication from the antirelativist transcendentalist.

Finally, the transcendentalist's uncritical commitment to neat structural elegance makes him oblivious also to the details of history. His allusion to the life-world and its contents need not be taken very seriously. As we have noted, Ricoeur criticises Husserl on this ground. On a comparable ground Hughes criticises Straussian structuralism. Hughes complains that Lévi-Strauss's abstract structuralism freezes the flow of history and finds (modern) logic in (anthropological) magic, where it is not, certainly not in the form sought after by the structuralist.[24] Taking cues from such intuitionists as Brouwer, Heyting, and Dummett one feels like asking, Why this insistence on *the* (elusive) unitary logic and not logics? I do not see good reason for forgetting that both synchronically and diachronically we have many paradigms of logic (that is, logics) and science (that is, sciences).

The "noisy events" of the external world, language and history, cannot be suppressed or ignored by any transcendentally strategic device. For, as I have tried to show, all these events are full of insistent human significance. Kisiel's reference to George Sarton in defence of the "essential history of mankind" is understandable.[25] In the latter's observation, "the history of science . . . the history of human thought and civilisation . . . is the indispensable basis of any philosophy." Kisiel hears the echoes of Husserl and his notion of "essential history" that transcends the "noisy events" of daily concerns. Sarton's "secret history" is the conceptual equivalent of Husserl's "essential history." It is true, as we have noted earlier (Chapter 2), that Sarton thinks that the unity of life manifests itself in three ways, (1) unity of nature, (2) unity of science and (3) unity of mankind. To my mind, in this "unity of life" or "unity of mankind" there is nothing very "secret" or essentialistic. All forms of life, human or otherwise, subject to the laws of nature, develop certain abilities, given which, the problems they encounter in the course of their living prove to be more or less similar, cutting across their territorial and cultural boundaries. And what is more, under these conditions, their attempted solutions also exhibit more or less similarity. This is what I have in mind when I speak of "human universals." Unlike the biolinguistic universals of the Chomsky-Lenneberg variety, they have nothing essentialist about them.[26] It is a well-known fact that, in spite of their geographical dispersal, linguistic and other cultural difference, or unevenness, people succeed in effectively communicating between themselves. Sarton himself, side by side with his unitarian scientific predilection, repeatedly speaks of the social roots of scientific historiography.

> Science never developed in a social vacuum, and in the case of
> each individual it never developed in a psychological vacuum.
> Every man of science was a man of his time and place, of his family
> and people, of his group and church; he was always obliged to
> fight his own passions and prepossessions as well as assail the
> superstitions that clustered around him and threaten to choke
> out the novelties. It is just as foolish to deny the existence of those
> superstitions as it is to ignore contagious diseases; one must throw
> light upon them, describe them, and fight them. The growth of
> science implies at every step the fight against errors and pre-
> judices; the discoveries are largely individual, but the fight is
> always collective. [27]

My understanding of the historiography of science is closer to the view
of Sarton quoted here. It takes due note of human fallibilism and the
corrigibility of science. A moderate form of transcendentalism can go
well together with human fallibilism, both theoretical and practical.
In fact, they do go together. This point has been persuasively argued
by, among others, Popper and Ricoeur in recent times. It has been
rightly pointed out by Ricoeur that there is no basic incompatibility
between the structural type and an "event" type of historiography.
History is indeed both a matter "of structure" and "of multiple events."
Ricoeur seems to be justified in affirming that "history is history only
to the extent that it has reached neither absolute discourse nor absolute singularity." [28] A similar view has been reiterated by Popper in
such later works as *Objective Knowledge: An Evolutionary Approach*,
where he argues that proto-Platonic transcendentalism and historical
growth and fallibilism of science go well together. He takes pains to
point out that the microstructure of scientific theory patently reveals
scientific fallibilism and that if it seems to be latent in the macrostructure
of metatheories it is only because of the relatively abstract level at which
the historian of science proposes to operate. The transcendental structure is not and cannot be unresponsive to the "noisy events" of the
microlevel. But the very purpose of the historian of science, working
at the transcendental or metatheoretical level, is defeated unless he
systematically, that is, deliberately, ignores these events and concen-
trates on their structural properties. This is a simple result of methodological decisions to operate at a macrostructural level.

If the life-world of the Husserlian is earnestly interpreted in a liberal,
not conservative, way, I think, many of the criticisms raised against
the ahistorical transcendentalism of the early Husserl can be substan-

tially met. The unity of the life-world is marked by diversity and histority. Diverse forms of life are present in it. Strictly speaking, even terms like "form of life" are somewhat abstract and transcendental. It is in and through actions and interactions of individual human beings that forms of life are brought into being and transformed historically. But the fact that we do not refer to each specific human being and refer only to his *form* of life does not mean that, on demand, we are not prepared to take due note of his specific presence and performance. Collateral to this point is the historical diversity of different forms of life. All forms of life, strictly speaking, are not assimilable under and subject to the "forces" of one uniform history. It is in this connection that one should bear in mind that "universal history," for example, is the product of the philosopher's philosophisation of history. Needless to say, there is nothing wrong about it. As I have just said, both the historian and the philosopher are free to choose their level of understanding and operation. But it seems to me that for understanding of history of science one would be well advised to look into the different forms of life, specifics of different cultures. High-level transcendentalism may make him somewhat blind to the "multiple-event-structure" of history. It is to be noted here that Sarton, who is never tired of speaking of the unity of mankind and the unity of science, never fails to look into the specifics and peculiarities of different cultures. I have already referred to this point (Chapter 2). True, different histories of science as embedded in different cultures exhibit some very interesting, at times even striking, parallelism. This induces one to speak of "human universals" and make use of the same. But one should not accord thick ontological status to them. Nor should these universals be construed as innate competencies of "human nature." In fact, there is nothing like *a* human nature. Human nature as evident from such different cultures and subcultures as science is highly uneven. For methodological or heuristic purposes the structural anthropologist and the transcendentalist historiographer may be required in some cases to ignore this cultural or subcultural unevenness. In fact, the Straussian and the Husserlian understandably often follow this approach. But these methodological devices, in spite of their usefulness in certain cases, must not be reified. If we pay due recognition to the particular "event-structure" of history or the concreteness and diversity of the life-world, this tendency toward transcendental reification may be suitably controlled and appropriately corrected.

The theses of anthropology and historiography of science that I am trying to defend do not demand that I deny all sorts of transcendentalism. As I have already tried to show, transcendentalism is of various types, strong and weak, very strong and very weak. For example, the Kantian form of transcendentalism appears to me very strong. Even stronger is perhaps its Cartesian form. In his bid to be fair to history the Hegelian form of transcendentalism becomes somewhat "weak." But, since by "history" Hegel means "philosophy of history," he is inclined to undercut the "event structure" of history and highlight its transcendental structure. In Husserl, as we have noted, there are two trends, one, rigorously transcendental and the other sensitive at least of the macroevent structures of the life-world. To my mind, neither of these two trends is theoretically enough equipped to be sufficiently fair to the highly uneven event-structure of the histories of science obtained in different cultures or forms of life.

The postpositivist era of Euro-American philosophy has witnessed the rise and fall of several forms of transcendentalism of varying strength or weakness. The two most instructive falls that have substantially contributed to the decline of positivism are (1) the unworkability of the project of unified science and (2) the realisation that the ("problematic") given cannot be explained by the ("unproblematic") given (of the same type or level). The fact that the philosophy of science of the Vienna Circle has not produced any historian of science of consequence is largely due to the joint effect of (1) and (2). Rightly understood, (1) and (2) are closely interrelated. The unity of sciences cannot be shown by and within the sciences themselves. For showing it one needs a somewhat transcendental structure of understanding together with a relatively higher-level language. One-dimensional given and one-dimensional (for example, *Tractatarian*) language beg something not given and higher-level (or, at least, relatively richer) language for their explanation and clarification (not establishment or constitution).

In this connection, I will briefly refer to two weak forms of transcendentalism, Popperian and Quinean, which appear to be theoretically well enough equipped to provide a sound "foundation" for scientific historiography. I even venture to suggest that the Kuhnian structure of scientific historiography is marked by a very weak form of transcendentalism — transcendentalism nonetheless. Let me clarify what I intend to say in defence of the weak or modest forms of transcendentalism with reference to the preceding three thinkers.

The basic similarity of different empiricist positions lies in their insistence that observational statements are more dependable than and corrective of higher level statements derived or induced from them. By implication, empiricists also agree on the point that for the construction of scientific theories scientists are obliged to rise above and go beyond observational statements that are known by various terms: protocol statements, basic statement, observation report, and so forth. According to Popper, science has no foundational structure beneath or beyond it. The acceptability of observational statements as falsifiers of the theories aiming to solve the problems of science is due to communal consensus: temporary consensus of the concerned community. In a way basic statements are communal or social and temporary in their efficacy. The higher-level scientific theories, essentially problem-oriented and conjectural in nature, are answerable to and falsifiable by the basic statements. Scientific theories and the corpus they form admittedly transcend the narrow scope and confine of basic statements. They are also more durable than the latter, despite their distance from the "empirical ground." Although falsifiable in principle, scientific theories are not in effect decisively and easily falsified. Good conjectures often survive their falsifying tests, the results of which enrich their contents. Even when the commitment of the scientist to falsify his theories proves to be successful, the resulting success turns out to be partial or marginal, and never total. A good hypothesis, entrenched well in a system of theories, cannot ordinarily be totally overthrown. Not only hypotheses and theories but also problems and arguments, according to Popper, are inhabitants of his World3. Compared to World1 (physical) and World2 (psychological), World3 is clearly transcendental. But in Popper's evolutionary scheme of thought all Worlds are more or less "causally open," doubly open, both upwardly and downwardly. Of the three Worlds the most transcendental and durable is World3. In spite of its admitted evolutionary and causally open character it has often been characterised as Platonic. Even if we discount the understandable exaggeration of this characterisation, it is difficult to deny that it is indeed necessary for Popper to posit a world like this in order to explain the historical and problematic characters of scientific theories. The interesting point to be noted is that Popper's transcendental world, World3, is not intended to make philosophy scientific or to impart rigours to science, but only to preserve and show the historical and yet durable nature of scientific theories.

Popper's and Quine's common commitment to Neurath's image of science as a floating boat appears to me of more than casual significance. That science as a boat cannot be constructed or deconstructed all at once is clear to both of them. Neither establishment nor disestablishment of science is a matter of instant understanding of history. It is time taking and gradual. In spite of Popper's rejection of Quine's methodological holism and preference for "piecemeal engineering," it is clear that he recognises the gradual and historical nature of the process of falsification, deconstruction and reconstruction of science. Even in the face of falsifying evidence or counterexamples theories are not thrown *totally* overboard. I take this point of Popper's as an unintended concession to the Duhem-Quine thesis to the effect that there is nothing in any observational statement or empirical evidence that can decisively change the history or the career of a scientific theory. That science faces the tribunal of experiences as a whole and that, even in the face of negative evidence, it can substantially preserve its corpus by redistributing the truth-values of its constituent statements seem to me extremely insightful and seminal. First, it shows the substantially and historically continuous character of science. Admittedly, change in one part of science animates, and has repercussion upon, its other parts. But this interanimation or repercussion does not affect the identifiable unity of the scientific corpus as a whole. To me this is a weak variety of transcendentalism without entailing any sort of antihistorism.

A similar, though considerably weaker, form of transcendentalism is evident also in Kuhn's understanding of history of science. I know very well that the very expression "transcendentalism in Kuhn" will raise many eyebrows, and I will not be surprised if the Kuhnian himself frowns upon my transcendental interpretation of Kuhn's historiography of science. The common objection that is likely to be raised is that incommensurabilism and transcendentalism cannot go together. My point is precisely the opposite. That is, incommensurabilism presupposes, however implicitly or remotely, some sort of transcendentalism. In support of my view I offer two basic arguments. First, in his writings, time and again, Kuhn highlights the importance of "the community structure of science." Science as such does not disclose its full implication unless it is viewed in relation to its social background. Incommensurability remains an incomprehensible concept unless there is some possibility of comparing different paradigms in respect to their structure and their stuff. Kuhn himself affirms that he wants to "emphasise the need to study the community structure of science." For without this, he fears, I think rightly, it becomes difficult to understand not only the criteria of recognising certain views as scientific but also those used in rejecting and grading some other views. The process of socialising nonscience (for example, myth, magic, and metaphysics) as science, of tolerating pseudo science as science, and of condoning deviations from and aberration of science is indeed very interesting. In each of these cases, the concerned social process performs the role of transcendental legitimacy. What in-itself is perhaps not yet scientific or has ceased to be so may be "saved" and certified as science by the authority (for example, academic community) of science. When Kuhn says, "Scientific knowledge, like language, is intrinsically the common property of a group or else-nothing at all."[29]

While Kant and Hegel are engaged in defending a universal transcendentalism in order to legitimise science, Kuhn is satisfied with showing that the legitimacy of science is not intrinsic to the structure of science itself but rooted in its affiliation to a *social* group or community, professional or political or religious. The same culture or society may extend recognition to more than one scientific theory or paradigm. Often it happens over a period of time, successively, not simultaneously. But this is not necessarily the case. There are historically available societies and periods in which more than one paradigm did enjoy simultaneous recognition. I think, given his interpretation of scientific historiography, that Kuhn perhaps will be disinclined to accept this view. The reigning paradigm, according to him, displaces all other contending or rival paradigms. To him the paradigm-shift is like a gestalt switch. His account of the gestalt switch needs to be taken with considerable circumspection, whose reasons he has been provided by himself. First, he argues to show that the paradigms, in spite of their historical shift, are interrelatable. When he speaks of the relative merits and weaknesses of the Aristotelian, the Newtonian, and the Einsteinian paradigms, clearly he commits himself to a definite standpoint, or conceptual scheme, wherefrom this view of his derives its meaningfulness. In relation to the paradigms compared and contrasted, the comparing standpoint or conceptual scheme is bound to be transcendental. However, this does not mean that this transcendental standpoint lies ever beyond the sweep of historical change, that is, criticism and correction. Second, his incommensurability thesis is not at all incompatible with the requirement of communication or translation. On the contrary, he affirms that the authors of incommensurable theories can and, in fact do, successfully communicate. For understandable reasons, for example, difference in linguistic situatedness, this communication turns out to be partial. Even in that case, the criteria used, implicitly or explicitly, for choosing or rejecting theories are found to be *more or less* the same: accuracy, simplicity, fruitfulness, and the like.[30] The reason for which the choice-parameters are not uniformly used is practical or normative-evaluative. If Kuhn insists on the personal factor in the use of the choice-parameters, it is not to deny the transcendentality of the parameters defining or constituting the comparative standpoint. If he speaks of nonavailability of any absolutely neutral language to be used for the purpose of comparing different paradigms, this is not to deny the possibility of communication between the inhabitants of different scientific communities or subcultures. The latter, though affiliated to different languages, can communicate. In this respect, Kuhn follows, up to a point, the Quinean thesis of interlinguistic translatability and the attending indeterminacy. Indeterminacy or underdeterminacy of translation or occasional breakdown of communication is not at all a proof of the impossibility of the either. Firmly footed in one's own conceptual scheme or language, when one communicates with others and translates their languages into one's own language, one does not either give up one's own standpoint or totally internalise others' conceptual schemes and standpoints. These arguments of Kuhn are clearly, though weakly, transcendental in implication. In his historiography Kuhn is not a pure descriptivist or narrativist. His historical narration of science has a definite structure of its own.

Much of what I have said is intended to show that transcendental historiography of science in its stronger forms devours science or reduces it to a shadowy dance of macro-events. Criticism of transcendentalism does not mean its total rejection. On the contrary, it purports to show two things: (1) negatively speaking, the stronger variety of transcendentalism tends to deny the reality of history together with the empirical richness of science, and (2) positively speaking, without some modest form of transcendentalism, meaningfulness of history and therefore also of history of science cannot be rationally vindicated.

When I speak of typologically different paradigms of scientific knowledge — magic, metaphysics, science, and superscience — their partial incommensurability poses no unsurmountable difficulty for making communication between their protagonists possible. In spite of their cultural and historical distance they can (in a sense) meet and converse, that is, communicate. This process of communication is bound to be loaded with interpretation. One might say that it is not that the authors of different paradigms communicate but that they are made to do so (in a make-believe way) by the historian of science. From this one might hastily conclude that it is only the historian who, strictly speaking, is the real transcendentalist and not those whose theories and practices he tries to explain. This is true only in a limited sense. Even the scientist of today is capable of understanding the science(s) of yesterday. He can also partially anticipate sciences of tomorrow. He can do so because there is something in his understanding that does not confine his competence to the contemporary time. His ego is not a prisoner of his time (history) and place (society). Egology cannot be completely sociologised, nor sociology egologised, however transcendentally one might try to construe the ego. In every time and place other times (histories) and places (societies) are effectively present, though incompletely. Interfusion of cultures, like interfusion of meanings, is a sedimented social reality in which we live, but of which, without reflection, we are not aware. Even on reflection, it is not possible for one to get to the fullness of meanings of other sciences embedded in alien cultures. This is what I tried to argue earlier by drawing a distinction between internal rationality and external intelligibility. For example, the contemporary historian, familiar with modern science, can undoubtedly understand the magic of the past. But his understanding of it is bound to be different from the magician's own understanding of magic. To a certain extent, this difference accounts for partial interface and partial incommensurability between the scientific achievements of different cultures.

Complete commensurability presupposes a very strong form of transcendentalism. Understandably enough, the transcendental subjectivity that tries to do away with the incommensurability of different paradigms of science found in different forms of life or cultures is claimed to be itself free from all presuppositions. If different cultural presuppositions of different scientific paradigms are accorded strong recognition, it is feared, their unification under a transcendental philosophy as rigorous science is ruled out. In plain language, if cultural diversity together with scientific diversity is taken as a recalcitrant datum of history, its assimilability under and reducibility to some transcendental structural unity proves impossible. Therefore, it is not surprising that Hegel makes *historical* diversity intelligible by bringing it under a *philosophical* unity. He maintains that history, unless philosophised, remains meaningless and only as scattered data of the past. A similar trend is discernible in Husserl. The facts of experience viewed from the natural standpoint and under the aspects of different "shapes" of corporeality, linguisticality, and histority prove to be unityless and meaningless. It is only in terms of the meaning-bestowing (or interpretive) capacity of presuppositionless transcendental subjectivity that facts of experience are lifted above the disjoined cussedness of the natural standpoint and brought together into a meaningful unity. To meet the rightly anticipated objection that this "transcendentally constituted meaningfulness" is purely a priori and hardly historical, the Husserlian feels rationally obliged to refer this unity to the life-world wherefrom, he claims, this unity in fact originates. Had the originary unit lent by the life-world been sufficiently unifying, the hermeneutic or the meaning-bestowing role of the transcendental subjectivity would have been superfluous or merely ratificatory, not really constitutive.

The ambivalence of Husserl, I have tried to show, has been convincingly demonstrated by Heidegger and Gadamer. The comparable ambivalence of Hegel was fully exploited by Marx. What Marx, Heidegger, and Gadamer have tried to do in common is this: Putting real human beings of flesh and blood at the centre of the historical drama and highlighting their interpretive and creative role they seek to explain the grounds of the increasing convergence of and communication between different cultures. Their historism, not without traces of weak forms of transcendentalism, allows them to recognise simultaneously (1) the *diversity* of human culture and of subcultures such as science and (2) the historical trends of their growing *unity* (largely due to the increasing influence of science and technology). The points to be mainly noted in this connection are (a) that antipresuppositionalism entails a strong form of transcendentalism and aims at a total rejection of scepticism and relativism and (2) that historism, without being averse to diluted forms of transcendentalism, tries to explain the growing unity of diverse cultures and different scientific research programmes. Defenders of (b) are opposed to and try to undercut the transcendentalist programme of achieving a unitary and unquestionable "rigorous science." For, having taken the lesson of recorded history of human cultures and different sciences, they are reconciled to the sensible conclusion that whatever is human in its origin is indeed questionable and corrigible. However, this sober realisation in specific errors and even crises and trying to remove those causes through both individual and collective efforts. This positive attitude often expresses itself in the philosophies of peaceful coexistence, meaningful cooperation, continuous dialogue and even universal conversation. I speak of "even" in the context of "universal conversation" because, I feel, universal conversationalism (à la Derrida and Rorty) is strong transcendentalism in the reverse.

The reason for which sciences could not be unified remains operative in making the programmes of "universal conversation" very difficult to work out. For cultures, like individuals, have their distinct, though interfaced, personalities or identities. The need of conversation is rooted in this distinctness of personality, individual as well as cultural. The "human universals" that make said conversation possible rule out complete universalisability of that ongoing conversation. Like the nature of man, that of history, science, and history of science, ultimately authored by man, is and will remain open-ended forever.

EPILOGUE

•••••••••••••

Anthropological Rationalism without Essentialism

I

I THINK WE HAVE REACHED THE POINT WHEN WE ARE EXPECTED TO recapitulate and supplement briefly the basic points we have tried to establish in this work.

One of the main weaknesses of contemporary philosophy of science is its distance from historiography and anthropology of science. Barring the insightful few, the common run of the analytic philosophers of science seem to be unwilling to review their anthropological and historiographical presuppositions. Failure to see science in its synchronic perspective gives a false impression, that scientific activities and conclusions are necessarily abstract and autonomous. A sort of false consciousness seems to contaminate science, giving the impression that it is primarily a matter of experimental laboratory and lecture theatre and has very little to do with the people who are not dons or qualified students. I have tried to show that the rigours of science are not antithetical in relation to the life-world.

Descriptive chronicle or narrative historiography has its necessity as well as limits. Descriptive details and narrative continuity are, at least partially, corrective of the miseffects of excessive theorisation. Respect for details saves history from its being swallowed up by philosophy. At the same time, it is to be noted that descriptive details cannot become meaningful unless they are conceptually colligated and that the proclaimed continuity of narratives becomes difficult to follow without some hidden theoretical threads.

For the preceding considerations I am not opposed to the idea of accepting ideal types in history. Idealisation and typification of historical details are not intended to take away their specific features. Specificity and ideality can well go together. Whenever the historian speaks of different periods of history, he introduces, often prereflectively or unconsciously, the heuristic concept of ideal type. That periodisation of history involves an element of "arbitrariness" is likely to be conceded by the working historian himself. For he knows best that between the scopes of different (and even successive) ideal types there are bound to be many deliberately ignored details.

Perhaps I owe an explanation of my choice of the *scientific* domain of history to the exclusion of many other possible domains, economic, literary, and so on. By this time it is perhaps clear to us that in the public mind the image of science is mainly earth-bound. Even many informed people are of the view that since science is empirically founded, its history is bound to be concerned with foundational details. Pleas for taking leave of the narrative history of science are frequently refused on the alleged ground that too much of narration and too little of theorisation are likely to degrade history into philosophy (if not metaphysics) of history.

The debate on the relative importance of factual details and theoretical idealisation in history may be carried on indefinitely, not necessarily as a useless exercise. The issue is comparable to the theoretician's dilemma within science itself. It is not easy to decide in the field of scientific theory-construction whether observational terms or theoretical terms are primarily important. The question cannot be answered in an abstract way. It depends upon the level of narration or theorisation we have in mind. Positively speaking, whether one narrates or theorises one must have a definite point of view wherefrom one is to gaze on his historical horizon, understand, and write it. There cannot be a privileged point of view.

Every point of view has a relatively obvious *positive* aspect that is indicated by the details chosen by the individual and every point of view has also a *purposive* aspect which is not so obvious. Only when the concerned historian's chosen details are closely looked into, we can discover in and through them the telos of the author. This duality underlying every historian's point of view is symptomatic of the dialectical character of his reason. No social scientist, be he a historian of science or an anthropologist of science, can escape this duality or dialectics of reason. He can neither disregard facts nor dispense with relatively abstract theories. He is well advised to free himself of both fact-fetish and theory-intoxication. Determining how facts and theories can be shown to be interwoven was the main object of this critical inquiry.

II

In order to understand clearly the import of the last point I have introduced some ideal-typical concepts: Primitive Society, (Time 1); (PS[Tl]); Medieval Society, (Time 2); (MS[T2]), Contemporary Society, (Time 3), (C3[T3]); Future Society, (Time 4), (FS [T4]). Also I have used four other concepts, Magician (M), Philosopher (P), Scientist (S), and Superscientist (SS). These terms are the designations of the "wisemen" of the preceding four ideal-typical societies. Similarly, in order to designate "the best form of knowledge" available in the said types of society, I have used four terms, *magic, philosophy, science,* and *superscience.* All these ideal-typical concepts underlying the said terms, though necessary, are not sufficient for the purpose of having a clear understanding of history. This has been made clear in this way: Understandably history is never history in general. It is of *this* or *that* society or culture. It may also be of *this* or *that* subculture, such as science or economics. No society is "primitive" or "contemporary" in an absolute sense. What is "science" in one culture is "magic" in another. This shows that the meanings of these concepts are culture-bound and that their general understanding remains bracketed. So when "we" say something as scientific "they" may use the term "magic" to designate it. Although this "internal" view of science and magic, for example, has nothing very objectionable in itself, it is bound to give rise to questions. Cannot we, being situated as we are within a culture and being committed as we are to our own internal view of it, understand an *alien* culture? Because of our internal commitment are we prevented from understanding different and distant cultures? Are all of us, irrespective of our diverse cultural affiliation, condemned to be shut up or enclosed within our own culture?

Every form of human understanding, irrespective of its domain and level, is grounded in some conceptual framework. Alternatively, one might say, every form of understanding is embedded in a culture. Though culture is a *complex* totality, it, like conceptual framework, is a totality nonetheless. If its internal constituents are closely examined, they exhibit both homogeneous and heterogeneous elements. This basic factor, in turn, is rooted in human nature, which is partly free and partly determined by the presence, ideas, and actions of other human beings. Human freedom can be neither narrowed down to zero nor given a completely unfettered form. This dual or dialectical character of human freedom is at work in both our thought and our action.

Consequently, the problems that we encounter in our practical intercourse with and understanding of fellow human beings within our own culture are evident also in our dealings, communications and praxis vis-à-vis the peoples belonging to other cultures, other times, and other places. If we remain critically close to our own practical consciousness, it becomes gradually clear to us that the problems of intercultural communication, like those of intracultural communication, are not really intractable. As a matter of fact, in visiting and living in other cultures or even reading books about them, we are more or less reliably *informed* of their people, customs, languages, ways of living, and so forth. What we thus gain through personal experience or theoretical study may be regarded not only as *information* but also as *comprehension* or understanding. True, our information may turn out to be wrong and our understanding on scrutiny may prove misunderstanding. But that is a problem not peculiar to intercultural communication and understanding.

It is also present within our own culture. If we bear in mind the systematically ambiguous (free-unfree) character of individual human nature, the possibility of misunderstanding is to be found within our own selves. It is not merely a figurative expression when we say, for example, "I failed to get myself right." What is meant here is this: all the contents of my thought and action that I am objectively obliged to own are not subjectively available as a total whole to myself at any particular point of time. There are always certain things *in* me *of* which I am not author or owner, at least not consciously. That partly explains why I ask a friend or psychoanalyst what seems to be "wrong" with me.

This excursion into individual psychology helps us to understand the problems and themes of intracultural as well as intercultural human relationships. Besides, it shows the human roots of the issues concerned. When I say, "I belong to Bengali culture," this immediate sense of belonging is not inconsistent with my (not so immediate) sense of belonging to Indian culture and saying, "I belong to Indian culture." By extending this line of argument I may consistently both feel and say,

"I belong to Asian culture" and "I belong to an emerging global culture." In other words, one can simultaneously belong to more than one culture and subculture. For example, my professional commitment to philosophy, one subculture, is not inconsistent with my commitment to politics, another subculture, of the same Indian culture.

What is more: between different subcultures of the same type, say, Indian philosophy, Islamic philosophy, and Euro-American philosophy, despite the difference of their parent cultures, there is an affinity. This *affinity* (I am not saying *unity*) need not be necessarily contrived or imaginary. Cultural parallelism is not brought about or constituted by human thought. Our mind takes note of it. Maybe in the process it interprets that parallelism.

Another point that has been brought to light by our investigation is this: Between different adjacent cultures there cannot be any spatial or geographical gap. In the same geographical territory different cultures do coexist and often overlap. Like the maps of languages and dialects, the maps of culture, especially those of adjacent areas, are marked by intersectional fuzziness. Once this important point is kept in view, the problems attending intercultural communication do not assume alarming proportion or prove intractable.

On the contrary, a positive factor, often neglected, needs to be highlighted. A man *territorially* belonging to one culture may *spiritually* feel more akin to another culture. We often hear of Indophiles in Europe and Europhiles in India. A Mother Teresa, hailing from Albania, has been spending her lifetime in the slums of Calcutta identifying herself with the people of the place. Similarly, one can recall Albert Schweitzer's migration to and settlement in Equatorial Africa and his identifying himself with the culture of the people of that continent. In brief, in spite of the *local* cultural affiliation of a person, he may *authentically* belong to a *global* culture, or, in Tagore's word, become a spiritual articulation of the Universal Man. In a way this shows, among other things, that intercultural communication of ideas and ideals is not necessarily problematic.

A necessary word of caution: In view of the paradigm of global culture one must not forget man's local cultural affiliation. The possibility or even primacy of global, international, or intercultural consciousness does *not* negate the concerned man's local roots. Thus we find that every man's understanding of culture has at least two facets or levels, *internal* and *external*. That is how one man can understand both himself and his culture and others' understanding of him and his culture. The former may be said to be *internal intelligibility* and the latter *external intelligibility.* I understand Indian culture in one way, maybe in several ways. But these are not the ways that it is generally viewed by an outsider. Even the most genuine Indophiles, living long in India, probably cannot get into the heart of Indian culture. Many objects, ideas, and ideals of this culture appear to them somewhat strange at best and meaningless at worst. It is no wonder that to the average European student of Indian culture its basic symbols are snake charmer, rope tricker, and naked *sadhu* (monk). Comparable difficulty is experienced by the Indian student of Western culture. He is easily overimpressed by wining, dining, and permissiveness of that culture. In no time he "discovers" facile confirmation of the critical and pessimist ideas of such writers as Spengler, Sorokin, and Toynbee, who think that the hallmarks of Western culture are materialism, consumerism, high incidence of divorce, mental illness, and crime (even among the educated and affluent sections of the society). In brief, self's view of other and other's view of self are bound to be different, despite their ability to understand each other. Negatively speaking, self and other cannot possibly arrive at a *completely identical* understanding of each other. For that presupposes that self can understand other without being rooted in his own culture or conceptual framework, however vague or indefinite it might be, and the converse.

My point is that cultural relativism is unintelligible unless it is assumed that every man in his understanding of other things and beings is logically bound to be more or less faithful to his own point of view. This is not a mere assumption but a hard fact of life. When it is said that one must assume or be faithful to one's own point of view it does not mean that the content of the said assumption or faith cannot be critically reviewed later on at least in some respects. Self-view is certainly reviewable in principle, though not dispensable in its entirety. One cannot jump out of one's own skin in order to get to others. This does not mean any sort of solipsism. What makes relativism intelligible also contains it and indicates its limits.

III

It is not that science or philosophy cannot be or has not been viewed autonomously. In fact, the positivist defends philosophy as a sort of science, trying to keep it as free as possible of metaphysical philosophy.

The metaphysical philosopher, in his turn, refuses to see his discipline enclosed within the narrow confines of science. But a critical appraisal of science and philosophy as metaphysics discloses the correct relation between the two. Metaphysics presupposes as well as anticipates what science asserts and discovers. Scientific assertions may confirm or refute metaphysical presuppositions. Although metaphysical philosophy and science, are related, their relation is dialectical, not unilateral or analytical.

A close examination of Collingwood's theory of absolute presuppositions makes it clear that they are neither absolute nor a priori. Influenced by Kant's notion of category and Hegel's of historical disclosure or gradual determination of Ideas, Collingwood tries to demonstrate that presuppositions are in fact culture-bound and developmental. If metaphysics as science of absolute presupposition has proved itself to be basically historical, it becomes difficult to escape the conclusion that natural sciences are even more deeply historical and owe their validity to the concerned culture. In a way Collingwood's theory anticipates Kuhn's sociology of science and the epoch-bound validity of every scientific paradigm.

Unless the different levels of presuppositions and the nature of their interrelationships are spelled out, we cannot show their connection with science and metaphysics. Broadly speaking, the scientist and the metaphysical philosopher operate at four levels of presuppositions: sensible, objectual, *generally* objectual, and *universally* objectual (often formulable in physicomathematical language and axiomatisable). If the intermediate levels are kept out of sight, the relation between the top- and bottom level presuppositions appears problematic, that is, undefinable. We need the help of concrete language and culture in order to see and show that different levels of presupposition are interrelatable, if not more or less interanimated.

Though in natural sciences and philosophy the levels of presupposition are hierarchically arranged it is not difficult to show in terms of ordinary language and the life-world that they are all somehow rooted in our "normal" cultural life. It would not, therefore, be correct to claim that any particular point of view—the psychological, the physical, the mathematical, or the metaphysical—occupies a privileged or vantage position to see and show the world or a part thereof. Similarly, no item of experience—nameable, describable, or valuable—can be given a privileged ontological status in the world of experience, sharply separating one from the rest.

Scientific and philosophical problems, like those of life, have no intrinsic or inviolable character of their own. It is only within the context of life or theorisation that we experience what is primitive to us and accordingly try to thematise and tackle it. For example, whereas some societies are poverty-stricken, some others are worried about their surplus food production and the resulting price crash. Since our problems are not universal, the question of seeking a "universal solution" does not make sense.

Analogously, it may be pointed out that our cultures and languages are not universal. If all of us had one universal language and belonged to one universal culture, most of the questions of intercultural communication, interlinguistic translation, and the attending problems would not have arisen at all. Most of our theoretical and practical problems are traceable to our affiliation to a particular culture, a particular language, and a position in this or that subculture, such as science, philosophy, or literature. When I *describe* this relativistic view, one must not think that the problems posed by relativism are overwhelming or insoluble. Even a pretheoretical descriptive view of our life as we live it is enough to convince us that though relativism or contextualism is present, yet *practically* we do succeed in more or less overcoming the resulting problems. One may even say that interhuman and intercultural relationships are bound to be problematic. This is not to deny our ability to solve or at least tackle the problems that arise.

Though we are familiar with or even committed to the "logic" and "science" of our time, that does not prevent us, certainly not the professionally competent ones among us, from understanding the so-called prelogic and magic of primitive society. History and anthropology would not have been possible if our rootedness in a culture or an epoch could make it impossible for us to transcend our limits of place and time. Firmly footed in one place, we can well see distant horizons. By moving a little we can push our horizon back. Similarly, in our epistemic enterprise, anthropological or historical, we can understand what is different and what is distant.

The question of relativism may be viewed in a different way. When the logician or the mathematician speaks of the "richness" of a language, he has in view something quite different from the richness of ordinary language alluded to and used by the litterateur and the ordinary language philosopher. Whereas by *richness* the former means "abstract, powerful and simple" properties of the concerned *constructed* language, the latter means something quite different, namely, "naturalness" and "complexity." Logicomathematical language is primarily intended to formulate and prove certain "things," such as problems and theorems. The purpose of ordinary language is endlessly diverse. It may be expressive, suppressive, affective, emotive, imperative, indicative, optative, and so on.

Although the preceding distinction is important, it must not be taken in an absolute sense, because we must bear in mind that there is an inseparable link among concept, language, and experience. However abstract a concept may be, it cannot be experientially rootless. Similarly, a language, however formalised it may be, cannot snap off all its links with ordinary language. And the latter, in turn, we must remember, is inseparable from the life lived by us. That our semantic ascent must not make us blind to how thickly or thinly it is related at every level to the life-world and ordinary language has been shown, in quite different ways, by Husserl and Quine.

Acceptance of the theory of culture-bound absolute presuppositions commits one to a sort of relativism and one may be criticised on that ground. *Per contra*, it should be borne in mind that rejection of the culture-bound and epoch-bound character of science or scientific philosophy tends to push us to a sort of metaphysical or transcendental philosophy that is said to be itself ahistorical and culture-neutral, yet lending validation to and legitimising all our culture-bound cognitive paradigms. This sort of transcendentalism obviously aims at removing or at least minimising the miseffects of relativism and contextualism. The principles of transcendental philosophy strongly claim for themselves immunity against criticism from the end of experience or life-world. Whenever a Kantian or a Husserlian speaks of criticism, he means self-criticism, internal criticism, criticism from within. Scrutiny reveals that whereas for Kant *critique* is essentially justificationist, for Husserl it is constitutive-explorative. In no case is *critique* allowed to have an infirming effect on our knowledge.

It is interesting to note that relativists like Quine also speak of internal reorganisation of science. According to the well-known Neurath-Quine thesis, the boat of science, if damaged, has to be repaired from within it and, what is obvious, the (critics or) repairers are required to remain afloat on it. In different ways both the metaphysical transcendentalist and the radical empiricist are defending a sort of internal criticism and, by implication, ruling out external criticism. Yet the difference between the two, particularly emphasised by the transcendentalist, has to be carefully noted. The empiricist's paradigm of science is physics, and he does not deny that there is an external world with various objects, both predictable and unpredictable, in it, which, if credibly experienced by or communicated to the scientist, requires the latter to revise and reorganise his cognitive system. The transcendentalist paradigm of science is metaphysics. Unlike the empiricist, the transcendentalist is not prepared to recognise naively the existence of the external world populated by imponderables. He finds that its reality is largely constituted by man's transcendental epistemic capacities. This transcendental attitude in its radical form amounts to refusal to learn from experience. For, it is argued, experience as such has nothing to teach us. It is by our internal-transcendental concepts and capacities that we transform "meaningless" experiences into meaningful and systematically interrelated objects. The transcendentalist test of rationality and meaningfulness is rooted in the human mind itself, its transcendental subjectivity, and not to be sought in the "abstract" correspondence between the separate objects of the world and the isolated items of our experience.

The controversy on the models of rationality defined in terms of correspondence or consistency, that is, systematicity, is not confined to that of the rationalist-empiricist and the metaphysical transcendental. With some variation it is also repeated by the empiricists themselves. It is clearly evident from the well-known controversy between Planck and Mach on the issue of the correct interpretation of the thermodynamical theory of entropy. Whereas the realist Planck stoutly defends the correspondence model of rationality, Mach takes immense pains to show how our theory-construction is a part of our overall strategy of adjustment to our environment. The language of science, he argues, cannot be totally separated from the surroundings of our life. In other words, whether the statement of Planck is true or not cannot be decided by us by disregarding the conditions under which we assert it. While Planck is primarily concerned with (correspondence) truth-conditions, Mach's main concern is adjustmental or systematic assertibility-conditions.

By analysing the latter position it is not at all difficult to show that our perception of *future* and the *needs* of the present are silently but influentially operative within our assertibility-conditions. In a sense our cognitive reason takes note of not only what is there (the realm of ontology and history) and what is happening around us (the realm of sociology) but also of what is ahead of us (the realm of praxiology and the spin-off effects of science in the form of technology). This discloses the "invisible" dialectical character of reason. Thus, in a sense, our science is both historical and futural.

IV

The issues that we face in understanding the relation between philosophy and science are conceptually repeated, with, of course, some variation, in understanding the relation between anthropology and history. Essentially, the problem is how we can best understand science as a subculture, that is, as a part of a culture. Generally speaking, the historian and the ethnographer are more concerned with the descriptive details of science. But the understanding provided by the ethnographer and the historian is often found to be unsatisfactory because of its alleged fragmentary character. The ethnologist, primarily concerned as he is with the principles of comparative study of different cultures as complex totalities, wants to eliminate the fragmentariness of descriptive ethnography. Anthropologists like Lévi-Strauss want to reconcile ethnographic details with ethnological principles. According to him, anthropology needs both data-details and necessary organising principles. The outcome is known to be structural anthropology. Details are really structured or structurable in principles. And that is how structural anthropology can help us well in understanding science as a part of culture.

The historian, like the anthropologist, can operate at two different levels, descriptive and collective, at least. To understand science its historian may decide to go into its details and describe them as faithfully as he can. Alternatively, he can use some principles to organise those details and make them more meaningful.

The basic question that has engaged my attention in this study is whether it is history or anthropology that provides us the relatively advantageous standpoint to understand science. Whereas historiographers such as Sartre claim that history is the basic human study that, rightly used, can help us best in understanding science, working anthropologists such as Lévi-Strauss reject this view and assert that it is structural anthropology, the most fundamental science of man, that enables us best to understand the different forms of human activities, including scientific ones. The Straussian view rests on the assumption that anthropology and its underlying analytic reason are simultaneously mindful of historical details, in the form of ethnographic data, and necessary organising principles. Lévi-Strauss's emphasis is on the totality of culture. And it is only within the totality that he is in favour of viewing and understanding science as an institution, because, he argues, cultural objects and activities derive their meaningfulness from their context. At the same time, he finds that the different traits of different subcultures of widely separated cultures exhibit some distinct uniformities. These uniformities or universals are, in his view, very "natural," not contrived or mere constructs of analytic reason. In spite of their differences, there are two important points of agreement between them. Both are opposed to the idea of aping the method of natural science in human science. Second, in different ways their approaches are prohistorical. It is on the question of primacy to be accorded to this science (history) or that science (anthropology) that they fall out. Lévi-Strauss explicitly criticises Malinowski's antihistorical functionalism. He points out that all the details of a cultural whole cannot be functional, certainly not equally, and therefore their meaningfulness must be gathered from the whole to which they all belong. This structural holism of Lévi-Strauss seeks to operate at a higher level: beyond the lower-level fragments of history alluded to by such anthropologists as Boas.

Like Lévi-Strauss, Sartre admits that the basic concern of the historian is individual. But whereas the Straussian individual is paradigmatically a complex whole, the Sartrean individual is a free human being. The starting point of man's cognitive inquiry is his existential individuality and not, as Lévi-Strauss suggests, his holistic cultural affiliation and identity. Though man is affiliated to culture, that affiliation cannot take away his freedom to know or determine the range of knowledge achievable by exercising that freedom. The reason he makes use of in knowing the world around him is said to be dialectical. It has two components, positive and normative. By his reason man wants to know both what is the case and also how to relate it to the end of his life. This purposive or ideological perspective of human knowledge imparts a dynamic character to whatever he knows. Man's encounter with the Other and his knowledge of it are bound to contain a dialectical character.

If this premise is true, then not only higher-level history but also lower-level ethnography is ultimately grounded in the individual man's consciousness. If ethnography, history, and anthropology, irrespective of their micro- and macrocharacters, are really grounded in man's consciousness, then Strauss raises the critical question: should we think man on his own is the author of all forms of human knowledge? The Straussian rejection of Sartrean extreme individualism is clear in the question. According to him, subject, goal, and method of both history and anthropology are identical. Their difference lies in the fact that whereas the historian deals with what is *consciously* social, the anthropologist goes deeper and is concerned with both the conscious and the *unconscious* elements of social life. In effect, Lévi-Strauss contests the Sartrean notion of the *transparent* consciousness of the individual human being. Marx is right in affirming that individuals are the real makers of history, but Lévi-Strauss, following Freud, points out that they do not necessarily do so in a conscious way. Our authorship of history is only partly conscious. And what we are determined to do by our social conditions is never entirely available to our consciousness. Therefore, Lévi-Strauss speaks of the necessity for the historian to move from what is socially explicit to what is socially implicit. This is a movement primarily confined *within* a culture. In contrast, the anthropologist's main concern is not his own consciousness, self-consciousness, or history as obtained within and made by his self. He wants to understand both self and the other, the latter from the point of view of the former.

This transition from Self to the Other would not have been possible if other cultures had not exhibited some relational structures. Strauss is obsessively concerned with the binary relational structures said to be evident in every culture. He finds these common structural features both in human systems (cultures) and in their linguistic systems (languages). He refuses to accept the Sartrean criticism that these structural universals are constructs of analytic reason. He accords them a "real" life, and this reality is said to consist in their *actual functional* efficacy. To say that language has a structure and life of its own is to affirm that actual uses of language, if recorded and coded, would exhibit the said structures. Whereas Lévi-Strauss affirms the substantial isomorphism between social structure and language structure, he is careful enough to concede that their correlation is not 100 percent positive. These differential features of separate cultures are partly responsible for his rejection of a universal "metaphysical view of history." He seems to be equally circumspect in his defence of linguistic universals. According to him, linguistic science, is, at first, that is, provisionally a priori, but *may* cease to be so a posteriori, that is, functionally. In a way he concedes that neither cultural universals nor linguistic universals are to be accepted as a priori valid. The question of their validity is open-ended and has to be decided in terms of their applicability to and consilience with actual field data, ethnographic, historical, and linguistic. Man's relationship with fellow human beings and the world at large is understandable both implicitly or symbolically and explicitly or in the light of details. To be precise, it must be mentioned that, according to Lévi-Strauss, even the "field data" or "details" are microstructured, not disparate and discrete. Microstructures test the validity-claim of macro-structures.

Whenever the question of validation, verification, or demonstration arises, the related questions that become inevitable are, valid for whom? verification for whom? demonstration to whom? If the answers to these questions are presented in an abstract and "objective" manner, Sartre feels, we achieve little that is precious. According to him, the question of validation of historical knowledge is essentially a matter of praxis, individual or group. Authored by human beings, historical totalities are judged in terms of their approximation to or distance from the intended goal. Since every human being is more or less irresistibly free, historical totalities always include fissures and frictions. Consequently, no totality can have a unified end in view. For the same reason the means chosen by different groups and individuals to constitute the totality are often found to be incongruent or conflicting. As a result of all these things, the intended goal frequently proves to be divergent, mixed up with unintended consequences, or even elusive. Like the unity of historical totalities, their goals are marked by opposite pulls and pushes. Dialectical unity of life cannot have any clear-cut analytic or unified goal.

Historical totalities are conceived by Sartre as extending the analogy of self-history. When from the question of self-history we move to that of understanding the Other, the Sartrean model is fated to face the problematic legacy of Cartesian dualism. If the individual cogito cannot be the sole constituent force for the totalisation of its own group or totality and faces opposition within it, how can it be plausibly credited with the capacity of constituting the Other, comprising other cultural totalities within it, as homogeneous or unified? Anticipating this pertinent and critical question, Sartre frames his answer mainly by emphasising the concept of *the unity of the opposites* as the heart of his dialectical reason. He realises, can almost see for himself, that there is no unified view or understanding in Contemporary Society, CS(T3), of the subculture "science" of Primitive Society, PS(T1). In fact, most of the contemporary historians of science would refuse to recognise the "science" of the primitive society as genuine science. They prefer the term *magic* for it.

Here a little refinement perhaps is necessary. Even the philosophical-minded historians like Sartre and Kuhn and anthropologists like Lévi-Strauss and Malinowski, all belonging to contemporary society, do not agree in their characterisation of the "science" of the primitive society. Even about the advisability of using the term *magic* they are not unanimous. *Our* views of their "magic" or "science" hardly coincide with *theirs*. Our assessment of their technology is not shared by them. Primitive classifications of things and beings are different from modern classification of the same. The point to be noted is that even the expression "the same" is bracketed. This suggests that from within a culture it is difficult to grasp other cultures truly. Even the term *true*, given the Sartrean conception of history, is bound to be bracketed, for truth or falsity of a view turns out to be context-bound. And *authentic*, a value-loaded term, usually takes the place of *true*. Highlighting this dilemma of the Sartrean view of history, Lévi-Strauss reiterates the necessity and rationality of *structural* anthropology. Unless we recognise *cultural universals*, the Sartrean dilemma cannot be resolved. Sartre's main mistake seems to lie in trying to defend a highly personalised and ideologised view of history. If every enterprise of understanding is value-loaded and goal-oriented, it is difficult to see our way through the thick of facts and to get down to the bottom-level ethnographic data of other cultures. Our view of them can be verified, at least partially, by comparing our views with theirs with "reference" to the concerned things and beings. But scrutiny reveals that the said reference is somewhat opaque. The effect of opacity can be minimised by repeatedly examining details, interpreting and reinterpreting details, and exchanging views with the persons close to the concerned cultural scene. Even then, it has to be admitted, "we" cannot replace "they," nor can our views replace theirs.

It is for this reason that Lévi-Strauss pleads for conceptual simplicity without disregarding empirical diversity. It is for the same reason that he prefers analytical reason to dialectical reason. In order to enable us to understand and write, however imperfect that writing may be, the history of the Other, we are urged to span the gap between Self and Other by analytical reason. According to Lévi-Strauss, Sartre's dialectical reason, being somewhat conscious of its own limits, tries to go beyond itself. It is nothing but a form, an *active* form, of analytical reason itself. Straussian analytical reason tries to assimilate Sartrean dialectical reason within it.

In fact, Sartre himself speaks of two forms of dialectical reason. According to one form, dialectical reason and analytical reason are antithetical, and, according to the other, they are complementary and compatible. Analytical reason may be viewed as reason at rest, dialectical reason as the creative or constitutive form of it. Reason in every man has two aspects, self-affirming and self-exceeding. In its self-affirming aspect man creates microstructures, smaller social aggregates with which anthropology is primarily concerned. In its self-transcendental aspect reason tries to form macrostructures, larger social aggregates.

This distinction must not be taken in an absolute sense. For microstructures are partly broken up and partly preserved in macrostructures. Conversely speaking, macrostructures nesting multiple microstructures within them are not necessarily isomorphic. Some sort of conflict between the two always goes on. One might say that it is inherent in the very nature of dialectical reason and symptomatic of the unity of the opposite tendencies in human nature. By this account of dialectical reason Sartre tries to show that simultaneously it answers the needs of the anthropologist and those of the historian. Since all structures, macro and micro, are products of human praxis, individual and group, their truth is disclosed and established through praxis itself. In the process structural totalities are detotalised and retotalised. It is a *continuous* process. Like the history of science, it knows no finality. The final *unity* of science is merely a *hope* of the scientist and not his achievement. Given Sartre's view of history, anthropology is transformed into history and, Lévi-Strauss complains, past events are updated and made contemporaneous with the period of the historian. On the other hand, Sartre fears that if history is allowed to be structurally anthropologised in the Straussian fashion, the very *process* character of history will be stilled, its human authorship denied, and history itself as history killed. Anthropology must not be allowed to be the killer of history.

This criticism of structuralism is unacceptable to Lévi-Strauss. The structuralist, having first distanced himself from the antihistorical functionalists like Malinowski, tries to rebut the criticism of ahistoricality against him. He argues that his account of past science is marked by *double* appropriation of history. To start with, he takes into account the ethnographic data about science and technology of other cultures and then brings them together into a meaningful structure or totality through generalisation. Later on, structural features of different cultures are compared, contrasted, and thus tested. If history is not introduced in this way at two different levels into anthropology, we are likely to repeat the error of Sartrean historiography. Lévi-Strauss complains that Sartre mythologises history, keeps it distant from us, and views the science of other cultures by applying criteria of our own science, that is, of our own time and place. By decontextualising the "science" of other times and places what we get is not their history but only its imported fragments and as elements of our own history.

Lévi-Strauss feels that this way of assimilation of the Other into Self gives us metaphysical history and not anthropologically verifiable history. He himself wants to show that anthropology and history, spatiality and temporality, are symmetrical. If history is accorded an asymmetrical primacy over anthropology, assuming that it would provide us a privileged view of past science, we commit an avoidable error. For historians' *selective* approach and *ideological* orientation, or chosen goal, are bound to emasculate the facts of history or the ethnographic data. History must not be construed as history *for* this or that person or group. When history is unnecessarily ideologised, it tends to be more propagandist than informative. Ideological history may serve the purpose of motivating people, but that does not mean the account it gives of the past is correct. However, this cautious formulation of history need not be taken as a plea for total value-neutrality.

Rightly understood, I think, structuralism and historism are not antithetical. The historian, in his reflective moments, can easily realise how often, may be unconsciously, he makes extensive use of such structural notions as year, century, and millennium. The time used by the historian is social or cultural and not physical and has no intrinsic metric of its own.

But the critic may raise the question, If we are intellectually bound to use structures in our history in general, and in our history of science, in particular, how can we assure ourselves that our structural accounts are correct? Along two different, but not necessarily incompatible, ways we may get down to the details of the concerned culture, the ethnographic data. If, for example, we want to know the correct, or at least the reliable, history of science in India, we must try to know more about the pertinent facts from the historian, the archaeologist, the philologist, and other specialists working in different empirical disciplines. Second, we may initially ignore the details and ascend to a superstructural height so that from that "vantage" point we may look at the details as parts of a unified whole, a meaningful totality. In the latter case the knowing subject is transcendental humanity and not this or that individual historian.

The suggested ways out represent two extreme views, neither of which seems to be humanly practicable, still less achievable. What as realist we should aim at is an integrated approach that takes due note of both *specific details* and *general principles*. We do need general principles in order to understand the details of history as a relational whole or meaningful continuum. The details are necessary in order to ensure that general principles do not turn out to be arbitrary, ad hoc, and unrelatable to the life-world. Reflection makes it clear that respect for both details and principles is not a mere methodological prescription. In fact, this is the phenomenology of our understanding, the faithful description of the ways that our mind actually works. Our mind by virtue of its cultural embodiedness is deeply committed to certain general principles. At the same time, the fullness and richness of our experience do not lend themselves to absolutely *neat* conceptualisation, *exhaustive* classification, and *infallible* interpretation. Consequently, our efforts to conceptualise the items of experience, their classification and interpretation, have to be carried on endlessly and critically renewed from time to time according to our informed needs.

V

The complementarity between structuralism and historism is not confined to the study of culture. Its validity can be illustrated from the study of language as well. In fact, it is instructive to note the view that anthropology may itself be rightfully viewed as a branch of semiology. Every culture with its all *signifying* subjects and *significant* objects is a system of signs and symbols. It is we, the human beings, who are capable of signifying and symbolising what in some sense or other we have *in* us. Different uses of signs — demonstrative, connotative, relational, and so on — are due to us. Different structures of signs — propositional, sentential, inferential, and so forth, are also due to us. Such concepts as "propositions-in-themselves" and "natural meanings" are abstract, bloodlessly realistic, and spurious. It is true that external objects, ideas, and fancies are not created or authored by us. But in an important way they are also to be found within us. Independently of their modes of being given to us we cannot speak of them meaningfully. Representations of the outer world in the inner world are rarely direct, literal, or picturesque. Therefore, every item of experience, when perceived or received by us, is more or less transformed or transfigured by our native interpretative capacity and activity.

In spite of the interpretative transformation of "objects" in consciousness, when we articulate them in and through signs and symbols, they are generally proved to be intelligible to others. Neither our reception of objects nor their articulation and communication are entirely passive in character. We give them meaning or sense. We cannot but do so. When man is defined as a semiotic being, what in effect is sought to be highlighted is the *spontaneous* character of his interpretative and constitutive activities. A sign cannot work as a sign unless there is some man-signifier or group of men-signifiers behind it. For example, a Red Cross sign (+), physically speaking, is indistinguishable from a plus sign (+). Similarly, the logical sign of implication is hardly distinguishable from what is called horse shoe ($\supset$) or arrow ($\twoheadrightarrow$). We can easily conceive some country where the Red Cross Society and its sign are completely unknown. In that country the physical Red Cross sign will not signify "anything" (that we will be able to understand). Analogously, a person who knows nothing of modern symbolic logic cannot understand why a horse shoe ($\supset$) should be regarded as something called implication. Things qua things are not *significantly* relatable. Their relational network or system is rooted in the capacity and activity of some human beings. Signs are signs only within a culture authored by some people for themselves as well as for some other people. To put it differently: sign is made possible by some selves and is communicable and understandable by other selves.

To say that the sign-signified relationship is simple and direct is to miss the role of the signifier and his acts, interpreting and signifying. What is more, a sign is always meant to serve some specific purpose or purposes. Besides, the author or the user of a sign, the signifier, has always in view some people for whom a sign may work as a sign.

This complexity of a semiotic situation is more theoretical than practical. If our sign-using practices are closely inspected, the components of the complex situation become clearly evident. When we repeatedly emphasise the social character of a sign, what we have in view is its relational character. Sign, like human action, needs some people who are socially and epistemically akin to the signifier. Similarly, an action fails to be significant unless its "internal" intention or its "external" expression, preferably both, proves somehow sharable by the fellow human beings of the actor.

Unless we can grasp the human capacity to signify and the way the signified thing or idea is understood by the people for whom it is intended, we are not able to explain the possibility of intracultural and intercultural communication, conversation, discourse, and dialogue. In complementary ways anthropology and history are both concerned with intracultural and intercultural communication.

But philosophers differ with regard to the nature of the signifier, the signifying man and his fellow human beings. Different theories of history and anthropology are traceable to different concepts of human nature. Reflection makes it abundantly clear that science as a subculture of human culture lends itself easily to semiological or linguistic analysis and understanding. Different concepts of science, empirist-realist, contextualist, and transcendentalist, are very intimately connected with different concepts of human nature, phenomenalist, phenomenological, and transcendental. Needless to say, these concepts are not necessarily exclusive or exhaustive. For example, the empiricist need not necessarily be committed to realism; he may be a radical phenomenalist. The contextualist may or may not be realist. Transcendentalism goes well with both idealism and realism.

There are still other ways of conceptualising scientific *activities* or science as an *institution*. The two ways we have highlighted are historical or fluxist and structural (anthropological). In two cases, what we are minimally required to account for is how scientific theories are validated or invalidated, accepted or rejected, supported or criticised. These questions cannot be settled, this way or that, unless the related questions of criteria of rejection or selection and evaluation of evidence, internal or external, are satisfactorily settled. The structuralists are of the view that science as a cognitive system is to be primarily judged in terms of its structural properties: how the signs and symbols of a particular science have been meaningfully totalised into a coherent structure. The rules of synthesis or structural totalisation have to be taken into account. According to this view, if scientific signs and symbols, constitutive concepts, and regulative ideas can be shown to be meaningfully structurable, then it favourably decides the method of validating science.

Kant's transcendental argument purported to vindicate science may be cited as an example of this variety of structural validation. And underlying this sort of transcendental structuralism there is a distinct view of human nature. The ultimate certification of science has to come from the transcendental self and its synthetic apperceptive capacity. There is said to be no tribunal above or beyond it. This sort of transcendental structural validation seems to put a stamp of finality on science or, to be more precise, on a particular paradigm of it.

All structuralists are not antihistorists. Some of them are not slow to point out that scientific views, be they called magic, philosophy, or science proper, though meaningfully structurable, need not be taken as final or conclusive. In the light of new negative findings or ethnographic data the constructed structure may have to be deconstructed and reconstructed. When, for example, Lévi-Strauss claims that his variety of structuralism is doubly historical, both regressively and progressively, he concedes that scientific structures can neither be arbitrarily constructed nor abruptly abandoned. Both at the stage of construction and at the stage of validation relevant facts and findings have to be taken into account. Ethnology or comparative anthropology, not adequately based upon and tested by ethnographic data, is bound to be abstract and a priori (in the bad sense).

It is not difficult to find out the concept of human nature presupposed by Lévi-Strauss. That man is endowed with transcendental capacity is evidently assumed by him. He chooses his data in the light of his native universals. But even then he feels rationally obliged to test his generalisations based on these data by further relevant data. Structural generalisations are made answerable to the new data. In this respect Straussian structuralism is definitely prohistorical and different from the Kantian model.

Even this modified version of structuralism represented by Lévi-Strauss is unacceptable to Sartre. He finds that neither Kant nor Lévi-Strauss adequately recognises the creative-constitutive capacity of human nature. The Kantian man is *universal* and so is his knowledge. The Straussian man is *universalisable* and so is his science. Sartre's man is existential and free. His freedom, though situational, is extendible. And his image of science, though mindful of positive facts, is end-conscious, if not ideologised. Besides, he believes in multiple images of science. This is a corollary of his historism and differential situatedness of existential human beings and their groups. The only concession he is prepared to make to the ideal of universal science is based on human freedom and the cultural convergence progressively emerging from that freedom. Praxis of (free) human groups, he thinks, will bring about an increasing convergence of human views and values.

Basically Sartre is a situationalist or contextualist. In the name of universalism he is not prepared to accept the view that what man creates, science, language, or art, will be really universal or even universalisable. He is not interested in any foundationalist view of knowledge or in the ideal unity of knowledge. From history we get only a continuous, progressive-regressive, primarily progressive, and continuous account of science. Till the modern time, the lived structures of human beings are found to be basically micro. The larger sociopolitical aggregates are more or less unlived and formal. The preceding forms of duality between historism and structuralism may also be illustrated in the field of linguistics.

While empiricists like Skinner and Quine think that language acquisition of children and of different language-speaking groups has to be explained in terms of stimulus-response and reinforcement, rationalists like Jakobson and Chomsky are of the view that without postulating linguistic universals we cannot explain these bewilderingly diverse empirical data. The structuralism of the latter is of two kinds, *substantive* and *formal*. Traditional universal grammar and Jakobson's phonological theory may be regarded as substantive. According to this view, the underlying syntactic structure of all languages is identical and comparable universals may be dug out by analysing the basic characteristics, for example, of designative (signifying) functions and connotative (signifying) ones. The *formal* theory of linguistic universals is relatively abstract. According to the formalist, the syntactic aspect of a grammar contains transformation rules mapping semantically interpreted deep structures into phonologically interpreted surface structures. Formal universals are claimed to be available also at the semantic level. For example, proper names of all languages designating objects are required to satisfy a formal condition of spatiotemporal continuity. Whereas formalists like Chomsky maintain that all languages in their depth are cut to the same pattern, that does not mean that there is any point-to-point correspondence between different languages or that there are rules for definite interlinguistic translation.

It is clear that Chomsky has liberalised and reinterpreted his position in the light of criticisms of his theory of deep-seated linguistic universals. By highlighting the issue of creativity and that of the absence of interlinguistic translation procedure, he makes some concession to what I call historism and contextualism. How proper names work can hardly be decided without taking into account the context of their uses. Not only descriptions, but even proper names are in the nature of a text or, etymologically speaking, a piece of textile. The elements from which a text is prepared or a textile piece woven are drawn from different sources and put to different uses.

It is not surprising that those who advocate the theories of linguistic universals and speak of a universal grammar are ordinarily found to be innatist in epistemology, because they fear that if they compromise on innatism in linguistics, then historism, contextualism, and anthropologism will take over the whole ground. The unitary model of language learning and knowledge of language will be irreparably damaged. In endless diversity the deep-structured unity of all natural languages will be forgotten.

This issue, time and again, has appeared in different branches of knowledge, from metaphysics and mathematics to history and anthropology. We find that some thinkers, such as Leibniz, Kant, and Husserl, are engaged in defending such theses as "universal mathematics," "scientific metaphysics," "universal history," and "universal rigorous science." We also notice that some others, such as Hume, Marx, Heidegger, and Sartre, are trying to highlight the diversity of human culture in all spheres: economic, political, moral, and so on. The basic point that has drawn my repeated attention in this respect is the fact that neither can the antihistorist ignore the historical features of different cultures nor can the prohistorist be blind to the structural similarities of different cultures. Whatever name is given to "science," it is difficult to deny for anybody, irrespective of his cultural affiliation, that there are certain activities that are cognitively kindred and provide information, if not comprehension, of what goes on within man and around him, and that their result is "testable" in some form or other.

In my study I have particularly examined the duality between "ideal" and "real" objects, between "logical" and "real" necessities, between "logical" and "real" grounds (of knowledge). In this connection, the views of Husserl have drawn my special attention. It is interesting to note that on these related subjects Husserl's views have undergone significant changes over his long professional career. Initially (1901), to him, phenomenology was a sort of descriptive psychology. Later on, he purged it more and more of the psychological elements, paving the way for pure phenomenology. He criticised the psychologism underlying the logical works of Sigwart and Wundt, who were very influential in Germany toward the end of the last century and the beginning of this century. He drew a sharp distinction between what is factually real and what is ideally real, between factual truth and ideal truth.

> The truth itself is . . . above time: i.e., it makes no sense to attribute temporal being to it nor to say that it arises or perishes. This absurdity is clearest in the case of the laws of truths themselves. If

> they were "real" laws, they would be reals for the coexistence and succession of facts, i.e., of such facts as are truths, and to these facts, which they govern, they themselves as truths would belong. . . . The law would [then] arise and perish in conformity with the law, a patent absurdity. . . . Such absurdities are unavoidable if the fundamental distinction between ideal and real objects, and the corresponding distinction between ideal and real laws is disregarded or misunderstood.[1]

Husserl's anxiety is understandable. If the knowing man is recognised as the author of knowledge, its validity-claim is to be left somehow or other to the knowing man himself. In that case phenomenology, whether it is regarded as descriptive psychology or epistemological criticism of psychology, fails to assume the dignity of pure logic or true science. Husserl is determined to show that what is true is absolutely so, intrinsically so, and has nothing to do with "man or non-man," "angels or gods" and their apprehension and judgment of it. "Logical laws speak of truth in this ideal unity, set over against the real multiplicity of races, individuals and experiences, and it is of this ideal unity that we all speak when we are not confused by relativism."[2] In the Husserlian ideal unity of knowledge there is no place for relativism, anthropological or historical. He explicitly rejects the anthropologism of Sigwart's logic. He seems to be impatient with the view that *unknown* truth is fictitious. The being of truth does not consist in its being known by man, angel, or god. "Our truth . . . remains in itself what it is, it retains its ideal being . . . in the timeless realm of Ideas."[3] It is clear that Husserl is seriously engaged in establishing true science. The essence of that science consists in its unity and in the validation of the grounds that make it possible. The grounded validations interweave isolated pieces of knowledge into a systematic unity. When this unity is found, Husserl claims, we go beyond the grounded validation and see their unity. And he calls this unity a theory of science; it is a science of sciences; it is logic.

Husserl's serious determination to keep logic, the best possible form of knowledge, free of psychologism, anthropologism, and relativism is understandable. But the question that remains unanswered is how a concrete shape is to be given to this Idea of science. Who can possibly make it possible? Husserl tells us explicitly that this "true and correct science is not our own [human] invention." In the same breath he adds that the science "is present in things, where we simply find or discover it."[4] What, in effect, Husserl asks us to believe is that the highest form of knowledge, though not our own invention, is found by us in the world of things. In other words, he has to demonstrate to us the unity of the world of things available to our experience and that of truths in themselves, timeless ideal beings.

Anybody who is interested in establishing all-comprehensive rigorous science is, of necessity, committed to give an account not only of ideal truths but also of the facts of the empirical world, including the fictitious objects. It is not that Husserl has not addressed himself to this problem. But the solutions he arrived at and offered in different phases of his long professional life do not appear to me satisfactory and critical.

In his earlier life the solution was framed in terms of ideal unity of truths, comprising regional unities of factual reals. In that picture individual man does not figure prominently.[5] There he is not mainly concerned with how the knowing subject, one's ego-pole, can possibly discover other things and beings, that is, objects, as meaningfully unified within himself.

In his later works, particularly in *The Crisis*, Husserl returns to this problem with vigor and determination. Here he claims to have found a satisfactory solution to the problem in terms of the principle of transcendental subjectivity as the constituted principle of all-comprehensive unity. But a close scrutiny gives rise to some basic difficulties. If for the sake of "ideal" unity "real" diversity of scientific objects, of historical and cultural facts, of fictions, of myths, and so on, are ignored, their "rough" edges suitably cut and polished, what we get is philosophy or metaphysics of history, including history of science and culture, but *not* history as we understand it. If the question of other human beings is brought into the picture, it becomes even more problematic. Glorification of theoretical "unity" does not necessarily call for downgrading of the tacticity of facts or even that of fictions. After all, fact-fiction dichotomy is not very easy to sustain. "Their" facts are "our" fictions and vice versa. All diversity of facts and fictions, I agree, can well be rolled into a meaningful unity, metaphysical or epistemic, but the cost factors, that is, the attending problems, have to be seriously taken into account by Husserl and his followers.

The first and foremost problem that disturbs me is the fact that, on the one hand, he asserts that, unlike Kant, he would not *presuppose* anything, objective or subjective, not even the unified principles of self-understanding and other-understanding, and, on the other hand, he endows the knowing subject with some transcendental capacities to transform the given objects of science, facts and fancies of different cultures, into a meaningful whole.[6] True, Husserl is aware of the paradox of treating human subjectivity both as a subject for the world and at the same time as an object in the world. How can other human beings, "objects" in the world, possibly be regarded by me as a part of our "common we"? Husserl's way of solving the paradox is to claim that objectivity of all objects, of things and beings alike, is provisional (*epoche*). Gradually, I start realising that I have in me a universal capacity of intersubjective constitution. Ultimately I see that my "ego-pole" and others' "ego-poles" are identically constituted. But who makes it possible? And how? The Kantian inspiration of the Husserlian way of solving the paradox is unmistakable. Like Kant, Husserl asks us to believe that the objective world was always concealed within our own subjective world and that it is only the regressive movement of our understanding that has enabled us to discover the concealed world as a part of our own universal being. However, Kant's transcendental reals, things-in-themselves, are not in any way constituted but presupposed. Husserl's antipresuppositionalism dispenses with things-in-themselves but commits him to postulate some transcendental capacities in every ego-pole that enables it to internalise or constitute all other ego-poles, "their" facts, fictions, and so on.

Second, it seems to me that Husserl's admiration for mathematics, especially the Leibnizian notion of universal mathesis, makes him somewhat blind to the insistent Otherness of the Other. He discards the propsychological logician's view that the drift of our thought from less general levels to increasingly more general ones is based on reasons of economy and simplicity. To him, this line of thinking is tainted by a sort of naturalism or presuppositionalism. The ideal logical laws are present in each thought as their inherent basement, guiding principles, and not as presuppositions. The laws of pure mathematics are present in all spheres of applied mathematics not as the distant ideals of the latter but as their own inner driving forces, as the drawing forces of truth. Husserl's laudatory references to the Leibnizian notions of *mathesis universalis* and *Ars Combinatoria* and Bolzano's science of logic give an idea of the direction of his own thought. To him, the unitary interconnection of things is inseparable from the unitary interconnection of truths. In this way Husserl makes use of Bolzano's notion of truths-in-themselves and tries to relate it to the truths of empirical propositions.[7] Thus the Platonist in him is never inhibited by the endless diversity of the thing-world from idealising and mathematising it. Only with the passage of time and as the result of deeper reflection does he seem to have realised the necessity of highlighting his commitment to phenomenology, that is, the necessity of returning to experience in search of the original sense of the ideal unity of knowledge.[8] There also one notices the vacillation of his position vis-à-vis the said two worlds. Whereas, on the one hand, he earnestly expresses his commitment to the man of psychology and anthropology and his experience as the starting point of his ideal of exact science, on the other hand, he keeps on systematically reminding us of the necessity and elegance of the mathematics of continua and analytic geometry. The Platonic ideal of geometrising the world of shadows never seems to have left him. Until and unless he can show the geometrisability not only of the physical world but also of the historical world, he does not feel that physics and history could be regarded as the original elements of the exact science of his dream.[9] Exaggerated fear of relativism and scepticism seems to have driven him to the extremity of Platonism, paying only parenthetic tribute to the acknowledged importance of the life-world. Had he been more seriously concerned with the reality of the life-world and its endless complexity and peculiarity, his commitment to the ideal of universal mathematics or pure geometry would not have been so uncritical.

Like Leibniz he finds everything in every being. He finds no gap between the intramonadic world and the intermonadic world. All worlds are claimed to be subjectively constituted. Anticipating the possible criticism of naturalism he speaks of "transcendental subjectivity" instead of "mere subjectivity." Similarly, to preserve the radical stance of his phenomenology, he speaks of criticism. Here, too, following the footsteps of Kant, by criticism he means internal criticism, that is, self-criticism. Curiously enough, in this proclaimed self-criticism the other, the external, things and beings, have little or no say at all.

My last major criticism of Husserl's transcendental philosophy centres around his hybrid concept of *historical a priori*. It betrays the inner tension between his commitment to the life-world and antipresuppositionalism, on the one hand, and to geometrisation of physics and idealisation of history and culture, on the other. The first point to be noted is that the transcendental philosopher himself is historically situated and belongs to a definite culture. The next question pertains to his transcendental subjectivity. Is he by virtue of this capacity lifted above his historical situatedness and put in cognitive communion with other human beings? Or should we take the more radical possible interpretation of this capacity, "the historical" (situatedness) itself, as "transcendental and ideal"? Husserl's proposed answers to these questions are bound to remind one of Leibniz and Kant. Whereas, according to Leibniz, the facts of history are objective and intermonadically sharable by virtue of their a priori availability, Kant speaks of the possibility of reviewing them as parts of a universal totality in terms of the unitary regulative Idea of Reason. Intermonadic sharability and intersubjectivity are kindred concepts. Husserl's concepts of transcendental subjectivity and constitution unmistakably bear the Leibniz-Kant legacy.

Like his predecessors, he affirms the possibility of unitary idealisation not only of natural objects but also of cultural ones. And, like them, he believes that this ideal science is rooted in some a priori capacities of the essential man. This man and his capacities know no boundary, natural, cultural or historical. On the contrary, the whole universe (with all that is natural, cultural, or historical in it as its different regions and shapes) is constituted by man's transcendental constitutive capacity. This capacity is claimed to be essentially unfettered and free. Nothing can block its progressive self-explication or horizontal expansion. More radically speaking, there is nothing, literally *nothing*, external to it that can possibly block its path of (transcendental phenomenological) progress. Nothing owes its sense to it.[10]

Husserlian "historical a priori" is hardly historical at all. It is admittedly a priori. If everything, every item of our unitary system of science (or knowledge), from fact and fancy to nothing, is constituted by (man's) a priori capacity, transcendental subjectivity, nothing in the world or even beyond it that can possibly, even minimally, deconstitute or reconstitute the system is left. In that case, one strongly feels, the system is *not* historical; it is metaphysical or transcendental in the *uncritical* sense. The life-world is given no critical say in the constitution of the system. The empirical turns out to be secretly transcendental. The former is allowed entry into the system only to play the inevitable second fiddle to the latter. It is a sort of getting the got, as Samkara, the Advaita Vedantin, would have perhaps liked to describe the situation. I find, to my dismay, that in the constitution of the transcendental phenomenological system of knowledge the life-world is assigned no *critical* say whatsoever.

I am not the only person to feel dismayed by this sort of situation. Dilthey criticises Kant on this very ground. Heidegger rejects Husserl's "enclosed" view of history based on internal time-consciousness and defends a view of history as "disclosure" of man as determined and individuated by time. Gadamer's and Ricoeur's criticisms of Husserl's theory of knowledge and philosophy of history seem eminently sensible to me and are akin to my own line of thinking.

Dilthey's Critique of Historical Reason, though fashioned after Kant's Critiques, is structurally very different from the latter. To start with, he rejects the Cartesian ideal of cogitolike certainty in knowledge. Engaged in search for a rational answer to the question, How is historically meaningful experience possible?, Dilthey finds that Kant's transcendental structure is unnecessary, if not contrived, and, what is worse, obstructs our path to the lived world where we can discover the answer. The lived life has a structure of its own. Time is in it. And its building blocks are not only cognitive but also affective, violative, and conative. It contains sedimented past as well as futural contents in the forms of desire, hope, and so forth. Kant's categories appear to him artificially clear-cut, exhaustive, and therefore unacceptable. By recognising *value* and *purpose* among his categories he succeeds in bringing valued past and solicited future into the heart of the lived present. Besides, it makes the structure itself historical or *developmental*. Human experience fails to be meaningful unless its *parts* and *whole* are both recognised as mutually complementary and equally necessary to each other. It fails to be *critical* and dynamic if the inner-outer distinction is pulled down and everything "outer" is unilaterally internalised by invoking some transcendental principle. Dilthey's categories of historical reason, despite the lack of clarity in their formulation, are worth recalling for understanding, to some extent, how and where Husserl, following Kant, went wrong. Husserl's own criticism of Dilthey and Brentano on the alleged ground of their failure to follow the important distinction between *descriptive* and *theoretical* psychology is rooted in his robust transcendentalism and resulting unwillingness to see that the elements of descriptive psychology are themselves theorisable and structurable. Dilthey's psychology is in fact the surface structure of a nonessentialist and antitranscendentalist anthropology.[11] With the steady emergence of cognitive psychology as a *respectable* discipline of knowledge the age of antipsychologism seems to be on the wane.

It is not that Heidegger is averse to use of the concept of structure. In fact, he does use it rather extensively. The fundamental concept of *Dasein* is itself said to be structured in the world. In a way it emerges from that structure. But the intelligibility of that structure is rooted in *Dasein's* capacity to thematise the structural and substructural components of the world. Thus Heidegger, somewhat like Husserl himself, faces the problem of solving the paradox of man's being-in-world and being himself an articulation of the world. But his solution of the paradox differs from Husserl's. First, he rejects the man-world dualism postulated by Kant. By criticising Kant's formal and empty principle of "I think" he points out that it has to be replaced by the concrete principle of "I think something." He argues to show that man's thought cannot be thought without being thought of something. And that "something" being a part of the world man's knowledge cannot avoid being both human and world-ly at the same time. Second, it is pointed out by Heidegger, evidently under the influence of Husserl, that to understand the fundamental struc-ture of being in terms of biology, psychology, and anthropology is not of much help, at least not in their traditional forms. In the process he critically refers to Dilthey and Bergson's "personalistic" approach to man (anthropology), mind (psychology), and life (biology). Their approaches, though philosophical, are not ontologically foundational. In this respect he stands closer to Husserl and Scheler. He prefers phenomenological understanding to their positivist formulations because the former pro-vides the resources necessary for delving into the depth of human ontology.

The central issue of all ontology is human ontology, and it is rooted in the phenomenon of time. It is through temporal determinations that man is disclosed and becomes available to us. However, before man's disclosure he must be deemed to have an a priori position within the structure of the world. But to speak meaningfully of this structure one has to first get into the being of man. It is in this sense that man is *primarily* a temporalised phenomenon. He is also structured a priori within the world. This hiddenness or concealment is more in the modern man than in the primitive man, and for that reason Heideg-ger emphasises the point of studying the structure of primitive man rather than that of his modern counterpart.

In any case man, despite his very nature of phenomenological disclosure or uncovering, can negate his transcendental structural roots, accounting for the further possibilities of his disclosure.[12]

Whereas Husserl prefers the primitive life-structure of man to the modern one for the authentic understanding of man as a phenomenon, as we have already noted, he is sceptical about the nature of the help available from traditional psychology, sociology and ethnology in the matter. He is very doubtful of the value of the scientific data provided

by these disciplines for the purpose of expounding an adequate analytic
of *Dasein*.

> We shall not get a genuine knowledge of essence simply by the syn-
> cretistic activity of universal comparison and classification. Subject-
> ng the manifold to tabulation does not ensure any actual understand-
> ng of what lies there before us as thus set in order. If an ordering
> principle is genuine, it has its own content as a thing *[Sachgehalt]*,
> which is never to be found by means of such ordering, but is already
> presupposed in it. So if one is to put various pictures of the world
> in order, one must have an explicit idea of the world as such. And
> if the "world" itself is something constitutive for *Dasein*, one must
> have an insight into *Dasein's* basic structuring in order to treat the
> world-phenomenon conceptually.[13]

What is true of social structure is also true of natural structure: the
structure of nature as found in the laws of natural sciences. Here also
the question of a priori truth comes up in a roundabout way. The
concept of truth as understood by Heidegger can in no way be independent of man. In and through man truth becomes what it is. The
question of truth and falsity without reference to man does not make
any sense. However, from this one must not conclude that truth is
relative to this or that man or that man is the measure of truth.

> To say that before Newton his laws were neither true nor false, can-
> not signify that before him there were no such entities as have been
> uncovered and pointed out by those laws. Through Newton the laws
> became true; and with them, entities became accessible in themselves
> to Dasein. Once entities have been uncovered, they show themselves
> precisely as entities which beforehand were already there. Such un-
> covering is the kind of Being which belongs to "truth."[14]

This conception of truth is evidently different from that of Husserl.
Heidegger strongly denies the concept of *truth-in-itself*. He is also
opposed to the concept of *eternal truth*. However, he is cautious enough
to remind us of his antirelativistic persuasion. The entities that are
captured in and made available to us by the laws of physics in and
through our being are not constituted by our being. They are grounded
in the world itself. But of this ground we can significantly talk only
through our own being's disclosure. It is our being that thematises
the entities of nature and projects them into nature. Even mathematical
formulation and projection are due to us. What is disclosed by our

projection is *"something that is a priori".* Heidegger goes to the extent of asserting that the paradigmatic character of mathematical natural science is not to be found in its exactitude or universality: "it consists rather in the fact that the entities which it takes as its theme are discovered in [the concerned sciences] in the only way in which entities can be discovered — by the prior projection of their state of being."[15]

On the one hand, Heidegger denies the *existence* of the unknown and eternal truth; on the other hand, he speaks of the a priori and structured existence of the entities represented by the laws of science. This anomaly or mixup of realism and idealism is due to the initial lack of explication of the concept of existence. Since, to him, the paradigmatic *existence* is human, he finds nothing wrong in defending realistic ontology in humanistic, seemingly relativistic, idioms. In the context of history he repeats this structural a priori argument. To him, the historical is in a sense, an existential sense, human. Yet he insists that the entities that are said to be historical have their own being. Though he assigns *primary* history to man, that does not prevent him from pointing out that what is thus disclosed in and through man has its being in the world itself "We contend that what is *primarily* historical is *Dasein*. That which is *secondarily* historical, however, is what we encounter within the world."[16]

In a very significant way Heidegger anticipates the basic ideas both of structuralism and of historism, especially the latter. Time and again he speaks of the existentially paradigmatic character of man. Equally he is emphatic in his assertion of the primary history of man. Negatively speaking, man's history is not parasitic upon the social structure to which he belongs or the ontological structure that he articulates or discloses. His repeated reference to the objective structures of the entities represented by the laws of science is indicative of his realistic sympathy. But his phenomenological interpretative idioms seek to hide it from our understanding. Here also his difference from Husserl is noteworthy.

Once we take the notions of *human freedom* and *phenomenological interpretation* seriously, then from Husserl via Heidegger we can traverse a long way and indicate the line along which Husserl's transcendental phenomenology can be shown to be criticisable and given a new constructive interpretation. Must we think, following Husserl, that the ideal of universal rigorous science, when fulfilled, shall yield us the only possible *unique* science? Is that unique science a matter of discovery or constitution? If man is really free, it is difficult to think how his discovery of the past and projects of the future must always be consistent. It is not a question only of this or that individual man, his past and his future, but also of this or that society, its past and its future. Since past and future are not without some present connecting them, the question of understanding the present also proves problematic or, one might say, creatively diverse. If we step out for a while from the world of philosophy of theorisation and take note of the ideas and actions of our fellow human beings, we are bound to be struck by the diversity of their approaches. Living in the same society and in the same age, some of us speak of our glorious past, inglorious present, and doubtful future. Striking a different note, some others find that the past was dark, the present is misty, and the future is going to be bright. There are still others who strongly disapprove this epochwise or culturewise qualitative judgment: Even in the literature of historiography we come across different types, optimist, pessimist, realist, determinist, indeterminist, and so on.

Both from the sociology of facts and from the history of theories we find plurality of philosophy, multiplicity of historiography, and endless variety of literature. Is it symptomatic of real human freedom or a proof of anarchy in the field of knowledge? If Locke and Kant are right, the Newtonian paradigm of natural science should have been the last. If Hegel is right, his philosophy is the only philosophy in which the ideal of philosophy finds its self-realisation. A similar, but not quite identical, tendency is evident in Husserl's own thought.

I find no compelling reason to think that a rational philosophy in order to be rational has to be *the* philosophy, or that *a* rigorous science in order to be rigorous must be *the* science, or that a meaningful cultural totality in order to be really meaningful is required to be unique. Can we wish away the multiplicity of rational, rigorous, and meaningful philosophies, sciences, and cultures? Interestingly enough, even those who have been arguing down the centuries about *the* science or *the* philosophy are not unanimous in their choice of the major premise (the true nature of Absolute-God-Man) or of the minor premise (singular details). Consequently their conclusions cannot be identical in import. In the face of these recurring and insistent findings, both theoretical and practical, are we justified in trying to defend the "finalistic" views on any branch of human knowledge?

Contrary to the popular belief, reflection reveals that the artist is not the only creative man among us, freely creating (what we often mistakenly call his) dream-worlds, that is, fictitious worlds. The scientists, who claim to be faithful to the earthly details of experience and rigorous experimental methods, are also coming up with *different* paradigms of rigorous science, not only in different periods of history but also in the same period. Not only phenomenological philosophers like Husserl are unhappy with the fast-spreading dreaded "diseases" of relativism and scepticism; philosophers of science like Popper are equally opposed to the prevailing methodological "anarchy" and the resulting retreat from the realist-objective image of science.

What, then, is the upshot of the debate between structuralism and historism, between the proponents of a unique ideal system of knowledge and those of multiple systems of (equally genuine) knowledge? The question may be radically formulated, as it has been, by Ricoeur in his critical remarks on Husserl's a priori sense of history: Is history incomprehensible "if it is not a unique history unified by a sense?" Or does history cease to have its sense "if it is not an unforeseeable adventure?"[17] The metaphysical philosophy of history is understandably associated with the names of Kant, Hegel, and Husserl. If we accept their transcendental views, the critic can rightly complain, *historical* details lose their singular event-or action-structures in the seamless unity of the unique system of *philosophical* sense. Unity swallows multiplicity. Philosophy devours history to gain its sense.

The opposite thesis is that history is nothing more or nothing less than story. Like story, it too has its plot, a thematic unity, but that does not take away the singularity of its details. On the contrary, the latter unfolds the plot. This storic view of history has been ascribed to historians like Fisher and Geyl and philosophers like Croce, Collingwood, Oakeshott, and Dray. Then, between unique philosophy of history, philosophies of history, history and story where do we stand? How can we understand correctly their interrelationships, if any?[18]

Ricoeur's answers to the questions are partly critical and partly reconstructive of Husserl's views on the subject. On the one hand, he finds good reasons to take history as "an undivided and harmonious whole," and, on the other hand, he finds equally good reasons to view history as "the plurality of men . . . communities and civilizations." The reasons that make the constitution of the *whole* possible are said to be logos, language, and discourse. The working historian's main concern with the "granular" or "quantic" aspect of historical events may be ascribed to his aim to see for himself and show others the singularity of every individual event. According to Ricoeur, the *unity* of history and the *singularity* of the events recorded or narrated in history are not antithetical. However, their distinction must not be blurred. The fact that a Hegel or a Husserl can phenomenologise or even logicise the events of history does not mean that they have no individuality. The details that make history possible are by themselves not historical, still less philosophically historical. The nature of our understanding is such that at one level it is more concerned with grasping the structural unity of the events, the meaning of history. At another level, at the storic level, the events are recognised in their full-bloomed individuality. Certain details are so transparent, almost intrinsically meaningful, that they need not be shown as parts of a whole to disclose their meaning. Starting from the other end one might say that the whole does not have an *absolute* meaning of its own that is not in any way relative to its parts. Ricoeur seems to be justified in rejecting the supposed juxtaposition between "universal history" and "absolute singularity." "Universal history" does not exist; neither do "absolute singularities" exist . . . "[T]he ambiguity of history is . . . its imperfection, and this will always hold it a little short of that which would complete it: short of the goal of the unity of meaning or the goal of singular works [events]."[19]

The goal of the storyteller and that of the historian as a philosopher are clearly not identical. History as story has no language of its own, whereas the philosopher has. Philosophers of different schools or ideological persuasions systematise differently the same details. The main point that Ricoeur successfully drives home against Husserl is that in the name of giving a unity-sense to history he is not entitled to destroy the transparent singularity of individual events. If he is allowed to do so, one fears, history of science tends to degenerate into philosophy of science and, what is worse, *the* philosophy of science.

To salvage the basic elements of the Husserlian position a rearguard strategic action can possibly be considered. After all, it is we who, in our transcendental subjectivity, are engaged in constituting the structures and the substructures of events, bestowing meaning upon them and thus unifying them into a whole. But this whole is in the nature of an ideal goal or an expanding horizon. The first point to be noted is that all our meaning-bestowing acts are not fulfilled. They are frustrated or remain unfulfilled. Once we go into the roots of the unfulfilled meaning-conferring acts, we start realising that there are, or at least may be, "somethings" in the life-world that can frustrate our acts. To say that the meaning-conferring capacity of transcendental subjectivity is destined to be successful is to rule out a priori that there is, or even possibly can be, anything in the life-world that may prove negative or recalcitrant. It is bound to remind us of Hegel's dilemma with the "negative" or "unsuccessful" events in the philosophy of history. His strategic explanation of the "apparent aberration" of reason in history is framed in terms of "the cunning of reason." What will be Husserl's response if our transcendental constitutive capacity, meaning-bestowing capacity, comes across a transparent event of the life-world that proves to be negative or frustrative of the said capacity? The orthodox Husserlian's expected response, "It cannot be so" or "The conditions of its very possibility are absent in transcendental subjectivity," amounts to trying to solve the problem by definition or skirting the issue.

To my mind, the phenomenologist need not resort to this desperate strategy. He has a more plausible way out, provided he takes the concept of life-world more seriously and in a creative and reconstructive manner. Every event is like a text, clear or opaque. Text has no unalterably intrinsic meaning of its own. It is true that the author of the text, ordinarily speaking, can understand it best. But his understanding is not the only possible understanding. Not only interpreters but also critics can discover new and different meanings of the same text. Every interpreter, every critic, as a free and creative agent, brings a new context to bear upon the text in question. To state it from the other end, the text itself is differently contextured. When this life-rooted or context-bound character of events is brought to the focus of our phenomenological attention, we find that it easily lends itself to different interpretations. It is in this sense that philosophers like Gadamer are warranted in asserting that the real unity of history is hermeneutic, to be found through interpretation and not through the microstructure of events or the superstructure of transcendental subjectivity. The hermeneutic turn given to phenomenology by Heidegger has been creatively extended by Gadamer and Ricoeur. Both have in different ways succeeded in loosening the tight transcendental grip of phenomenology on history, both history of philosophy and history of science.

Real historical unity is interpretative and not transcendental and phenomenological. Gadamer speaks of two aspects of this hermeneutic unity, personal and historical. In and through his interpretative acts the individual interpreter injects his own self-understanding into the text. But, in any case, the text has in it a sedimented past of its own, that is, historical meaning. Therefore, in the name of interpreting it one cannot arbitrarily vulgarise it, appreciatively or critically. In this sense hermeneutics is text-bound.

At one important point the parallelism between history and hermeneutics tends to break down. The liberty that the interpreter can take with the text in interpreting it is not unlimited. The histority of the text imposes this limitation, though somewhat flexibly. If historical texts could be interpreted in any way one liked, then they could be nothing more than mere foils meant for one's misuse. In this sense texts have their self-preserving meaningful character. The importance of the point may be negatively indicated in this way. If it is said that text has no meaning of its own, then it may be easily and even contradictorily used for ideological purposes. It is with this aspect in view that Marx critically refers to philosophers' diverse and contradictory interpretations of history. Sociology of class-contradictions is reflected in ideologised history. Unless, therefore, textual meaning's objectivity, however limited it may be, is affirmed, philosophers as ideologists of this or that interest-group are liberally given license to distort history. Second, the distortion may enter into hermeneutics through the *futural* consciousness of the concerned interpreter. If in the name of shaping the future the interpreter exercises his native freedom to interpret the text in an arbitrary manner, the text is again reduced to a mere foil for the articulation of the interpreter's biases and prejudices, regardless of its meaning. Another way of distorting, if not destroying, the meaning character of (historical) text is to idealise it in an absolutely transcendental vein. In the resulting metaphysics of meaning, one feels, text's own meaning is irretrievably lost.

When I refer to these possible limitations of historical hermeneutics, I am not saying anything against the basic principle of hermeneutics itself, which has been so painstakingly developed by Gadamer. On the contrary, positively speaking, hermeneutics pointedly brings to our notice the creative human aspect underlying the acts of interpretation. Both in the context of history, in general, and in that of history of science, in particular, the principle of interpretative creativity deserves our close and critical attention. It is not history alone that lends itself to storic representation. History of science too can be represented in a narrative fashion. If, in fact, it is not done so, it is only because of the understandably idealised and relatively abstract character of the latter. Analogous to the plot of the story both history and history of science have their own thematics, though of different levels. In science and history of science our starting point is some problem. In the light of our problems we thematise the concerned details and thus put them to test, internal-phenomenological or external-evidential. Rightly understood, there is no antipodality between what is phenomenological and what is evidential. Evidence may be self-evident, and what is external may be interpreted phenomenologically and internalised.

The issue of criticism and creative progress is so central to the history of science that no serious philosopher of the history of science can afford to ignore it. Hegel speaks of moving and receding horizons of knowledge as sceptical; *skepsis* is nothing but a historical resting place of knowledge. In a somewhat similar vein Husserl speaks of discovery or uncovering of new, hidden, and unseen horizons of knowledge. Horizonal expansion is nothing but creative discovery. But one must be very careful here: discovery itself is not creation or constitution. If the former is confused with the latter, no discovered context can serve any critical or falsifying purpose. Where, to my mind, Kant, Hegel, and Husserl have gone wrong is in their common a priori conviction that what is yet to be discovered is somehow—in a concealed or covered manner—already available within us, implicitly present in us. This view, taken seriously, makes no sense of the concepts of constitution, creativity, and discovery. What is thus discovered is extremely trivialised. Its informative or cognitive content becomes negligible, if not nil. Constitution turns out to be mere explicit articulation of what is already pregiven to us by the life-world. Creativity proves to be objectward journey of our *spontaneous* consciousness unobstructed by the principle of *corporeality* or inertia of materiality.

If what is being claimed to be newly discovered has to be given any cognitive significance, it must be accorded a sense of its own. The "newly discovered" may be a thing or a being of the life-world. It is a world from which the possible objects of knowledge are cut out by us and commonly shared by us. But do not our cutting efforts fail at times? Do we succeed in sharing all that we wish to share? If it is claimed that objects are unilaterally created or constituted by our understanding or transcendental subjectivity or interpretation, we deny their ontological dignity, that is, relatively independent status. The ontic becomes an epistemic or hermeneutic creature. Its in-itself character is ignored. Self is unilaterally declared to be the author of the Other.

This is a highly unsatisfactory, uncritical, and counterintuitive situation. We cannot foreclose the possible objects of our discovery. If the life-world holds out a promise to disclose some of its objects to us, we do not thereby attain the right or capacity of knowing a priori what those possible objects are going to be like. They may or may not answer our needs and intentions. They may turn out even to frustrate of meaning-bestowing capacity. More radically speaking, our cognitive capacity itself, empirical or transcendental, may be incapacitated by a transparently "hostile" life-world. To deny this entails unfortunate consequences, both historical and scientific.

Historically speaking, our life is full of dialogues, silent or articulate. Self-Other dialogue is the basic stuff of our life and accounts for the histority and creativity of life. Interhuman discourses of different sorts—material, somatic and spiritual—are indicative of our (human) interdependence, not (monolithic) unity. We talk to each other, we hear each other, because these capacities answer some of our basic needs. In the process of fulfilling the needs we partly succeed and partly fail, giving rise to new needs, new problems, calling forth new forms of problematisation, thematisation, and solution. The situation has been described as dialectical. The persons concerned are said to be continuously engaged in an ongoing and necessary dialogue. In spite of our numerous differences, we try to understand each other. Discourse and conversation are our ways of coming to a consensus or, if possible, unity on the matters of both views and values. It is through discourse and conversation that we try to minimise the duality between Self and Other and broaden the scope of our consensus or unity. We enlarge the area of our problematics and thematics, of our conversation and discourse. Consciousness of new problems gives rise to renewed thematic enterprises, followed up by new investigation, more conversation, more discourse. The question is, Can we reach the level of discourse or conversation that can be strictly regarded as universal?

Ricoeur's concept of discourse, Derrida's concept of conversation, and Habermas's concept of communication remind me of, and are in-indeed analogous to, Collingwood's question-answer method. This method is extremely important for understanding not only the realm of history but also that of nature. Our conversation, discourse, and communication, rightly probed into, are found to be exercises in questioning and answering. Unless our consciousness becomes problematic or interrogative, we do not read the book of nature, consult books of knowledge, or converse with others. True, all our meaningful questions, like significant hypotheses of science, are drawn out of past knowledge or new "disturbing" information. The meaningfulness or the informed character of our questions by itself does not guarantee that we are sure to have true and testable answers to them, because as questioner I have no easy access to the true answer. Besides, the answers to my questions are, in most cases, provided by other persons and other things of the world. Even when I myself find out answers to my question, I cannot guarantee its truth-value, because the basis of my self-proposed answer is provided by others and can also be disposed of by others. It is for this basic reason that we, in our quest for knowledge, are always in touch with others, learning from others' experience.

For the same reason, the scientist, having framed his hypotheses in the light of his problems, approaches nature and enters as deeply as possible into its structures and details to find out true answers to his questions. The scientist's understanding does not constitute nature in its entirety and complexity. True, the intelligibility of nature motivates and emboldens the scientist to consult nature in order to find solutions to his problems, answers to his questions. But that does not mean that all answers provided by nature would prove true and stand up to test. Therefore, the question of test and criticism always remains open-ended, though at different levels.

VI

Consultation and conversation are kindred activities. The scientist consults nature in order to ascertain whether his hypotheses are correct or merely fanciful. The historian of science is engaged in conversation with both the scientists and the historians of science of other times and places. The records and documents he consults in this connection are integral parts of the language necessary for making conversation intelligible and useful.

The historian of science communicates with people who can possibly help him in understanding his subject matter and shares certain things (language, content, and so on) in common with the latter. To designate these commonly sharable things we use such terms as "cultural universals," "family resemblance," and "human universals." Cultural universals are not universals in the strict sense. Between different cultures the objects and ideas that we can discover exhibit some family resemblance. Resemblance is weaker than identity, and it is difficult to claim that different cultures are *basically* identical. If the *kind* character of mankind literally true, the necessity of conversation and communication between the peoples of different cultures would not have assumed the problematic importance that it has. In that case our access to one universal transcendental structure of understanding could have provided us the grounds for understanding the history and culture of all peoples separated by space and time.

Different forms of life have in common some recurring elements. If for the moment we forget the problem of determining the meanings of those elements and the related *theoretical* issues, our life as we live it presents us some *practical* cues to go beyond the bounds of our forms of life or language-games. In fact, the very term *bounds* does not mean any observable physical boundary. Between cultures and languages, especially adjacent ones, there is no boundary, no buffer zone or neutral belt. So the relativistic connotation of the language-game-theoretic approach or that of *Lebensform* need not be understood in an exaggerated manner. However, at the level of theory this unfounded fear or prejudice persists.

It is in order to avoid the misleading association of "cultural universals" and *Lebensform* that I have preferred the expression "human universals." Negatively speaking, the ground rules underlying human universals are not innate. Second, what man is able to know in terms of these universals, though in a sense synthetic a priori, is not necessarily valid. The conditions or rules of knowing are not able to ensure the truth of what is known. Third, human universals do not enable us to universalise our conversation or discourse. They only open up, in principle, such a possibility as a sort of programme. But there is nothing in them that can guarantee its successful execution. Even our best conceived programmes are, in practice, destined to suffer reverses. Fourth, human universals are not split up by the fancied external-internal dichotomy. All humans may not *essentially* belong to one identical kind, but they have so many things in common that the same cannot be grasped by such antithetically paired concepts as external-internal. Human universals are not neatly and rigidly structured. They have their own history, although that history itself is in a way structured or, at any rate, structurable. So in the context of understanding human universals I am also opposed to the use of such antithetically paired concepts as structure-history.

Positively speaking, human universals are some programmatic presuppositions, from which we have no escape. These presuppositions are questionable, criticisable, and revisable centres of (repeatable) reference and work as provisional categorical framework. Second, they give us different sorts of intelligibility, primary (or internal), secondary (or external), tertiary (or internal-external), and so on. They are not identically and uniformly available to all of us. Third, human universals, ontologically speaking, are of different but interrelated grades: physical, biological, linguistic, and so forth. In our physical constitution, biological structure, and linguistic competence we have in common certain things that largely account for our physical similarity, biological needs and propensity, and linguistic (or communicative) performance.

The factors that work as enabling conditions for giving practical shape to our ("universal") capacities are numerous: needs, social situatedness, historical and futural orientation, ability to use language in different ways. Analysis shows that this list of enabling conditions is merely illustrative and not exhaustive. Besides, these conditions, though differentiated for the purpose of identification and naming, are functionally interdependent, interactive, and systematic. For example, our *needs* are historically determined, contemporaneously influenced, and futurally oriented. Similarly, it may be shown that history is projection of the past toward the future and yet available in the present. The language of life is inseparable from the life of the people who use it. It may be easily shown that none of these enabling conditions is self-propelling; each one works in and through human beings, their dispositions and actions.

The whole enterprise of understanding of man by man, of human situations by human beings, when critically and phenomenologically looked into, makes it increasingly clear that such traditional dichotomies as idealism-realism, internal-external, subject-object, fact-fiction, theory-practice, and corporeality-spirituality are untenable. Critical reflection also makes it clear that such uncritically accepted traditional trichotomies as past-present-future, here-there-nowhere and science-arts-technology are very ill founded. Without disclosing or taking into account the human roots of the said dichotomies and trichotomies we cannot give any reasonably definite and communicable sense to any of these terms. For example, the "external" world that irritates my nerve endings cannot be meaningfully talked about unless I assume that the source of irritation is not a part of my body and, therefore, is external. Obviously this is not a very satisfactory way of drawing the distinction between what is external and what is internal. Similarly, it may be shown that I, the knowing subject, am also a knowable (or/and known) object. Painstaking analysis convinces us that it is very difficult to draw boundary lines between arts, science, and technology. Where one ends and the other begins cannot be clearly shown or even seen. These distinctions are not only humanly rooted but also practice-oriented.

It is this practical interest in, and will to know, past human beings, their thoughts, and their actions that account for our historical enquiry. It is just not the pastness of past events that can *causally* rouse our interest toward the events of the vanished days. There must be something in us at present that motivates us toward the past, toward a particular area of past human thoughts and actions. It is the underlying thought elements of the actions of the historical agents that enable the present historian to enter into a useful conversation with them. This "thoughtful" conversation cannot be subsumed under, and is not expressible in, physical-causal terms. Causalism and conversationalism do not go together. What makes conversation necessary for the historian is his inability to know a priori the thoughts and thoughtful actions of the historical agents of the past. If the latter acted thoughtlessly, it becomes doubly difficult for the historian to recapture them. The spatiotemporal distance and difference between the historian and his subject matter explain not only the necessity of conversation across cultures and centuries but also the nonavailability of the literal, that is, uninterpreted, past. In a way, paradoxically enough, the space and time that keep the historian away from his subject matter also account for how he can possibly get to it. Therefore, space and time must not be understood in the analogy of a gulf, wall, or barrier. The right analogy would be a bridge that is simultaneously separative and connective.

When the historian of the Kantian persuasion exclusively highlights the principle of "I think," he equates history with thought-history. And whatever seems to be thoughtless is denied a place in history. This Kantian bias of "rational history" had a strong impact on Hegel, who asked us to believe that the irrational has no place at all in history, that is, historically unexplainable. Obviously this romantic rationalism of Kant and Hegel created a lot of problems for the anthropologist of the nineteenth century who, having decided to study the "irrational" rites, rituals, myths, and so forth, of "savage" people, could not find his way to their human roots. Either he had to conclude, as Hegel did, that the so-called irrational things were inverted or concealed rationality, "the Cunning of Reason" itself, or he had to pronounce unilaterally, as Comte, Frazer, and Tylor did, that the alien cultures of the "savage" peoples were irrational and prelogical, at worst, or metaphysical and prescientific, at best.

The progression from Kant's "I think" principle to Husserl's "I can" principle definitely marks a constructive step toward making philosophical anthropology possible. Kant's "I think" principle (of *Pure Reason*) was narrowly defined in order to provide a transcendental justification for, a stamp of finality on, the Newtonian paradigm of the European science of the time. Given this justification, any other scientific paradigm of any other non-European culture was destined to be pronounced prelogical and prescientific.

Partly it is to Husserl's credit to liberalise the definition of rationality in terms of "I can." Kant's "I think" principle was suited only to certify scientific knowledge of Nature (constituted by understanding). The scope of Husserl's principle of constitution, of "I can," is much wider. It includes not only science-world but also life-world, including its so-called nonrational (cultural) forms.

To be fair to Kant, it has to be admitted that Husserl's "I can" principle was explicitly anticipated by Kant's *Critique of Practical Reason*. The universalisability requirement of moral law ("I ought") is based on man's supreme rational ability embodied in the ("I can") principle. But Kant's "I can" is intended to sustain only the "I ought" of the moral life. Husserl's "I can" has a larger horizon to gaze at and constitute, which includes not only cognitive and moral domains but also other domains, say, of fiction, fancy, and myth. This marks Husserl's departure from Kant's tripartite Reason, on the one hand, and resolve to "return to the naivete of life," on the other. Whether one can really return to the unaffected simplicity of the life-world is an old question long debated by the classical rationalists and empiricists in the European philosophical tradition. Heidegger's resolve to "return to the grounds of metaphysics" is also indicative of his intention to get close to our own existence, leaving our essence, if any, as far behind as possible. To go further back, Hume reminds us that there is nothing more *practically* reliable than sedimented history in the forms of tradition and custom. Self or mind, essential or existential, continues to be elusive forever. Therefore, Hume argues, to ask for a cogitolike certificate from that Self for *theoretical* vindication of science is bound to prove futile and invites sceptical reaction.

It is interesting to recall here the forgotten but deep debt of the phenomenologists to such phenomenalists as Hume. If we want to go beyond experience, the passage lies through experience. And except the passage itself there is no other guiding power, nothing transcendental or a priori, to take us to the destination beyond experience. Strictly speaking, experience presents us no idea of destination beyond or behind experience. This point of antitranscendental and transparent experience has been rightly emphasised by Kierkegaard and Nietzsche in their own simple but profound ways. They are bound to remind us of the Humean principle that there is nothing beyond and behind what we perceive. But reflection reveals that "what we perceive" is not itself perception. The former is in the latter as its content. Experience by its very nature is expressive of its content. There is no gap between the two. This view of the early existentialists is a step beyond Hume. This is the beginning of breaking up of the Humean fork, the division between matter and form of experience.

The fact that we can move in our consciousness from one matter of experience to another indicates that there is something in the former that enables us to pass on to the latter. This "something" has been variously interpreted and named, *telos*, *logos*, and so on. It is a contentward (but not necessarily an objectward) dynamic principle. This is Husserl's principle of intentionality, which seeks to combine the "synthetic" with "the a priori," the "historical" with "the a priori." I deliberately say that "Husserl's principle . . . seeks because closer scrutiny of his views on the subject shows that intentionality of consciousness gives no guarantee that its content would necessarily lead us to the point of intended object." True, every consciousness is consciousness of "something." But, at times, phenomenological reflection reveals that the said something, though a (sense) content, has no (noematic) *objective* correlate. In a sense one can be conscious of something (say, a mermaid, a mythical being), yet, truly speaking, consciousness cannot reach out to it as an object. Perhaps more central to our argument here would be the following example. Though our prereflective consciousness of raven, generally speaking, intends something black, in some exceptional (in this matter, Australian) cases, the intended "something" turns out to be not only not-black but, "strangely enough," white. To assert that the intended object may not *turn* up at all or prove chimerical altogether is counterintuitive. Therefore, to save the situation a line of argument has been developed highlighting the difference between *content* and *object*, *sense* and *object* (or *reference*), without giving up the basic principle of intentionality of consciousness. Unless this rearguard argument is used and pressed, it is difficult to reconcile the concept of intentionality with the *negative* or *frustrative* experience of the life-world.

Husserl's simultaneous commitment to the concept of a priori and to that of the life-world imparts added seriousness to the problem of reconciling "the historical" with "the a priori." We have noticed how Landgrebe, for example, has tried to bring about this reconciliation in terms of Husserl's own concept of intentionality. He wants to show that the a priori of phenomenological reasons is not fixed, but horizonally open and futurally oriented.[20] But the problem with Landgrebe's otherwise promising reconciliatory bid is that the a priori possibilities he speaks of are boundlessly free and destined to be factually self-fulfilling. Given this formulation, I have tried to argue that there can be no possible fact that can be deemed counterexample to the a priori possibilities of phenomenological reason. Because every "fact," every "example," according to this construal of Husserl's position, is bound to conform to what seems to me *fixed* a priori possibilities, despite Landgrebe's affirmation to the contrary. I fail to see how phenomenological reason, marked by intentionality, can really be regarded as *open* reason. For it is never open to refutation or nonfulfillment; it is open only to self-fulfillment.

It is for this reason that I have tried to offer a more plausible but critical construal of Husserl's concept of the historical a priori, bringing it close to a particular interpretation of the life-world that is not necessarily obliging or obedient to the possibilities envisioned by transcendental subjectivity. In no small measure Husserl himself is to be held responsible for the ambiguity of his view on this very crucial point. At times he speaks of a priori validity in terms of apodictic evidence based on eidetic intuition and it is said to have nothing to do with inductive generalisation. Unrestricted generality and strict essential necessity are mentioned as the hallmarks of the a priori. At the same time, it is conceded that all a priori is not self-justifying, self-founding or self-fulfilling. Whereas the constitutive a priori is claimed to be self-founding, the ontic a priori is not described or credited that way. But unless the latter is allowed to have a self-contained say, positive or negative, it is accorded no critical character whatsoever. Given the orthodox interpretation of Husserl in terms of "unfailing intentionality" and "essential structuralism," I find his phenomenological theory of history syncretic and hybrid in character.

All the "levels" of the life-world—scientific, prescientific and perceptual—are said to be carved out from one and the same *basic* life-world. In addition, it is claimed that because every item of the life-world being pregiven in transcendental subjectivity, the latter cannot encounter any opposition from the former. If one accepts this formulation of the relation between transcendental subjectivity and the life-world, the latter ceases to be historical and becomes an obliging and uncritical partner of the a priori structures of transcendental subjectivity. It is this uncomfortable perception of Husserl's fundamental position that draws my attention to some critical-constructive elements of Mohanty's interpretation of Husserl.

If one wants to take seriously Husserl's assertion to the effect that all riddles and problems of the world have to be solved within the world (of consciousness), one cannot logically *assume* right from the beginning that all worlds are reducible to, or articulations of, one unique world. Phenomenological reason cannot be regarded as really *open* if the constitutive principle of transcendental subjectivity is supposed to be already informed of all possible life-worlds, including all their structures, macro and micro. If "the constitutive" and "the constituted" are destined a priori to be *homogeneous*, one is led to believe, in spite of the phenomenologist's avowal to the contrary, that there is a sort of preestablished harmony between the two. If to preserve the *unity* of all life-worlds it is affirmed, à la Husserl, that within the *basic* life-world all *other* life-worlds are neatly nested—nesting and nested worlds are essentially *isomorphic*—one does not know how to draw a valid distinction between phenomenological reason and unreason. The a priori ideal of *essential* unity underlying transcendental (*subjective*) constitution and transcendental (*objective*) reduction leaves no room whatsoever for *unreason*, lest it subvert that much cherished *essentialist* ideal. Husserl is a follower of Kant and Hegel in this respect. His unitary (or unificatory) ideal of all-comprehensive rigorous science (as philosophy) recognises neither *criticisable* empirical sciences nor their *corrigible* history. When "the critic" and "the criticised," "the corrector" and "the corrected," turn out to be of the same origin and constitution, criticism and correction are bound to be shadowy and sham.

Against this rather counterintuitive background of science and history it is no surprise to see Heidegger's pleading for a *revelatory* view of the historical life-world in place of Husserl's *unitary* one. True, the former's notion of *continuous* disclosure of man as ontic, or worldly, relatedness, making knowledge possible, owes much to the latter's notion of *unitary* but horizonal expansion of the world of knowledge. The unitary model of knowledge, besides its straitjacketing effect on the given, gives the distinct impression that *all* the diverse things we know are mere self-explication, explication of what is already present in the self in essential form. The continuity model, in contrast, dispels the "concealed" thesis of "preestablished harmony," highlighting the creatively disclosive nature of man, and tries to show that the very possibility of human knowledge, science, and history is rooted in his being-in-the-world, ontic relatedness. In the field of knowledge emphasis is thus shifted from "transcendental constitution" to "ontological interpretation." Without interpreting and reinterpreting himself continuously man has no mysterious or anonymous transcendental capacity to enable him to know the "fixed and a priori" structures, if any, of the world and of himself as a part of it. Besides, what lends a distinct prohistorical orientation to Heidegger's thinking is his recognition of the primacy of the practical and affective modes of consciousness, relegating cognition to a secondary position. Knowledge is not a solo enterprise and achievement of being. It is an unending outcome of being's many-sided relatedness with the world and others.

Although one takes due note of these positive features of Heidegger one is likely to admit that he has at least partially succeeded in introducing an element of this-worldliness in the transcendental historism of Husserl. But the old question raised against the latter still remains unanswered and applies, though not identically, to the former: Can *Dasein*, being grounded as it is in the world-structure, rise above it and be the free and creative author of history of his own destiny? On the one hand, *Dasein* is a part of his social milieu, and, on the other, in his *care, anxiety,* and *death-consciousness* he is existentially lonely and authentically futural. *Dasein's* histority is qualified, qualified by his being-in-the-world and being-with-others. This qualified history is creatively disclosive and not negatively restrictive. Situated in the present, *Dasein* "appropriates" the past and makes it present, and, what is more, its anxiety and care both "throw" it to the future and, at the same time, bring the future back to "now," giving it a *present* life.

The many-sidedness of Heidegger's ontological hermeneutics has proved very influential mainly through Gadamer and his followers and has substantially contributed to making good the weakness of the transcendental hermeneutics of Husserl and his orthodox followers. The Heidegger-Gadamer tradition of hermeneutics is not "suspicious" of the empirical or the historical. On the contrary, it is positively "respectful" to each. That "awkward" facts and "inconvenient" findings are no roadblock to the possibility of transcendental philosophy has been rightly brought out by the defenders of ontological hermeneutics. When the transcendentalist develops due respect for historical details and ethnographic data, notwithstanding their occasional "irrational" or "negative" characteristics, the resulting structure of philosophy becomes rich (in diversity) and not monotonous and easily predictable. The fear of imponderables, fictions and myths, must not be allowed to impoverish transcendental philosophy. To achieve this goal what the transcendental historiographer is called upon to do is to reduce his enthusiasm for and, if possible, give up his commitment to, essentialism.

One of my main objectives in this study has been to vindicate anthropology and history of science in terms of a modest transcendental philosophy that is free of essentialism. Transcendental philosophy fails to be critical if it is found to be committed to essentialism and its allied thesis of apodictic evidence. In a very important sense it seems to me that Popper is right in asserting, drawing heavily upon the available history of science and philosophy, that the structure of scientific knowledge knows no rockbottom or absolute foundation; it may be "founded" either strongly or not so strongly. When Husserl speaks of the need of continuous self-criticism of all-comprehensive rigorous science, he too in his own way concedes its incomplete or "growing" character. But his firm commitment to essentialism and apodictic evidence makes it difficult for him to be self-critical in a serious sense. It is against this composite background of phenomenology and analytic philosophy that I find antiessentialism and antiapodictical ideas of such defenders of ontological hermeneutics as Gadamer, Ricoeur, and Mohanty interesting and instructive. Gadamer's emphasis on *interpretation* and *reinterpretation*, Ricoeur's on *singularity* of the event-structures, and Mohanty's *antireductionist* account of the life-world provide constructive cues for understanding anthropology and history of science from a new, creative, and critical point of view.

Rightly understood, there is no *absolutely authoritative* history of science or anthropology of science. If any transcendental philosophy stakes its claim to have for itself that unique –"the"– character, it is bound to come to grief. For the basic plank of this sort of transcendental philosophy, the essential or God-like infallible nature of man, is just not available. Man may well pretend to be a "self-critical" and "growing" God, but he can never be an all-knowing infallible God. And therefore his programme of a unique transcendental philosophy based on this undisclosed assumption is destined to ignore the details of history of science and emasculate the facts of multiple life-worlds. However, my criticism of a particular form of transcendental philosophy is not to be taken as a sweeping stricture against the very possibility of transcendental philosophy as such. On the contrary, I have tried to show, among other things, that without a transcendental philosophy we cannot clearly understand the true nature of anthropology and history. And, what is more, I have also indicated the hidden transcendental assumptions underlying some influential forms of philosophy of science and history of science that are ordinarily regarded as far from transcendentalism. For example, Quine's philosophy of science and Kuhn's historiography of science hardly disclose their transcendental backdrop. The point of my contention may be illustrated also by referring to Popper's philosophy and historiography of science.

Popper's Kantian inspiration is unmistakable. For example, when he speaks of the necessity of explaining the known in terms of the unknown, he echoes Kant. For him the starting point of any scientific investigation is some problem. The actual nature of the problem suggests the possible solutions that the scientist wants to capture in his conjectures or theories. Theories always go beyond the empirical domain of the problem in question. Though in the light of refuting evidence theories are susceptible to falsification, in effect, falsification rarely turns out to be total. Theories, though, transcend the domain of the empirical given, and are answerable to the latter. Viewed in this way, the Popperian image of science formed in terms of conjectures and refutations remains always more or less transcendental at the top and ill founded at the bottom. No amount of empirical evidence can ensure it a rock-bottom foundation. Nor even innumerable survivals through evidential tests can ensure its immortality, its permanent acceptance. Even his "proto-Platonic" World3 (of theories, arguments, and so on) is causally open to the forces of World2 (of psychology) and World1 (of physics).

Quine's theory of science has often been referred to as naturalist, physicalist, or even reductionist. In spite of his well-known rejection of the Russellian theory of types, recognition of physics as the paradigm of science, and methodological holism, I find numerous protranscendental elements in his philosophy of science. His mature characterisation of philosophy as self-reflective physics is very significant. Negatively speaking, physics qua physics is not *quite* aware of what it is like. An element of conceptual disengagement is necessary for the scientist to understand what he is engaged in. For example, body qua body does not even know what "irritation of nerve endings" is or means. Only in the cases of living bodies does the expression make sense. But the living bodies, if *anesthetised*, cannot have "irritation." To answer the simple question "whether 'irritation' is a *thing* or an *experience*" what one needs is embodied mind or mentalised body or self (whatever name we give to it). This regressive analysis, even before it is fully stretched out, starts making it clear to us that we ourselves, our knowledge of things and beings within and around us, are not of one *sort*. To build the boat of knowledge, to keep it afloat and going, and, if necessary, to repair it, what is needed is not only timber but various other *sorts* of things (not ordinarily mentioned because of their triviality in the boat-building context). For a methodological holist such as Quine to even liken science to boat is instructive. Why cannot the boat builder do his job, constructive or destructive, all at once? Why is he obliged to proceed in a piecemeal way? The plausible answers to the questions have, to my mind, definite transcendental implications. All elements of the structure or system of scientific knowledge are not equally open or answerable to, and modifiable by, experiential interrogation. Though, in principle, they are all subject to the experiential forces of interanimation, in practice we find that by experience the knowing body is more animated than what it has known, physics or mathematics. No element can be eternal. But certainly some are more stable, less open to empirical effects, or in a sense more transcendental than the rest in the structure of science. This is the point where even empiricists like Popper and Quine are conceptually obliged to espouse a modest form of transcendentalism.

A similar point is evident in Kuhn's understanding of the structure of scientific revolution. Whether a corpus of knowledge is scientific or not cannot be exclusively decided from within itself. What I mean is this: some sort of external recognition based on objective criteria is necessary to identify the corpus in question as scientific and distinguish it from the corpuses that do not satisfy the concerned criteria.

Besides, the point to be noted is that "science"-defining criteria are culture-bound and cannot be universalised. This consideration also applies to the case of definition or determination of what exactly a "revolution" is or means. Given one set of culture-bound criteria, a mere "transition," a transition from an internal point of view, may be alarmingly pronounced as "revolution." *Per contra*, given another set of criteria, even what is "revolution," revolution from an internal standpoint, may be calmly described as "transition" or "local anomaly." In order to unbracket the crucially bracketed concepts in the context—revolution, transition, internal, external, and so on—we need a transcendental or metatheoretic point of view. Otherwise the scientific paradigms of different cultures and epochs cannot be meaningfully compared, mensurated, and graded. To affirm, as Kuhn does, that scientific paradigms are incommensurable or to defend the opposite, that is, the commensurability thesis, the underlying logical requirement is identical. In brief, both incommensurabilism and its negation presuppose, implicitly or explicitly, some sort of transcendentalism. When the presupposed transcendental point of view is robust and allowed to work unilaterally, the conclusion that is forced upon us is this: all incommensurable paradigms are *essentially* articulations of, or at least can be viewed as, fragmented expressions of the concerned transcendental presupposition. Given this sort of robust transcendentalism, the paradigms are denied their singularity or internal, that is, culture-bound or epoch-bound, rationality. Evidently this is not the sort of transcendentalism that will be acceptable to Kuhn. In his scheme of scientific historiography different paradigms are allowed to retain their singularity together with internal rationality and, at the same time, they are said to be comparatively surveyable from a particular, in this case Kuhnian, point of view. Clearly this historiographical point of view is metatheoretic and transcendental. It may be pointed out here that Kuhn himself has not entered into the more philosophical question whether his own standpoint is reversibly criticisable in terms of the historical contents of the paradigms surveyed and studied. However, I do not propose to get into that larger question at this stage. For I have already critically mentioned it in the context of Kant and Husserl.

The point I want to highlight is that any philosophical understanding of science as a subculture demands that we view it as a part of a definite historical culture, and, what is more, the scientific subcultures of separate cultures, separated by space and time, have to be studied from a transcultural or transcendental point of view. Transcendentalism is not a retreat from or antithetical to factual empiricism or realism. On the contrary, to grasp the fuller meaning of the latter the former is methodologically indispensable. This pressing and practical truth becomes increasingly transparent to us only when we start philosophically reflecting upon what the working anthropologist and the professional historian are actually doing in their efforts to understand science. Since these efforts themselves and their outcome know no permanent boundary, theoretical or practical, our philosophical reflection, despite its transcendental character, remains an open-ended quest forever.

References

Introduction

1. See, for example, Joseph Agassi, "Towards an Historiography of Science," *History and Theory*, Beiheft 2 (1963).

2. I have examined some of these issues in D. P. Chattopadhyaya, *Individuals and Societies: A Methodological Inquiry* (Calcutta: Allied Publishers, 1967); enlarged 2d ed., (Calcutta: Scientific Book Agency, 1973).

3. Paul Radin, *Primitive Man as Philosopher* (New York: Dover, 1957). See, also, A. R. Radcliffe-Brown, *Method in Social Anthropology*, ed. M. N. Srinivas (Chicago: University of Chicago Press, 1958); Joseph Agassi, *Towards a Rational Philosophical Anthropology* (The Hague: Martinus Nijhoff, 1977).

4. See, for example, Gerhard Funke, "Phenomenology and History" in *Phenomenology and the Social Sciences*, ed. Maurice Natanson (Evanston, Ill.: Northwestern University Press, 1973).

5. Edmund Husserl, *Cartesian Meditations*, tr. Dorion Cairns (The Hague: Martinus Nijhoff, 1973), 151-57.

6. See D. P. Chattopadhyaya, *Individuals and Worlds: Essays in Anthropological Rationalism* (Delhi: Oxford University Press, 1976); see also my book, *Induction Probability and Scepticism* (forthcoming).

7. R. G. Collingwood, *An Essay on Metaphysics* (Oxford: Oxford University Press, 1940); see, also, Michael Krausz, ed., *Critical Essays on the Philosophy of R. G. Collingwood* (Oxford: Clarendon Press, 1972).

8. The philosophers whose works on these points appear to me very seminal are Husserl, Cassirer, and Popper, and their common Kantian background is very instructive in this context.

9. Claude Lévi-Strauss, *Structural Anthropology*, trans. Clair Jacobson, Brooke Grundfest Schoepf, and Allen Lane, (London: Penguin Books, 1969), and *Structural Anthropology*, vol. 2, trans. Monique Layton (Harmondsworth: Penguin Books, 1978); Jean-Paul Sartre, *Critique of Dialectical Reason,* trans. Alan Sheridan-Smith, ed. Jonathan Ree (London: New Left Book (NLB), 1976).

10. My further research in this crucial area may be found in my book, *Induction Probability and Scepticism* (forthcoming).

Chapter One

1. Wilhelm Windleband, *A History of Philosophy*, vol. I. (New York: Harper & Row, 1958), 23-24.

2. D. P. Chattopadhyaya, *Environment Evolution and Value: Studies in Man Society and Science* (New Delhi: South Asian Publishers, 1982), chap. 10.

3. F. A. Von Hayek, *The Counter-Revolution of Science* (Glencoe, Ill.: Free Press, 1952), 30.

4. Michael Dummet, *Truth and Other Enigmas* (London: Duckworth, 1978), 365-74.

5. Edmund Leach, "Models of Man," in *Man and the Social Sciences*, ed. William Robson (London: George Allen and Unwin, 1972).

6. Imre Lakatos, "Methodology of Scientific Research Programmes" in *Criticism and Growth of Knowledge*, ed. Imre Lakatos and Alan Musgrave (Cambridge: Cambridge University Press, 1972).

7. Thomas S. Kuhn, "Reflections on My Critics," in *Criticisms and Growth of Knowledge*, ed. Imre Lakatos and Alan Musgrave (Cambridge: Cambridge University Press, 1972), 271.

8. Martin Heidegger, *Being and Time*, trans. J Macquarrie and E. Robinson (New York: Harper & Row, 1962) 431-33, 445-49.

Chapter Two

1. Michael Dummett, *Truth and Other Enigmas* (London: Duckworth, 1978), 424.

2. F. H. D. Heinemann, *Proceedings of the Xth International Congress of Philosophy* (Amsterdam: Reidel, 1949).

3. W. V. O. Quine, "Two Dogmas of Empiricism," *Philosophical Review* vol. 60 (1951): 20-43.

4. J. W. N. Watkins, "Between Analytic and Empirical," *Philosophy* 32 (1957).

5. Hilary Putnam, "The Analytic and the Synthetic," in *Mind, Language and Reality: Philosophical Papers*, vol. 2 (Cambridge: Cambridge University Press, 1975).

6. Karl R. Popper, *Conjectures and Refutations* (London: Routledge & Kegan Paul, 1962), 75-93. Here I follow Popper's account and interpretation of the problems and suggested solutions. Works of S. Sambursky and Marshall Clagett are noteworthy in this connection. The results of the historical research of Charles Singer (*A Short History of Scientific Ideas, 500 to 1900* [Oxford: Clarendon Press, 1959]) and of George Sarton (*A History of Science* [Cambridge: Oxford University Press, 1966]) are substantially in accord with Popper's interpretation of the problem-situation at the time.

7. Singer, *Short History*, 26.

8. Popper, *Conjectures*, 82-83.

9. Singer, *Short History*, 24.

10. Singer, *Short History*, 27.

11. Sarton, *History of Science*, 295. See also Alfred Weber, *History of Philosophy*, trans. Frank Thilly and R. B. Perry (New York: Charles Scribner's Sons, 1925), 22.

12. Satya Prakash, *Founders of Science in Ancient India* (New Delhi: Research Institute of Ancient Scientific Studies, 1965), 605.

13. Bibhutibhushan Datta, *The Science of the Sulba* (Calcutta: Calcutta University Press, 1932). See, also, Bibhutibhushan Datta and Avadesh Narayan Singh, *History of Hindu Mathematics* (Bombay: Asia Publishing House, 1962).

14. Umesh Mishra, *Conception of Matter* (Allahabad: Allahabad University Press, 1966).

15. Sarton, *History of Science*, 255, see, also, 17-18: "Each settlement had its men of genius, its dullards, and its great majority of 'average' people."

Chapter Three

1. G. W. F. Hegel, *Philosophy of Nature*, trans. A. V. Miller, foreword J. N. Findlay (Oxford: Oxford University Press, 1970), xxiv; see also 6-13. In their own ways both may be interpreted as descriptive metaphysicians despite their proevolutionary stance.

2. Gerd Buchdahl, *Metaphysics and the Philosophy of Science* (Oxford: Basil Blackwell, 1969), 678; see, also, 512-30.

3. Stephen Toulmin, "Conceptual Change and the Problem of Relativity," in *Critical Essays on the Philosophy of R. G. Collingwood*, ed. Michael Krausz (Oxford: Oxford University Press, 1972), 218.

4. M. Minnaert, *The Nature of Light and Colours in the Open Air*, Eng. trans., new ed. (London: Dover Publications, 1954).

5. John Herivel, "Christian Huygens" in *Encyclopaedia Britannica* (Chicago: Helen Hemingway Benton, 1974).

6. Albert Einstein and Leopold Infeld, *The Evolution of Physics* (Cambridge: Cambridge University Press, 1971), 112.

7. Ibid., 120-21.

8. Karl R. Popper, *Objective Knowledge* (Oxford: Oxford University Press, 1972), 119.

9. Karl R. Popper, *Conjecture and Refutation* (London: RKP, 1962), 197.

10. J. J. C. Smart, "Quine's Philosophy of Science," in *Words and Objections*, ed. D. Davidson and J. Hintikka Amsterdam: Reidel, 1975), 4.

11. W. V. O. Quine, *Word and Object* (Cambridge: Harvard University Press, 1975), 3-4.

12. W. V. O. Quine, *The Ways of Paradox* (New York: Random House, 1966), 222-224.

13. Ibid., 222; see, also, 23-24, and Quine, *World and Object*, 275.

14. Michael Dummett, *Truth and Other Enigmas* (London: Duckworth, 1978), 425.

15. D. P. Chattopadhyaya, *Individuals and Societies: A Methodological Inquiry* (Calcutta: 1975), 131-32, 216-17; see also Quine, *World and Object*, 58-9.

16. Ninian Smart, *Reasons and Faiths* (London: 1958); see also, W. T. Stace, *Mysticism and Philosophy* (Philadelphia: 1960).

17. Albert Einstein, *Ideas and Opinions* (London: 1973), 336. See, also, 294, 301, and 322; and Albert Einstein, *Sidelights of Relativity*, 1923, quoted from H. Feigl and W. Sellars, eds, *Readings in the Philosophy of Science* (Minneapolis: University of Minnesota Press, 1953), 190-92.

18. Popper, *Conjectures and Refutations*, 184-92.

19. Alfred Tarski, "Truth and Proof," in *Fundamental Problems in Philosophy*, ed. Oswald Hanfling (UK: Basil Blackwell, The Open University Press, 1972), 275-78.

20. Max Planck, "The Unity of the Physical World-Picture," in *Physical Reality*, ed. Stephen Toulmin (New York: Harper Torch Books, 1970), 14.

21. J. W. Gibbs, *Elementary Principle in Statistical Mechanics Developed with Special Reference to the Rational Foundation of Thermodynamics* (New Haven, Connecticut: Yale University Press, 1948).

22. Planck, "Unity," 23.

23. Ernst Mach, "The Guiding Principle of My Scientific Theory of Knowledge" in ed. Toulmin *Physical Reality*, 39.

24. Ernst Mach, *Knowledge and Error*, trans. Thomas J. McCormack and Paul Foulkes, ed. (Erwin N. Hiebert, 1976), 15, 120.

25. Popper, *Objective Knowledge* (Oxford: Clarendon Press, 1972), 70, 261; see, also, 266-72.

26. P. F. Strawson, *The Introduction to Logical Theory* (London: Methuen, 1963), 175-79; see, also, 3-4, 9-12, 211-15.

27. W. Sellars, "Presupposing," *Philosophical Review*, 63 (1954): 197-215.

28. L. Linsky, *Referring* (London: RKP, 1963), 85-99.

29. Michael Dummett, *Truth and Other Enigmas* (London: Duckworth, 1978), 25-8; see, also, xiv-xix.

Chapter Four

Materials used in this paper were presented at Friday Seminar, Calcutta, and at Premnath Memorial Lectures at Punjab University, Chandigarh. I am grateful to those who criticised and commented on the paper. Special thanks are due to Arthur Danto, Columbia University, who read an early draft of this paper, and Erwin Heibert, Harvard University, who discussed with me some of the issues raised here.

1. Jean-Paul Sartre, *Critique of Dialectical Reason*, trans. Alan Sheridan-Smith, ed. Jonathan Ree (London: New Left Books, 1976), 817-18. For the purpose of exposition and interpretation of Sartre's thought I have relied, in this paper, almost exclusively on the *Critique*. The other well-known works of Sartre that I have occasionally consulted in this connection are *Being and Nothingness*, trans. Hazel E. Barnes, intro. Mary Warnock (London: Methuen & Co., 1974); *Search for a Method*, trans. and intro. Hazel E. Barnes (New York: Vintage Books, 1968); and *The Psychology of Imagination*, intro. Mary Warnock (London: Methuen & Co., 1972).

2. Claude Lévi-Strauss, *The Savage Mind* (London: Weidenfeld & Nicolson, 1974), 249. For the purpose of exposition and interpretation of Lévi-Strauss's thought I have relied, in this paper, mainly on *The Savage Mind* and occasionally on *Structural Anthropology*, trans. Claire Jacobson, Brooke Grundfest Schoepf, and Allen Lane (London: Penguin Press, 1969), and *Structural Anthropology 2*, trans. Monique Layton (Harmondsworth: Penguin Books, 1978).

3. *Philosophical Writings of Peirce*, selected, edited, and introduced by Justus Buchler (New York: Dover Books, n. d.), 98-119.

4. Ludwig Wittgenstein, Philosophical Investigations, 3d ed., trans. G. E. M. Anscombe (New York: Macmillan, 1968), remarks 30-1, 39-43, 139, 198-9.

5. R. Jakobson and M. Halle, *Fundamentals of Language* (The Hague: Mouton, 1956).

6. John von Neumann and Oskar Morgenstern, *Theory of Games and Economic Behaviour* (New York: John Wiley & Sons, 1964).

7. D. P. Chattopadhyaya, *Individuals and Societies: A Methodological Inquiry*, 2d ed. (Calcutta: Scientific Book Agency, 1975), 12-17, 29-35; see, also, 184-8 on the structure of kinship.

8. Cf. Gerard Radnitzky and Gunnar Anderson, eds., *The Structure and Development of Science* (Dordrecht and Boston: Reidel, 1979); Paul Feyerabend, *Science in a Free Society* (London: Verso/New Left Books, 1978).

9. Hans-George Gadamer, *Truth and Method* (New York: Crossroad, 1982), 235-74.

10. See, for example, Emile Durkheim, *The Elementary Forms of the Religious Life*, trans. J. W. Swain, intro. Robert Nisbet (London: George Allen & Unwin, 1976), 270-383, 377ff; and Emile Durkheim and Marcel Mauss, *Primitive Classification*, trans. and intro. Rodney Needham (London: Ghen & West, 1970).

11. D. P. Chattopadhyaya, *Environment, Evolution and Values* (New Delhi: South Asian Publishers, 1982), 108-22.

12. Lévi-Strauss, *Savage Mind*, 256. See, also, his *Structural Anthropology* Penguin, Allen Lane Penguin, 18, 23-25.

13. W. H. Walsh, *Philosophy of History* (New York: Harper & Row, 1960), 59-64.

14. See, for example, in Imre Lakatos, ed., *Inductive Logic* (Amsterdam: North-Holland Publishing Co., 1968), J. Hintikka's "Induction by Enumeration and Induction by Elimination," 191-216, and R. Carnap's response, 218-20.

15. See, in this connection, H. Stuart, Hughes's paper, "Structure and Society," in *Claude Lévi-Strauss: The Anthropologist as Hero,* ed. E. Nelson and Tanya Hayes (Cambridge: MIT Press, 1970), 22-46. The main complaint of Hughes, himself a professional historian with considerable philosophical competence, is quite like that of Sartre: that Lévi-Strauss is basically anti-historical, opposed to the ideal of progress as ordinarily understood, and a Rousseauite naturalist.

16. Ibid., 7-8.

17. John Plamanetz, *Karl Marx's Philosophy of Man* (Oxford: Clarendon Press, 1975), 219-26. See, also, Karl Marx's *Grundisse,* trans. D. McClellan (London: Macmillan, 1971), 120-21 and 134-35.

18. D. P. Chattopadhyaya, (8) supra, Chap. 4.

19. (12) supra, Part II.

20. D. P. Chattopadhyaya, *Individuals and Worlds: Essays in Anthropological Rationalism* (New Delhi: Oxford University Press, 1976), Chap. 9.

Chapter Five

1. Charles Hartshorne, Paul Welss, and Arthur Burks, eds., *Collected Papers of Charles Sanders Peirce, 1933-1958* (Cambridge: Harvard University Press) 5:313-14.

2. D. P. Chattopadhyaya, *Individuals and Worlds: Essays in Anthropological Rationalism* (New Delhi: Oxford University Press, 1976), Chap. 2.

3. M. A. K. Halliday, *Language as Social Semiotic: The Social Interpretation of Language and Meaning* (London: Edward Arnold, 1979), 40, 44, 51; see, also, 37-38.

4. D. P. Chattopadhyaya, "Development of Language," in *Individuals and Societies: A Methodological Inquiry* (Calcutta: Scientific Book Agency, 1975), 182-84.

5. Otto Jesperson, *Mankind, Nation, and Individual from a Linguistic Point of View* (Oslo: Instituttel for Sammentignende Kulturferskning, 1925), 607; see, also, 16-17.

6. P. F. Strawson, *Logico-Linguistic Papers* (London: Methuen, 1971), 171-2, 176.

7. Joseph J. Kockelmans and Theodore J. Kisiel, eds., *Phenomenology and the Natural Sciences: Essays and Translations* (Evanston, Ill: Northeastern University Press, 1970).

8. Ibid., 67.

9. D. P. Chattopadhyaya, *Individuals and Worlds: Essays in Anthropological Rationalism* (New Delhi: Oxford University Press, 1976), 77-78, 96-97, 194-95.

10. Paul Ricoeur, *Husserl: An Analysis of His Phenomenology*, trans. E. G. Ballard and L. E. Embree (Evanston, Ill.: Northeastern University Press, 1967), 170.

11. Paul Ricoeur, *History and Truth*, trans. C. A. Kelbey (Evanston, Ill.: Northeastern University Press, 1965), 63-73, 200-05.

12. D. P. Chattopadhyaya, "Unity of the Physical World and Human Freedom," in *Journal of Indian Council of Philosophical Research* 4, no. 1 (000): 139-68.

13. H. G. Gadamer, *Truth and Method* (New York: Crossroad, 1982), 213.

14. Ibid., 333-36.

15. Giorgio Tagliacozzo, et. al, eds., *Vico and Contemporary Thought* (Atlantic Highlands, N.J.: Humanities Press, 1976).

16. Gadamer, *Truth and Method*, 341.

17. Jacques Derrida, *Writing and Difference*, trans. and intro. Alan Bass (London: Routledge & Kegan Paul, 1978), 291.

18. Jürgen Habermas, *The Theory of Communicative Action*, trans T. McCarthy (Boston: Beacon Press, 1987), 396-99.

Chapter Six

1. Eric H. Lenneberg, *Biological Foundations of Language* (New York: John Wiley & Sons, 1967), 374-79.

2. I. Kant, *Critique of Pure Reason*, trans. Norman K. Smith (New York: Macmillan, 1973), B157.

3. Ludwig Landgrebe, *The Phenomenology of Edmund Husserl*, ed. and intro. D. Welton (London: Cornell University Press, 1981), 36-37.

4. Edmund Husserl, *The Crisis of European Sciences and Transcendental Phenomenology: An Introduction to Phenomenological Philosophy*, trans. and intro. David Carr (Evanston, Ill.: Northwestern University Press, 1970), 216-19. See, also, 106-8, 330-32.

5. Ibid., 178. See, also, 123-25.

6. D. P. Chattopadhyaya, "Models and Metaphors in Arts, Science and Mathematics," in *Mind, Language, and Necessity*, ed. D. P. Chattopadhyaya and P. K. Sen (Delhi: Macmillan, 1981). See, also, my book, *Knowledge, Freedom, and Language: An Inter-woven Fabric of Man, Time, and World* (Delhi: Motilal Banarsidass, 1989).

7. J. N. Mohanty, *The Possibility of Transcendental Philosophy* (Dordrecht: Martinus Nijhoff, 1985).

8. Husserl, *Crisis*, 145, 46.

9. Ibid., 147.

10. Landgrebe, *Phenomenology*, 199.

11. Mohanty, *Possibility*; see, for example, Essay 15.

12. D. P. Chattopadhyaya, *Individuals and Worlds: Essays in Anthropological Rationalism* (Delhi: Oxford University Press, 1976).

13. Husserl, *Crisis*, 70-71. See, also, his *Logical Investigations*, trans. J. N. Findlay (London: Routledge & Kegan Paul, 1970), vol. 1, 292, and vol. 2, 865; *Cartesian Meditations: An Introduction to Phenomenology*, trans. Dorion Cairns (The Hague: Martinus Nijhoff, 1973), 116-20.

14. Mohanty, *Possibility*, 98.

15. Husserl, *Crisis*, 137-41. See, also, 349-51.

16. Husserl, *Logical Investigations*, vol. 1, 56-7, 66, 145, 189. See, also, vol. 2, 524-26.

17. Husserl, *Cartesian Meditations*, 154-55. See, also, Martin Heidegger, *Being and Time*, trans. J. Macquarrie and E. Rabinson (New York: Harper & Row, 1962), 447-49; Joseph J. Kockelmans, *Heidegger and Science* (Lanham, Md.: University Press of America, 1985); see, also, Michael Allen Gillespie, *Hegel Heidegger, and the Ground of History* (Chicago: University of Chicago Press, 1984), 149-64.

18. H. G. Gadamer, *Truth and Method* (New York: Crossroad, 1982), 318-24.

19. Joseph J. Kockelmans and Theodore J. Kisiel, eds., *Phenomenology and the Natural Sciences* (Evanston, Ill.: Northwestern University Press, 1973), 83-84. See, also, in particular, Kisiel's paper, "Husserl on the History of Science."

20. Kant, trans. Norman K. Smith, *Critique of Pure Reason* (London: Macmillan, 1973), A 371.

21. Hegel, *Greater Logic*, quoted from Kockelmans and Kisiel, *Phenomenology and the Natural Sciences* (Evanston, Ill.: Northwestern University Press), 360.

22. S. Stuart Hughes, "Structure and Society," in *Claude Lévi-Strauss: The Anthropologist as Hero*, ed. E. Nelson Hayes and Tanya Hayes (Cambridge: MIT Press, 1972).

23. Kockelmans and Kisiel, *Phenomenology*, 68, 69.

24. Lenneberg, *Biological Foundations*, 375-379, 402-408.

25. George Sarton, *History of Science* (New York: Norton Library, 1970), xiii-xiv.

26. Paul Ricoeur, *Truth and History* (Evanston, Ill.: Northwestern University Press, 1965), 76.

27. T. S. Kuhn, *The Structure of Scientific Evolutions* (Chicago: University of Chicago Press, 1962), 210.

28. Ibid., 198-202.

Epilogue

1. Edmund Husserl, *Logical Investigations*, trans. J. N. Findlay (London: Routledge & Kegan Paul, 1970), 110.

2. Ibid., 140.

3. Ibid., 149.

4. Ibid., 62.

5. Ibid, 145-46, 72, 264-66, 352-53.

6. Edmund Husserl, *The Crisis of European Science and Transcendental Phenomenology*, intro. and trans. David Carr (Evanston, Ill.: Northwestern University Press, 1970), 173-183; see, also, 377-78, 382-83.

7. Husserl, *Logical Investigations I*, 107-08, 218-20; see, also, 222-29.

8. Edmund Husserl, *Experience and Judgment: Investigations in a Genealogy of Logic*, rev.-ed. Ludwig Landgrebe (Evanston, Ill.: Northwestern University Press, 1973), 44-46.

9. Husserl, *Crisis*, 22-74, 301-02; see, also, 322-25.

10. Ibid., 349-51; see, also, 377-78, 392-95.

11. H. A. Hodges, *The Philosophy of Wilhelm Dilthey* (London: Routledge & Kegan Paul, 1952), 220.

12. Martin Heidegger, *Being and Time*, trans. John Macquarrie and Edward Robinson (New York: Harper & Row, 1962), 40-62, 72-75.

13. Ibid., 77.

14. Ibid., 269.

15. Ibid., 414.

16. Ibid., 433.

17. Paul Ricoeur, *Husserl: An Analysis of His Phenomenology* (Evanston, Ill: Northwestern University Press, 1967), 170.

18. D. P. Chattopadhyaya, *Individuals and Societies: A Methodological Inquiry*, 2d ed. (Calcutta: Scientific Book Agency, 1975).

19. Paul Ricoeur, *History and Truth* (Evanston, Ill.: Northwestern University Press, 1965), 76-77.

20. Ludwig Landgrebe, *The Phenomenology of Edmund Husserl*, ed and intro. Dohn Welton (Ithaca: Cornell University Press, 1981), 199-200.

INDEX OF NAMES

INDEX OF SUBJECTS

A NOTE ABOUT THE AUTHOR

D.P. Chattopadhyaya is Research Scientist and Professor at the University Grants Commission, Calcutta, India.